THE BOOK OF
GARDENPLANS

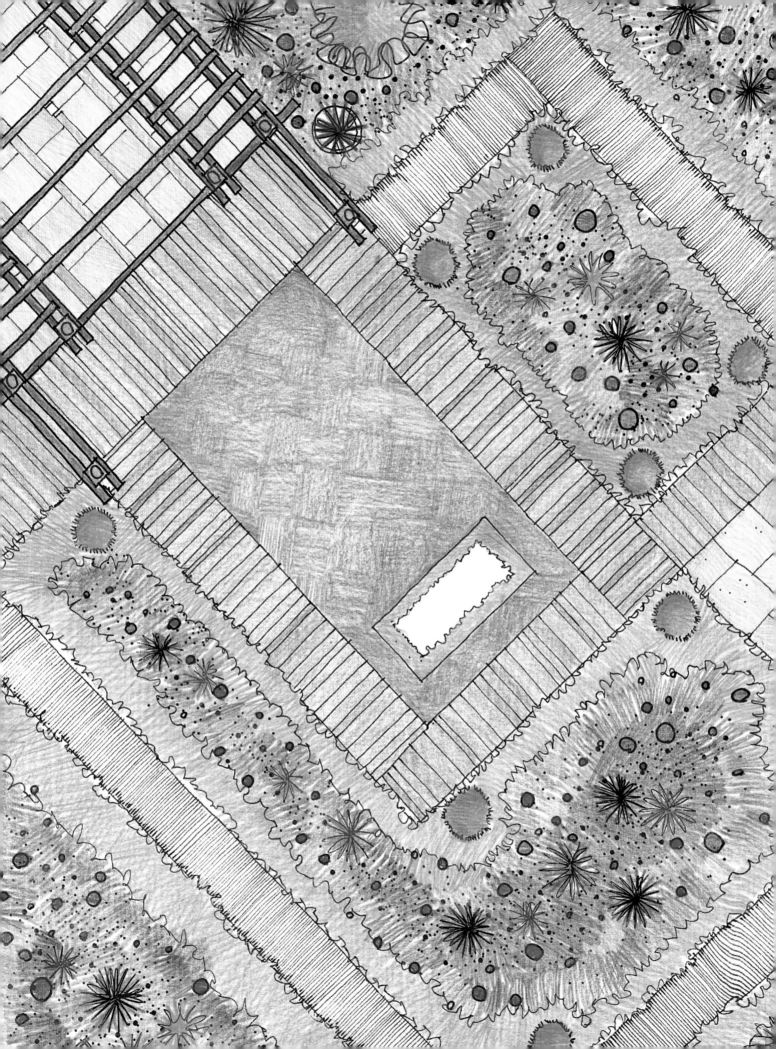

THE BOOK OF
GARDENPLANS

General Editor: **Andrew Wilson**

MITCHELL BEAZLEY

The Book of Garden Plans

First published in 2004 by Mitchell Beazley,
an imprint of Octopus Publishing Group Ltd,
2–4 Heron Quays, London E14 4JP
Reprinted 2004, 2005
An Hachette Livre UK Company
www.octopusbooks.co.uk

First published in paperback in 2008

ISBN 978 1 84533 360 7

A CIP record of this book is available from the British Library

Executive Art Editors Christie Cooper, Sarah Rock
Commissioning Editor Michèle Byam
Editors Jodie Jones, Theresa Bebbington, Catherine Emslie
Designer Geoff Borin
Picture Researcher Giulia Hetherington
Production Gary Hayes
Indexer Sue Farr

Set in Frutiger

Printed and bound in China by
Toppan Printing Company Limited

How to use this book 6

Introduction 8

Themed Gardens 16

Urban Gardens 44

Informal Gardens 86

Small Gardens 126

Water Gardens 174

Formal Gardens 192

Country Gardens 216

List of Designers 252

Index 254

Acknowledgments 256

Contents

How to use this book

In the majority of cases, each design is given an individual page. However, some designs are displayed across two pages in order to clarify the message or to include additional supporting information. For example, the work of those designers who open each section is illustrated in this way.

The various sections are designed for ease of reference, determined by size or garden type. Initially it may be most appropriate to refer to the section or sections that most closely reflect one's own garden. However, many designs in other sections may well contain ideas that can be easily interpreted or transferred to another scale or garden type. It is important to look at a range of design ideas with an open mind rather than to look for a specific garden because it resembles ones own.

Each design is shown as a plan with some additional visual support. Often, if the garden is not yet built, this support will be in the form of one or more of the drawings identified in the introduction. Where the gardens have been realized, photographs of the completed scheme are used. In some cases photographs from existing gardens showing planting or construction of a similar vein have been used to support or explain the design ideas.

The individual designers responsible for the work shown have been invited to briefly explain their gardens, providing information on their inspirational sources, briefs from the garden owners, or the character and context of the sites on which they have worked. Additional information, in bullet point form, helps to clarify why gardens have been created in a particular way, providing insight into the design process and into the final proposals. A typical page layout is shown on these two pages to help the reader navigate the book.

Garden designer's name or name of design practice.

The main details of the featured garden, showing the approximate size or dimensions, the soil type, aspect (orientation), and any key features within the garden.

Garden plan drawing, showing the layout or design of the garden, often in relation to the house, and the shape of the site.

A Garden with Outlo

Michael Day

dimensions: **10 x 15m (33 x 49ft) approx.**
soil: **alkaline**
aspect: **southeast facing**
key features: **slope from house down to boundary wall**

S

The owners wanted a low-maintenance garden that provided good outlooks from the house, and integrated the garden with the downland landscape beyond. They were keen to incorporate timber, especially sleepers, and climbing plants, and also requested a pond and a small seating area sited to catch the evening sunshine.

The site was dominated by a high boundary wall which, in the lower part of the garden, hid views of the landscape beyond. In addition, an oil tank on a concrete base was visible from all points in the garden and needed to be screened.

Existing concrete pavers were replaced with reconstituted stone slabs and shingle, the colour of which was chosen to compliment the paving but contrast with the house brick. From the terrace,

reclaimed railway sleepers form steps down the garden and provide a material contrast to the timber decking. The changing levels were enhanced by alternating the direction of the decking boards from one level to the next, and handrails were made high enough to lean on and wide enough to rest a glass on.

In the lower garden, a new pond became the focus of interest, distracting the eye from the high boundary wall. On three sides the pond was constructed using concrete block walls but the fourth side was a beach area to encourage wildlife.

The oil tank and a new storage shed have been screened using planed, ornamental fence panels with a pergola above providing another support for the clients' much-loved climbers.

above *The photograph shows the changing levels of decking and the handrails, made high enough to lean on and look at the pool below.*

below *The axonometric shows more clearly the pond in the lower garden, with a beach area on one side to encourage wild life.*

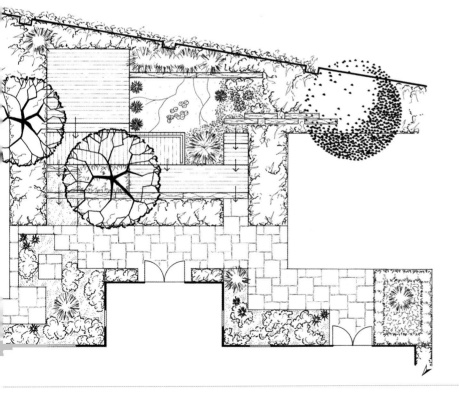

The following pages contain approximately 140 designs produced by 72 garden designers from Britain and other countries. Many of these schemes will not have been seen publicly before, providing an array of design solutions for many different sites and garden owners.

The designs are shown in plan form, illustrated, where possible, with sketches and three dimensional drawings. Completed schemes are also supported by images, showing either general views or details of planting, paving, water features, or sculpture. Where schemes have remained on the drawing board supporting images have been selected to explain or support the designer's thinking. What the book hopes to show is the wealth of creative and imaginative thought that designers bring to bear on the sites and gardens on which they work.

Introduction

How designers communicate

Although we converse freely and exchange ideas and concepts through language and text, this can be limiting, particularly when explaining or describing more complex shapes, patterns and forms. For designers who work in three dimensions, visual communication is often more efficiently descriptive and easily accessible. The visual or graphic communication of design ideas enables the designer to work quickly and effectively, using measured or scaled drawings for accuracy. Garden designers use two broad categories to communicate ideas: technical or architectural drawings, and freehand or sketched drawings.

For the client, freehand drawings are more readily appreciated and understood. Often in sketch form, such drawings seem more realistic, perhaps communicating the mood or atmosphere of a garden more effectively. However, technical or architectural drawings have their place in the creation of successful gardens,

and this book is dedicated to such work. This introduction explains the techniques used by the garden designer, thus enabling the drawings within to be read and explored with greater confidence and understanding.

Scale

Even the smallest garden is larger than the largest sheets of paper that a designer might use. The use of scaled, or scaled down, measurements allows large dimensions to be reduced in proportion to fit onto workable and practical sheets. Small gardens, perhaps those in urban areas, will usually be drawn at a scale of 1:50, meaning that the drawn garden will be 1/50th of the size of the actual garden.

For larger suburban or country gardens, designers might adopt a scale of 1:100, 1:200 or 1:500, meaning that these gardens will be drawn at 1/100th, 1/200th or 1/500th of the true size.

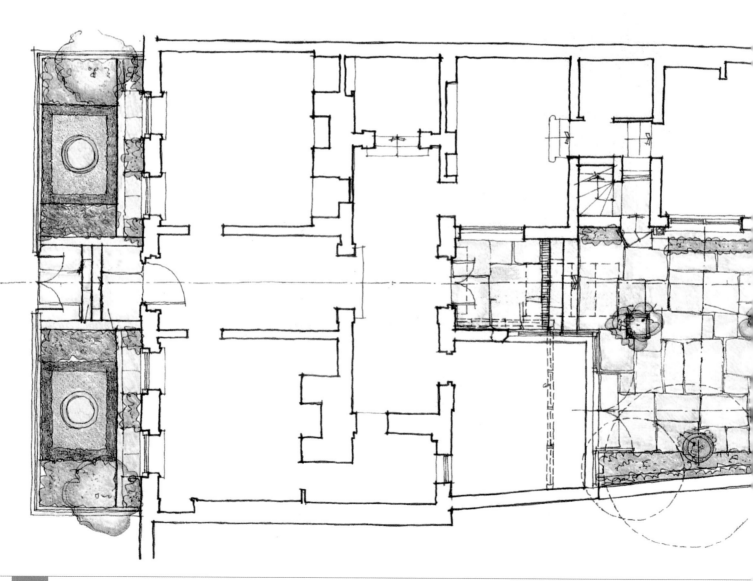

The Plan

When garden designers create their work, the plan drawing is the focus of the design process. To be able to understand these drawings one has to imagine being able to float above the garden looking down, as a bird might when flying overhead. This enables us to see the space laid out as a pattern.

The designer finds this useful as objects can be placed with great accuracy within the boundaries of the garden, an important consideration in recreating the design in reality. However, for the lay person, this view is often difficult to understand as it is not the way in which we would normally perceive and view the garden.

The plan is two dimensional, communicating length and breadth. The use of scale enables these dimensions to be read and understood accurately. The information on heights is missing in these drawings, and designers need to consider other means of communicating the third dimension.

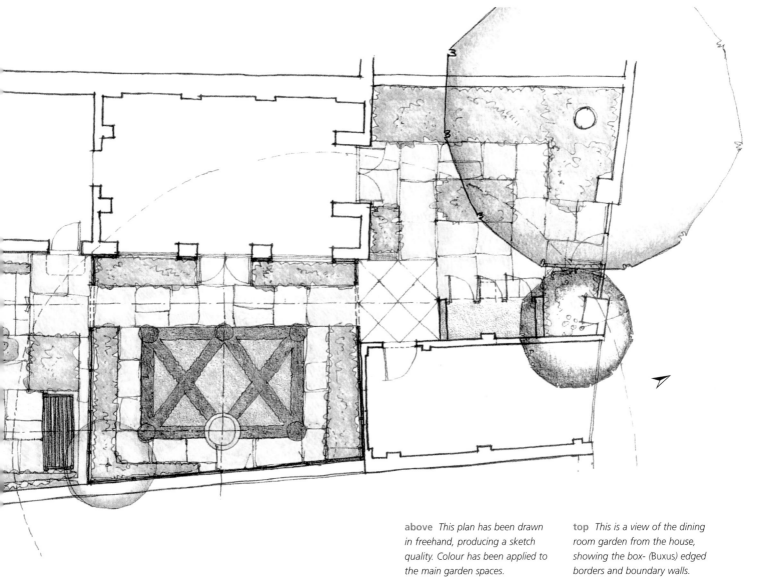

above *This plan has been drawn in freehand, producing a sketch quality. Colour has been applied to the main garden spaces.*

top *This is a view of the dining room garden from the house, showing the box- (Buxus) edged borders and boundary walls.*

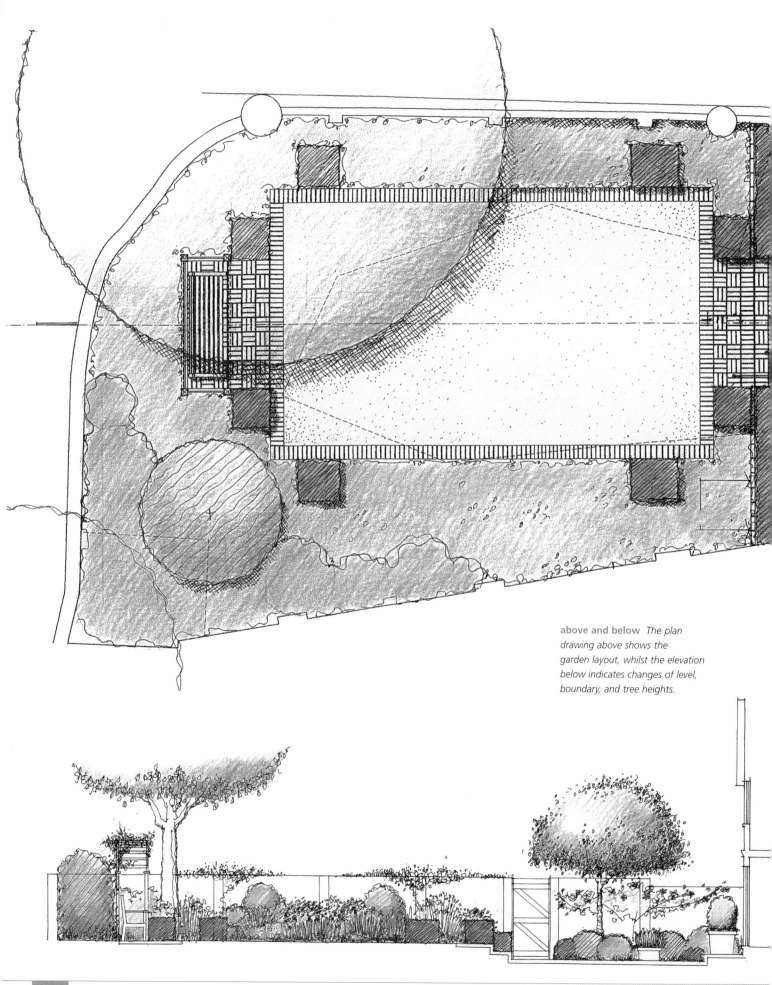

above and below *The plan drawing above shows the garden layout, whilst the elevation below indicates changes of level, boundary, and tree heights.*

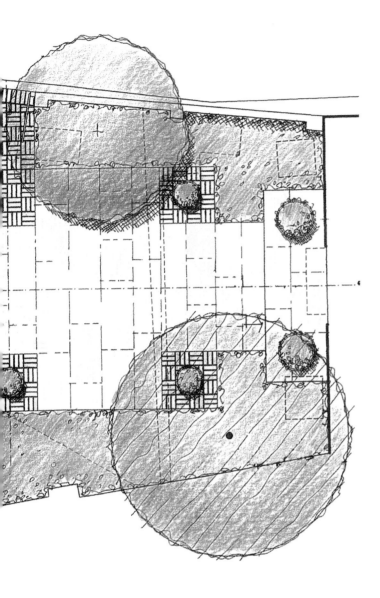

By using different line thicknesses, often called line hierarchy, a sense of the relative heights of structures, planting and artefacts can be suggested. Colour, and in particular light and shade, can also produce a more realistic and tangible sense of three dimensional form and height.

Designers use continuous, uniform line to suggest or indicate hard materials and constructed elements. This can produce an engineered or architectural quality to drawings. A more broken, organic line suggests soft materials or planting. When used together the results can be atmospheric and visually seductive, communicating the mood or character of a garden.

Many designers use annotation to describe and explain the changes made during the design process, or to provide additional detail.

The elevation

The elevation is normally used to support or explain a plan drawing. It provides the vertical dimensions or height that cannot be communicated in plan drawings. Although the elevation still does not produce a view that we would normally see, it is a more realistic drawing that enables us to understand scale.

Elevations are not to be confused with perspectives, which show a receding height over distance. In the elevation, heights remain measurable to the scale indicated, no matter how far away they might be from the viewer. The hierarchy of line is used to indicate this distance and, again, those elements close at hand will be drawn with a heavier line than those elements in the distance.

Changes of level can be illustrated clearly with the elevation and therefore steps, slopes or ramps, and retaining walls can be explained or highlighted. The garden designer uses them to indicate anticipated heights of trees or boundaries, to provide a sense of scale or, for example, to show the new landscape against an existing house.

The section

The section or cross section is an unusual drawing as it shows a slice through a design, a view that we would not normally see. Although often used on more technical drawings to indicate foundations that lie below ground, sections can also be applied successfully to the explanation of level changes, steps, or retained ground.

In this book of design drawings, they are often used in association with the elevation, producing sectional elevations.

The axonometric

The drawings discussed so far show two dimensions with clarity but the axonometric allows a measured three dimensional view to be developed, explaining form and spatial relationships with ease.

By angling the plan drawing on the drawing board, the designer can produce a series of vertical heights at important junctions or corners on the design. Although the resulting drawings must be viewed at a given angle, the effect when shading or colour is applied can be realistic and informative. In general, designs which are regular, rectilinear, or which involve a proportion of constructed or architectural elements will work best. Changes of level, especially regular steps, can be communicated effectively using this technique. An example of an axonometric drawing can be seen on page 7.

The perspective

There is a range of methods by which perspective drawings can be produced and a number of perspective views that designers may find helpful in illustrating their work.

For more formal and accurate drawings, designers might produce what is known as a constructed perspective. In these drawings elements within the design are related together with great accuracy, producing a clear and organized illustration.

Free hand perspectives produce a more sketchy image in which the designer is aiming to suggest the character and personality of a design. Accuracy is perhaps therefore less important than the atmosphere or quality of a designed space.

The simplest type of perspective drawing is known as a single or one point perspective. The drawings produced show lines perpendicular to the viewer, converging on a single vanishing point on the horizon. A more complex form of perspective drawing is the two point perspective in which the object, or in this case the garden, is viewed at an angle. This produces two vanishing points and can produce a much more realistic quality or effect. It is normal in perspective drawing to use what is termed the eye level. This approximates to the height at which one would view the garden if one were to walk through or stand in the space.

A bird's eye view would produce an image similar to a plan but the converging lines of the perspective would introduce a more realistic quality. In effect such a view would still be a one point perspective. The illustration on page 15 shows a bird's eye view, used here because the garden space is so restricted. One might imagine viewing the garden from a balcony above.

Each of these drawing techniques can be seen in this book. Designers often select the drawn approach that best explains their work. In addition, as graphic skills develop, they begin to symbolize or identify the particular style and approach of the designer – in other words, a personality emerges from the drawn or coloured work.

left and above *The drawing above is a one point perspective to show the view into a tiny space, similar to that to the left, as clearly as possible.*

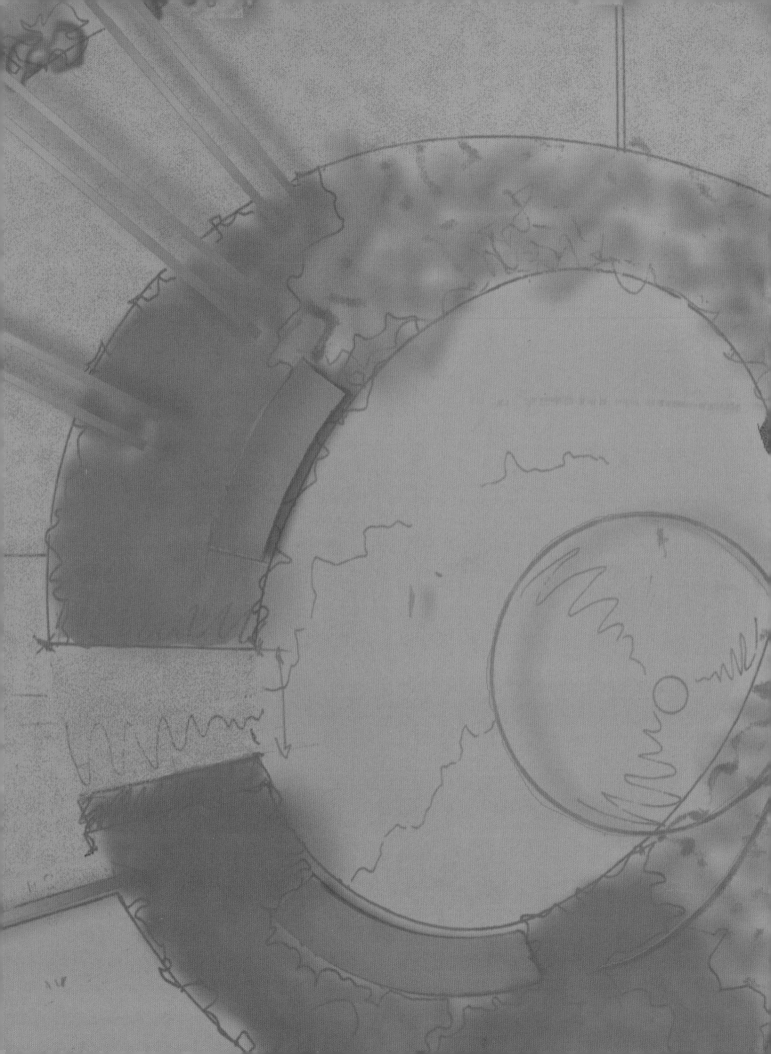

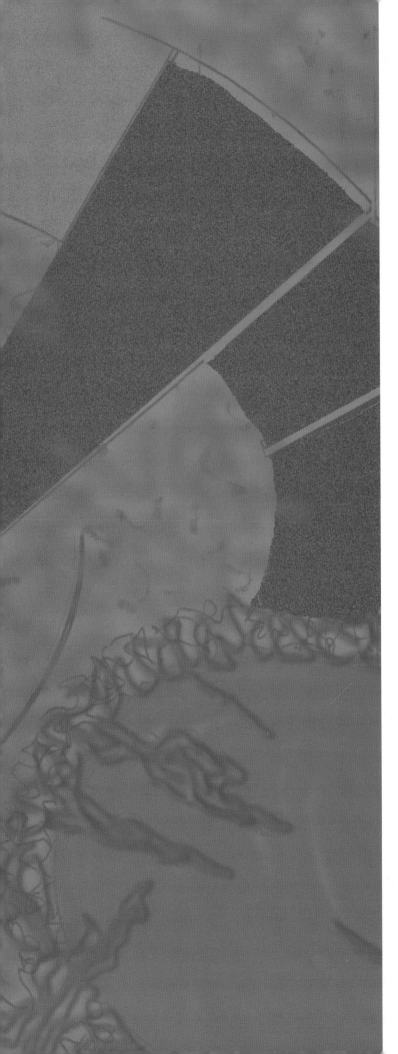

A range of gardens with an identifiable theme or concept has been included in this section. They vary in scale but illustrate imaginative and unusual design thinking, working with a less practical approach than most garden owners would be used to.

Many of these gardens have been created for shows and exhibitions in which it is important to innovate, communicate ideas powerfully and effectively, or utilize new technology. For many years the Chelsea Flower Show in London was the ultimate venue for designers, even though the bias of the show remains horticultural. More recently, design based shows or exhibitions have become much more prominent with ventures such as Chaumont in France or Jardins de Métis in Canada providing international showcases for contemporary design.

In the world of fashion, ideas conveyed on the catwalk eventually percolate into the high street. So with gardens, the designs featured in the major shows of the world eventually spread into the domestic scene. The gardens featured here demonstrate how ideas can be applied directly to the domestic garden, to stunning effect.

Vladimir Sitta's Fire Garden, which opens the section is one such scheme, using flames as a central element. The overall treatment of this town house garden in Sydney is simple, with planting acting as a dark backdrop to the lively fire dance.

Themed Gardens

"Fire Garden"

Vladimir Sitta/ Maren Parry

dimensions: **9 x 8.5m (30 x 28ft) courtyard only**
soil: **imported**
aspect: **west facing**
key features: **camphor lauer tree, building as backdrop**

The owner's brief was to provide something exciting and yet tranquil at the same time. The site was dominated by one large tree in the confined space, but otherwise there were no contraints placed upon the development of the plan.

Planting was confined to the perimeters of the space and a variety of hard materials incorporated to create dynamic interest at ground level. Split granite slabs were laid along radiating lines, together with a fire line of concealed gas jets which introduce a sense of high drama as dusk falls. Slates were laid around the base of the mature tree and the planting embraced it, helping to anchor it within the new plan. Within this deceptively understated scheme, a bronze egg on a white marble cross created another focal point, particularly when highlighted by flames from the fire line.

The planting was predominantly green and relied on texture and tone for its interest. Key plants included *Pleioblastus pygmeus*, *Chimonobambusa quadrangularis*, *Bambusa multiplex* 'Alphonse Karr', *Lomandra hystrix*, *Eustrephus latifolius*, *Shibataea kumasasa*, *Phyllostachys nigra*, *Osmanthus fragrans*, *Aspidistra elatior*, *Pandorea jasminoides* 'Lady Di', *Cissus rhombifolia*, and *Trachelospermum jasminoides*.

above *A daytime photograph of the Fire Garden highlights focal points, such as the bronze egg on a white marble cross, and the predominantly green planting. Granite slabs conceal a row of gas jets that spring into life after dark.*

right *The plan of the complete garden, together with a sketch depicting a vertical slate feature situated against a perimeter wall.*

below *At night the concealed fire line dominates the garden, highlighting nearby planting and the one large tree.*

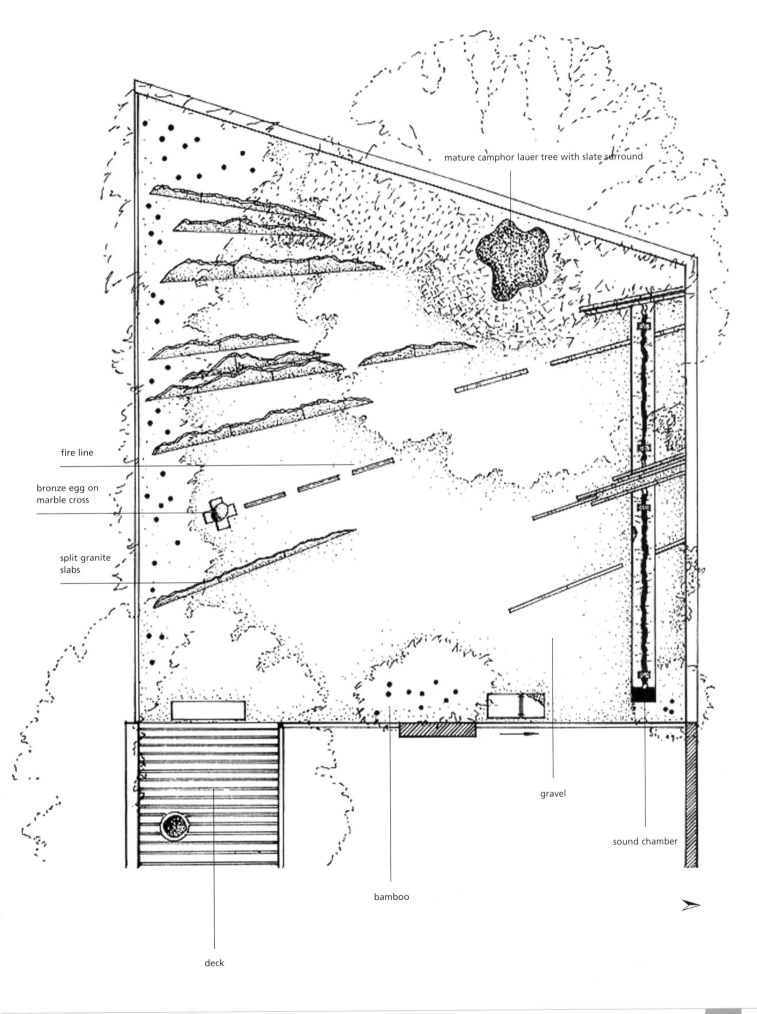

mature camphor lauer tree with slate surround

fire line

bronze egg on marble cross

split granite slabs

gravel

sound chamber

bamboo

deck

"The Peace Garden"

Arabella Lennox-Boyd

dimensions: **4000sq m (1 acre) approx**

soil: **London clay**

aspect: **northeast facing**

key features: **hedging, winding paths**

left *A double hedge of common hornbeam (*Carpinus betulus*) has been planted in the centre of "The Peace Garden". In this image hornbeam has been used in clipped hedge and pleached form.*

The brief for this garden, "The Peace Garden", at the Imperial War Museum, London, was to give an existing circular paved space a sense of belonging and context within the surrounding landscape of lawn and established trees. The concept was one of reflection inspired by "The Peace Garden"'s Himalayan roots. A cold environment at high altitudes limits the flora of the Himalayas, but plants such as birch trees thrive in these conditions. Several birch species were chosen for their striking bark, including *Betula ermanii* and *B. utilus* var. *jacquemontii*, and they were grouped in areas of long grass which allude to woodland. Mown grass and gravel paths wound through these groups. The size of each group was made up of sacred numbers important in Buddhism – 6, 7, 8, 12, 16, 21, 37, and 49.

Shelter, privacy, and a sense of inner sanctum was provided by a double hedge of hornbeam at the centre of the garden. The existing trellis structure within the hedges around this space was planted with climbing plants, and the existing beds replanted with shrubs and perennials to bring flowers into the garden.

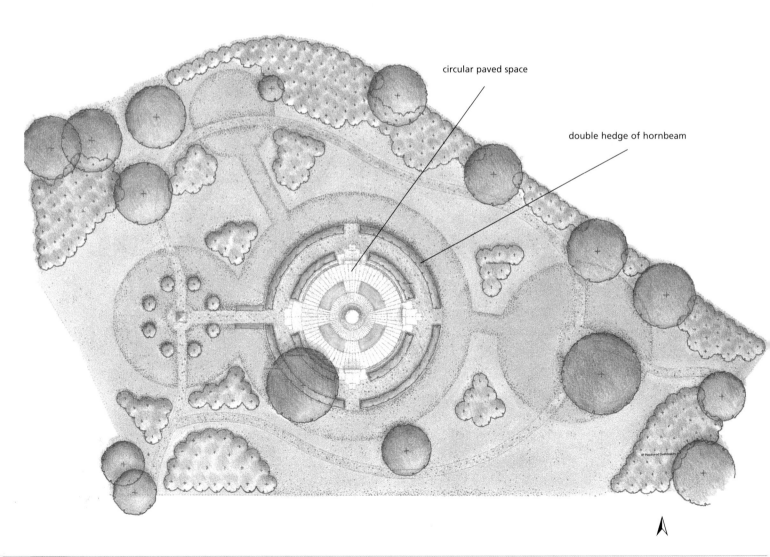

circular paved space

double hedge of hornbeam

Post Colonial Garden

Balmori Associates

dimensions: **125sq m (1344sq ft)**
soil: **n/a**
aspect: **north facing**
key features: **trellis, espalier wall, companion planting**

The sociable client uses the garden for frequent entertaining, but the space was very limited and had several changes of level. The garden is sandwiched between the house and the tall wall of an adjoining property. The driveway must also fit and function within this limited amount of space.

A single material, bluestone, was used for paving throughout the garden, dressed in a variety of stone patterns, textures and sizes. This helps delineate the various areas of the garden without visually distracting from the garden as a whole. Trellis was used to further carve up space in the garden, creating a series of rooms, and create a garden ceiling of sorts, supporting climbing plants.

Espaliered plants softened the blank face of the neighbour's wall. These walls were dimensioned in order to create interesting surfaces to train plants against, and introduce subtle perspective shifts. Perspective is further maximized by manipulating the depth of the borders so that they broaden towards the centre and taper at either end to create the illusion of a grander scale.

A companion planting strategy provided maximum diversity and variation within the garden. Thus, every plant had a seasonal, colour-coded companion alongside, and each pairing combined one culinary plant with an aesthetic counterpart for structure and a year round display. The aim, in this garden for entertaining, was to create a scheme for harvesting so that the produce might be given as gifts.

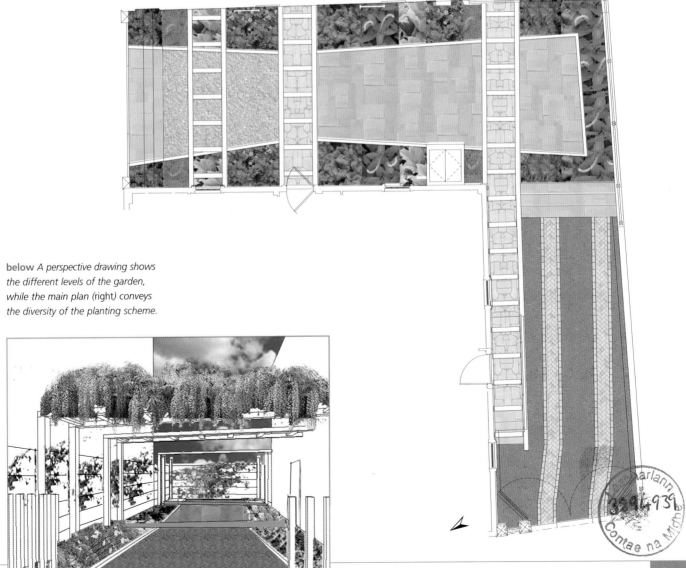

below *A perspective drawing shows the different levels of the garden, while the main plan (right) conveys the diversity of the planting scheme.*

left and below *A prominent aspect of this garden is the drift-style planting and flowing shape of the lawn. The garden plan conveys the stylish simplicity and gently flowing lines of this design. A staggered wall runs along the length of the garden.*

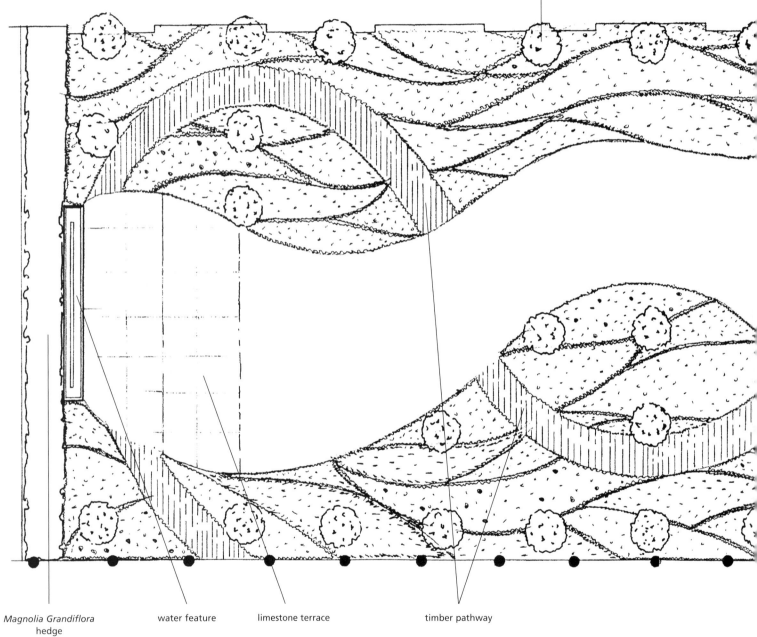

Carpinus betulus

Magnolia Grandiflora
hedge

water feature

limestone terrace

timber pathway

"Sanctuary Garden"

Woodhams Landscape

dimensions: **18 x 6m (59 x 20ft)**
soil: n/a
aspect: n/a (show garden)
key features: **water features, rendered wall**

This contemporary show garden was designed to be a peaceful and tranquil place, somewhere to relax and recharge the senses away from everyday life. Water was a key feature of the garden, as the source of life from which the plants grow. The water wall also added both dynamic visual appeal as well as sound to the top of the garden.

A geometric grid of *Carpinus betulus* combined with the clear, symmetrical lines of the limestone terrace area added form to the garden, and complemented the organic shape of the lawn and drift-style planting. The reflective pool on the limestone terrace contrasted the main water feature – the water was perfectly still and highlighted the tranquillity of the garden.

The backdrop for the garden was a *Magnolia grandiflora* hedge, which created the perfect focal point for the main water feature made from polished stainless steel. This feature had been designed with a glass disk that represents the sun, and when lit at night resembles the moon. The rendered wall that runs the length of the garden was staggered, giving movement and depth; it also provided additional shelter and allowed for prominent placement of the sculptures by Stephen Cox. Timber pathways leading through the trees allowed for easy maintenance of the planting areas, which were made up of grasses and rolling drifts of silvery mounds with burnt orange tulips pushing through them, providing a lush carpet of different textures and colours.

stepped out wall

limestone terrace

zinc lined reflective pool

right *The main water feature can be seen towards the back of the picture with a glass disk strategically placed so that it represents the sun during the daytime, and the moon after dark.*

Roof Terrace and Water Feature

Robert Myers – Elizabeth Banks Associates

dimensions: roof garden 20 x 2m (70 x 6ft)/water feature
3 x 1.8m (10 x 6ft)
soil: imported loam aspect: northeast facing
key features: "water table", pool/waterfall, pool

The owner's brief was to design two spaces within a residential development: an eye-catching water feature in the ground-level reception area, and a roof garden for outdoor dining and relaxation as an extension of a top floor penthouse apartment.

The roof garden (*see plan below*) was designed as a series of connected spaces, using timber decking, stone, water, and planting. At the north end of the terrace was a timber-decked "chill-out" zone. A gold-inlaid "water table" added water to the scene, and a shallow pool was crossed by stepping stones outside the study, leading to a dining area consisting of pre-cast concrete tables. The dining area was enclosed by pot plants and a fig tree trained against an adjacent wall. From here dramatic views over London were framed by a tree in

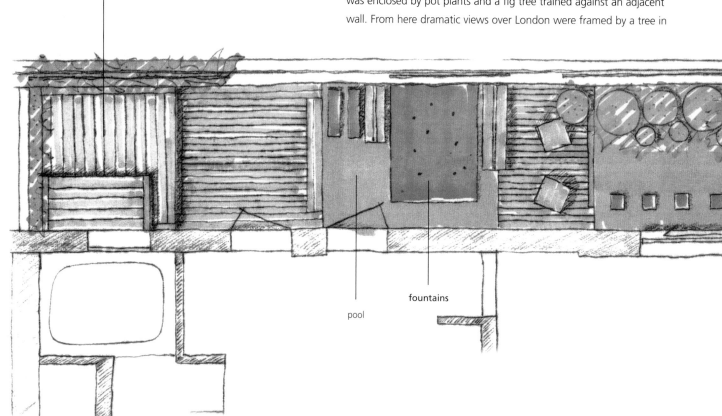

"chill out" zone

pool

fountains

right *The male fern (Dryopteris filix-mas) is one of several ferns growing in the raised beds that form part of the water feature.*

far right *With its strap-shaped, glossy fronds, the hart's tongue fern (Asplenium scolopendrium) contrasts sharply with the lance-shaped fronds of the male fern.*

a planter at the south end of the terrace. In the projecting bay of the living room was a private sunny spot, where a timber seat surrounded by planters created a space for quiet contemplation.

The design for the water feature created a stylised waterfall using granite blocks set against the back wall of the space. There was a shallow pool in front, while the rear wall was clad with granite planks, and the side walls were up-lit with recessed uplighters.

right *In the water feature bamboos and ferns grow in plant beds set alongside slate paddle stones in a shallow pool in front of an eye-catching waterfall.*

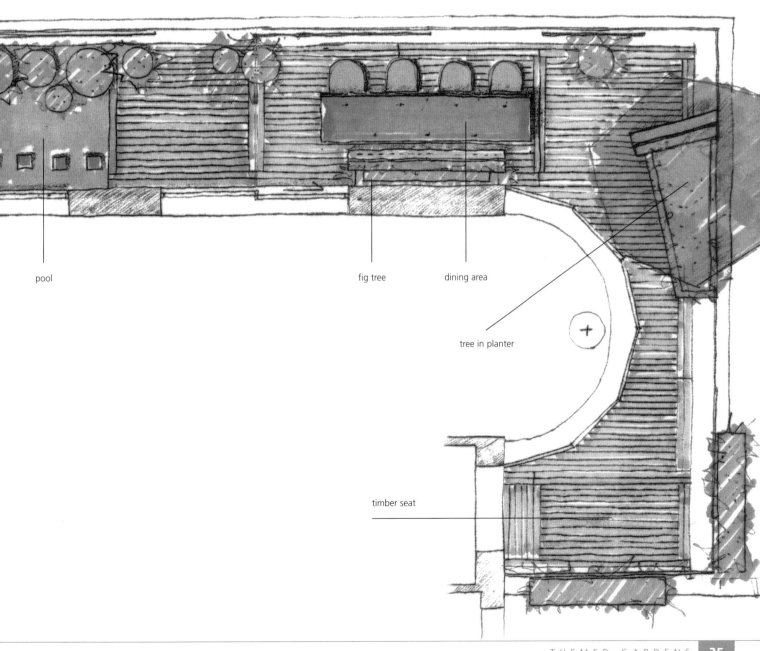

pool

fig tree

dining area

tree in planter

timber seat

"The Moon Garden"

Naila Green

dimensions: **11m (36ft) diameter**
soil: **chalky**
aspect: **south facing**
key features: **a steep slope with good views of the sea**

This garden is part of a tourist venue in Devon, southwest England, and the owners wanted a series of gardens to interest visitors. "The Moon Garden" is one of a number of garden rooms. Its evolution illustrated the point that not only is it fun to work with a theme but, because it restricts the materials and colours to be used, it can actually make the design process a lot simpler.

In keeping with the lunar theme, the hard landscaping was formed into circles and crescents and a combination of materials were selected for their colour and texture. The prevailing colour scheme of silver, grey, white, black, and blue determined the choice of materials which, where suitable, were sourced locally. This included the napped flint used for the high circular walls enclosing the garden. Circles of silver-grey pebblework were used to create walkways, surfaces for seating, steps, and an arched entrance to a grotto. The crescent pool was decorated with blue mosaic tiles in a design depicting the night sky at midnight on January 1, 2000.

Immediately behind the pool a raised bed followed the curve of the pool. Its front face was covered with a sheet of stainless steel, a material in keeping with the overall colour scheme but in contrast to the surrounding natural stone. Reflections, including the mosaic pool floor, were distorted by the curve creating an exciting effect.

Continuing the theme, the planting scheme was based on blue, silver and white plants, which in practical terms meant using foliage colour to provide a silver and glaucous base for white and blue flowers, including blue agapanthus and white lavender.

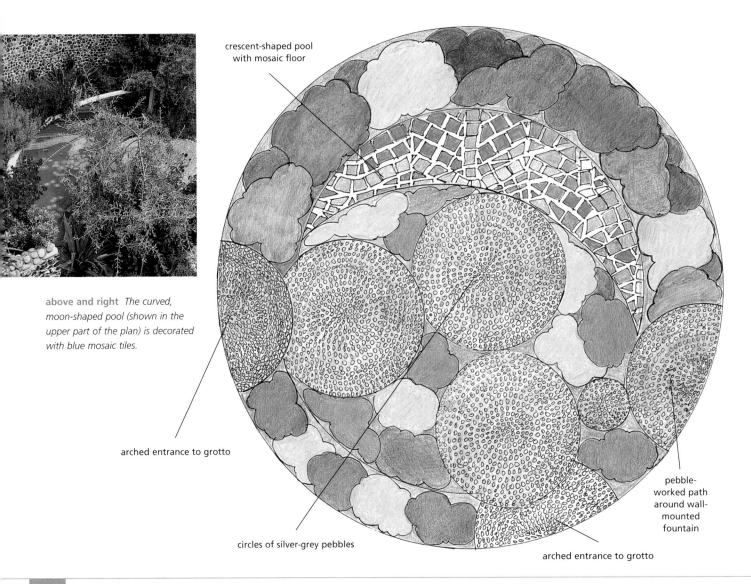

above and right *The curved, moon-shaped pool (shown in the upper part of the plan) is decorated with blue mosaic tiles.*

crescent-shaped pool with mosaic floor

arched entrance to grotto

circles of silver-grey pebbles

arched entrance to grotto

pebble-worked path around wall-mounted fountain

"Square Roots Garden"

Barbara Hunt – Hunt Design

dimensions: **12.5 x 12.5m (41 x 41ft)**
soil: **neutral/loam**
aspect: **south facing, entrance area in half-shade**
key features: **topiary, geometrically shaped pools**

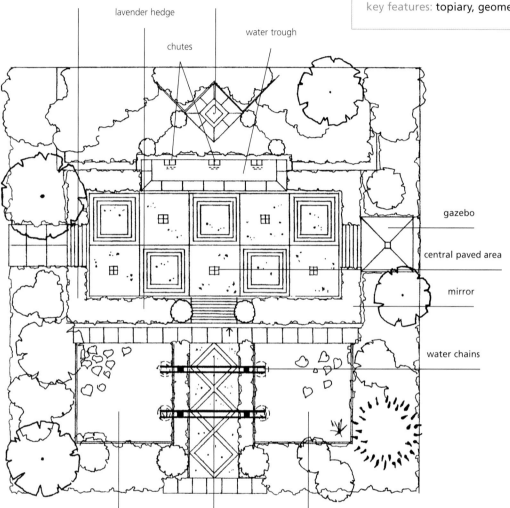

mirror

lavender hedge

fountain

chutes

water trough

gazebo

central paved area

mirror

water chains

pool   arch   pool

above In the "Square Roots Garden" the upright common hornbeam (Carpinus betulus 'Fastigiata') has been used as one of the garden's key plants.

The aim was to produce a formal garden in a contemporary style, on a low budget and using reclaimed and modern materials. The geometry of the square was the theme for this garden, which employs traditional elements of formal design, structured levels, topiary, geometrically shaped pools, and tromp l'oeil.

At the entrance, a path of linked squares of granite setts were laid on the diagonal to convey a feeling of movement, exerting a physical pull into the garden. Water trickled into the pools from stainless steel chains, suspended from the arch. The central area was surrounded by a lavender hedge. The paving comprised squares within squares, using a combination of reclaimed crushed concrete and blue "chocolate slab" stable pavers, each one divided into a grid of squares. The silvered cube fountain, made of glass-reinforced plastic (GRP) with an aluminium powder coating, positioned to provide a main focal point, was reflected in angled mirrors and thus appeared as four cubes rather than one. Water flowed over the cube and emerged from three chutes, in fact, old ridge tiles, into a long water trough, edged with reclaimed swimming pool copings. A timber substitute, made from recycled polystyrene, was used for the gazebo and arch.

Evergreens provided a solid base to the planting, which was essentially a foliage scheme, enlivened with silvers and lime greens. Key plants included *Magnolia grandiflora* 'Gallissonnière', *Lavandula angustifolia* 'Vera', *Phyllostachys aurea*, various hostas, and astilbes.

Experimental Show Garden

Bernard Trainor Design Associates

dimensions: **152sq m (500sq ft)**
soil: **n/a**
aspect: **n/a (show garden)**
key features: **corrugated steel and stucco walls**

This plan was for a show garden for the San Francisco Landscape Show and, as such, afforded an opportunity for experimentation in new territory. In trying to create a garden that didn't conform to typical designs, sustainable landscape issues, urban food production, and land art all influenced the development of the plan.

The hard elements of the garden brought together the use of corrugated steel and stucco walls painted in distinct, bright colours that "crash" together. Within this framework, the planting contributed another strong structural element, including architectural specimens, such as *Phormium* 'Dazzler'. Despite the constraints imposed by the dark building where the show was staged, which limited the selection of plants, the planting was experimental, bringing together diverse specimens, such as *Olea europaea* 'Manzanillo', *Centranthus ruber*, *Anigozanthus* species, and coastal meadow planting.

Seen as temporal art, landscape installations afforded an opportunity for experimentation. The designers set out to enlighten both themselves and the general public with these temporary installations. By trying new ideas, they were quenching their thirsty curiosity and perhaps creating models for future projects. These experiments have in fact led to new concepts in built landscapes. It has been interesting for the designers to see and hear the public's response to the installations. It can be a love-hate affair. However, like all of the arts, how else do you discover new concepts without dabbling in new directions? The designers recommend experimentation – you will make mistakes, but good things will eventually come from the bad.

left *The vibrant slabs of colour are intended to produce a sculptural but clashing effect, alongside which the planting plays a secondary role.*

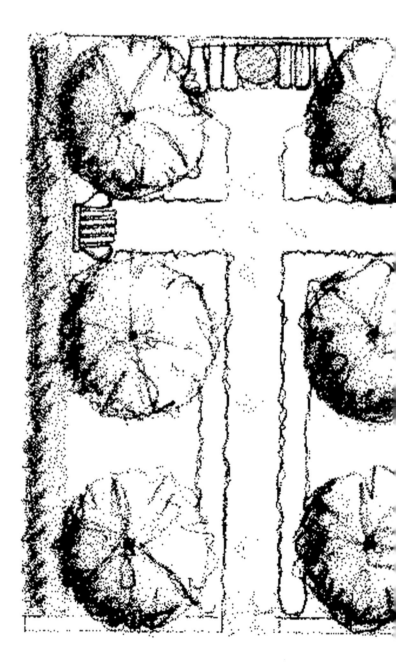

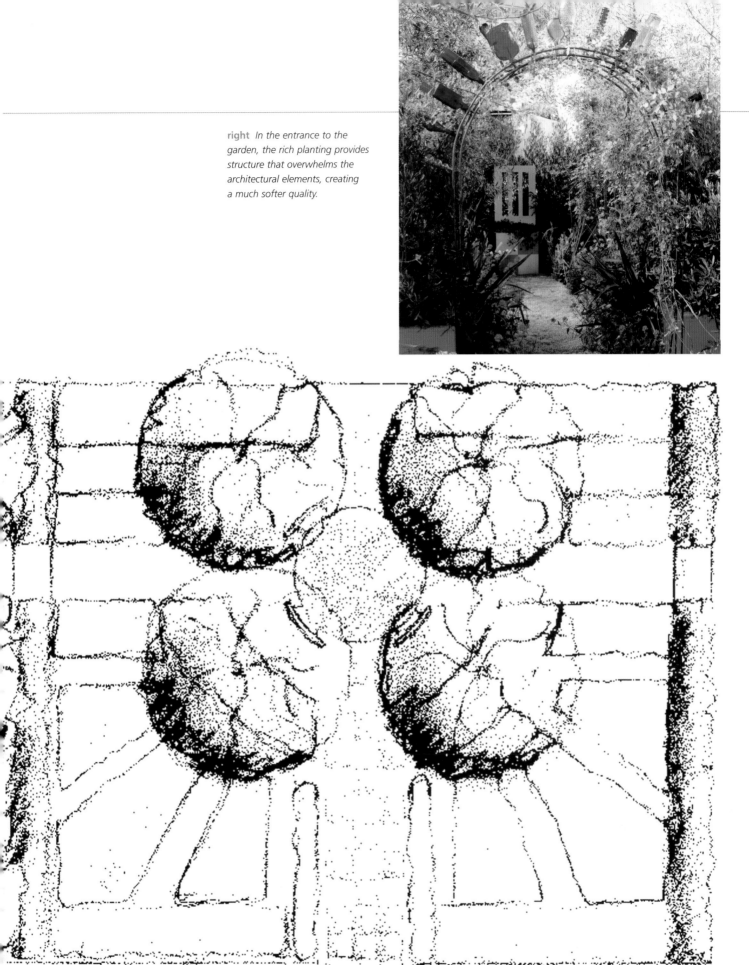

right *In the entrance to the garden, the rich planting provides structure that overwhelms the architectural elements, creating a much softer quality.*

"Millenium Garden"

Olin Partnership

dimensions: **22,500sq m (5.56 acres)**
soil: **imported soil**
aspect: **open**
key features: **ornamental grasses, native pairie plants**

right and below The "thumbnail" sketch (right) brings the design to life, and creates a sense of scale. The sectional elevation below shows the shallow soil depth over the roof.

This project was an invited competition to design a small portion of Millenium Park, to be constructed on top of a new underground car parking area and railway tracks in Chicago. The garden was conceived as a celebration of the culture and landscape of Chicago, conveyed in a collage of six interconnected gardens inspired by some of the city's cultural institutions. A large central space is flanked by intimate garden areas to the east and west.

This is a rooftop park and thus weight constraints had to be carefully observed. This affected the depth of soil which could be used over different parts of the roof, and in turn influenced the placement of rootballs for the large trees.

In the central "Grass and Sky Garden", the large open lawn and composition of ornamental grasses evoked the grassland prairie origins of the area and provided space for visitors to sit, relax, or play. Among the smaller gardens, the "Prairie Garden" was a stylized prairie scheme composed of various native prairie plants within a matrix of native grasses. In contrast to this naturalistic representation, the "Impressionist Garden" took its cue from the colourful Impressionist paintings in Chicago's famous Art Institute, which were echoed in specific colour combinations of ornamental plants.

While the garden was intended to be a unique place within the larger Millennium Park, its generous paths and spaces flowed effortlessly into adjacent areas. It was physically and visually connected to the park through a consistent use of paving and selected furnishings, and was connected to the larger context of the city through the particular garden themes, materials, and plants.

Reclamation Garden

Alistair Baldwin

dimensions: **8 x 8m (26 x 26ft)**
soil: **well-drained sandy loam**
aspect: **seating alcove faces due south**
key features: **pergola, seating alcove**

The garden was designed to bring together reclaimed architectural elements, laid out in crisp geometric shapes, and bold sweeps of grasses and perennials, taking their inspiration from patterns and rhythms found in nature. The result was a garden of changing views, where paths were concealed amongst the drifts of plants. Two structures provided spaces of different scales: the pergola for group socializing, and the seating alcove for more intimate occasions.

The reclaimed English oak pergola adjacent to the house was under-paved with cleaned, reclaimed Yorkshire stone. The seating alcove, also in reclaimed English oak, was topped with a dome of galvanized wire, threaded with worn blue beach glass. The paths were constructed using reclaimed steel treads from escalators, and the boundary fences were made from Victorian window frames, from which all the original glass has been removed, and the top row of panes replaced with blue glass.

The planting in this garden was designed to respond closely to the prevailing conditions, in order to minimize plant failure and maintenance. Key elements included three clumps of closely planted *Betula papyrifera*, clipped box balls, and *Yucca filamentosa*. This strong structural framework was complemented by a mixed planting, which included a selection of ornamental grasses, *Eryngium* x *tripartitum*, and *Euphorbia characias* subsp. *wulfenii*, together with fragrant *Perovskia atriplicifolia* 'Blue Spire', *Thymus vulgaris*, and *Salvia* x *superba*. Understated colour came from *Knautia macedonica*, *Verbena bonariensis*, and *Heuchera* 'Palace Purple'.

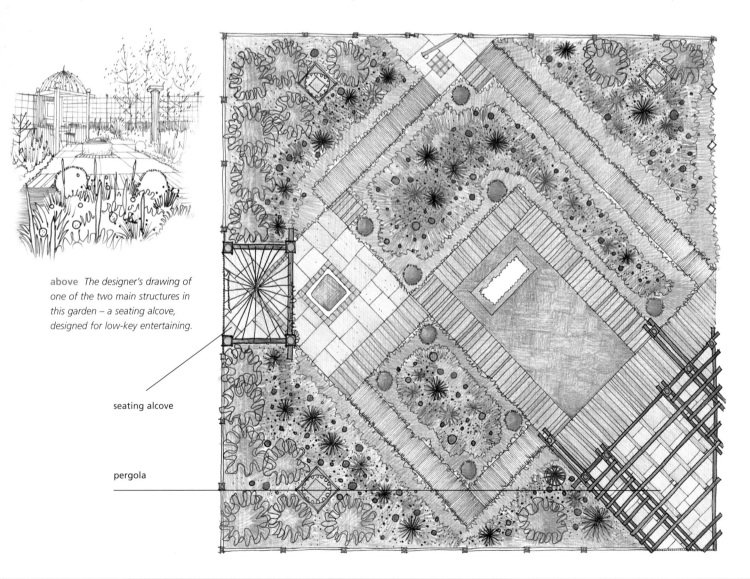

above *The designer's drawing of one of the two main structures in this garden – a seating alcove, designed for low-key entertaining.*

seating alcove

pergola

Julie Toll

dimensions: 8 x 9m (26 x 30ft)
soil: loam, free draining
aspect: southwest facing
key features: woven living hedge and arbor

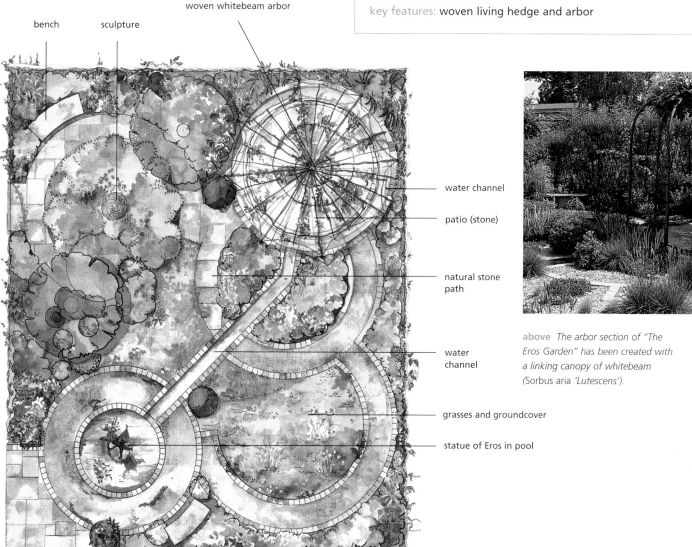

bench

sculpture

woven whitebeam arbor

water channel

patio (stone)

natural stone path

water channel

grasses and groundcover

statue of Eros in pool

above *The arbor section of "The Eros Garden" has been created with a linking canopy of whitebeam (Sorbus aria 'Lutescens').*

The aim was to create an enclosed, very green space with somewhere sheltered to sit, protected from overlooking upstairs windows. Water with sound and living structures were to be incorporated wherever possible.

A living hedge of woven willow, *Salix viminalis*, enclosed the garden. This was woven during the winter when the rods were set in the ground while still very flexible. It grows so vigorously that it has to be pruned two or three times a year, and thus is not an option for a low maintenance garden.

The arbor was created with whitebeam, *Sorbus aria* 'Lutescens', using trees trained when young so that they could be bent over and woven into an overhead canopy of linking branches. The structure

is maintained by spur pruning. For an extended season of interest, white wisteria is trained up each trunk, and again pruned regularly to avoid overwhelming the trees.

A water rill surrounded the terrace arbor and ran through the garden to a pond in the opposite corner. The water flowed over a series of little waterfalls giving a pleasing rippling sound. Other features included a woven willow globe placed within the planting, and a bold statue of Eros on a plinth above the pool, which recalls the famous London landmark in Piccadilly Circus.

Planting set in gravel replaced the lawn. Festuca, both gold and blue, thyme, white and pink thrift, and variegated sisyrinchium formed the backbone of the planting in the gravel.

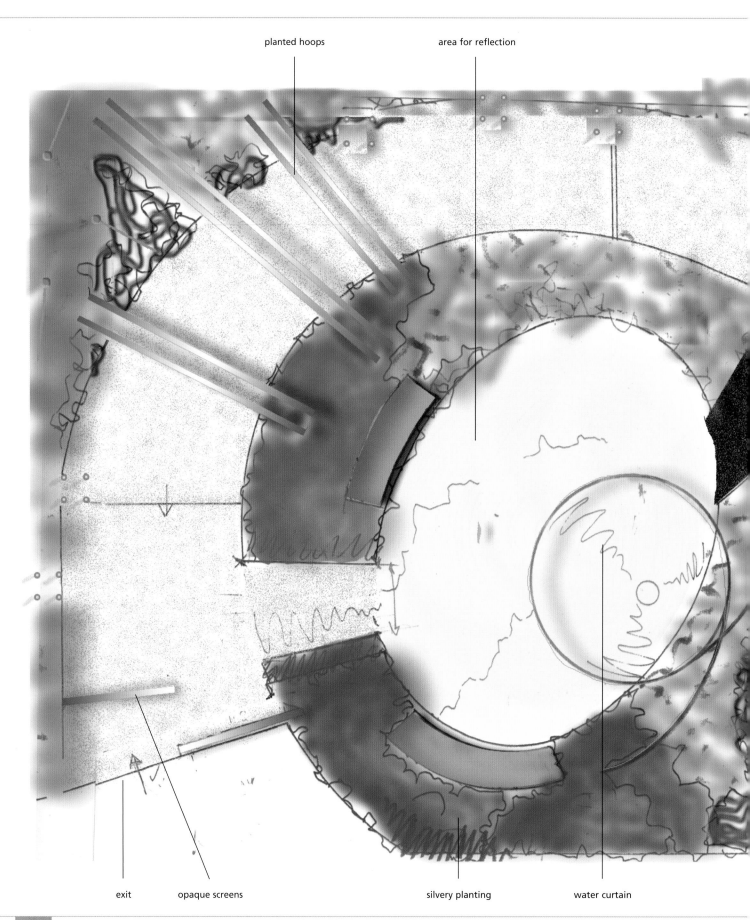

planted hoops

area for reflection

exit

opaque screens

silvery planting

water curtain

"Life's Journey Garden"

Julia Fogg/ David May

dimensions: **5 x 10m (16 x 33ft) approx.**
soil: **neutral and free draining**
aspect: **southwest facing**
key features: **water curtain, galvanized steel arches**

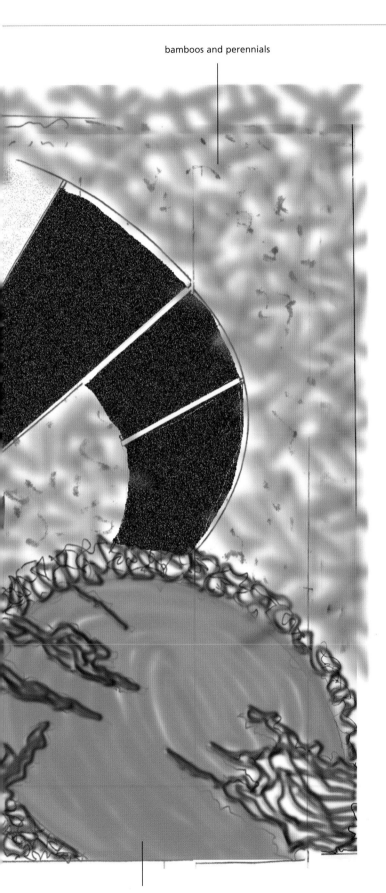

bamboos and perennials

entrance

This garden was conceived as an uplifting walk on a metaphorical journey through life, following a tightly spiralling pathway that conceals what lies ahead along much of the way. Although in fact a show garden, the design translated well in a domestic setting.

Hard landscaping materials throughout were predominantly industrial, including resin bonded surfaces, bound rubber granules, gravel chipping mulch, and steel edged steps. These contrasted strikingly with the various areas of dense planting. Three connecting pairs of arches, made out of galvanized steel hollow sectional tube, supported a selection of climbing plants, and the same material was used for poles which support a removeable set of colourful banners, which are intended to be changed to suit the season.

The use of bound rubber granules in the early sections of path created a colourful, bouncy surface that recalls the energy and enthusiasm of childhood. The surface became harder as the journey continued, but at the heart of the garden lay a hidden area for reflection, within which a water curtain created a feature which was simultaneously constant and continually changing. Here, predominantly silvery planting and sparkling textures were intended to recall a starry "Heaven on Earth", and comfortable benches encouraged visitors to sit and rest a while.

Opaque screens symbolized the end of this journey and the start of another, blocking the final outcome from view until the actual moment of departure from the garden.

right The connecting arches are made from galvanized steel tubes; the same material was used for the poles that support the removeable blue banners.

Jungle Area Garden

John Moreland

dimensions: **34 x 40m (112 x 131ft)**
soil: **neutral to acid**
aspect: **northeast facing, subject to cold easterly winds**
key features: **split level with jungle area**

This Cornish site has spectacular sea views, but its open aspect makes it susceptible to cold winds which can cause severe damage to plants in early spring. The rear garden is on two levels running behind a recently built house, and the plan evolved to incorporate an upper "laid-out" lawn area from which granite steps led to a lower "jungle area", and a gravel play beach was created for the owners' seven-year-old daughter.

An existing hexagonal summerhouse was relocated to integrate it into the planting. A custom-made playhouse in the play beach and duck boards across gravel were all stained dark teak to match both summerhouse and decking areas, which in turn echo the colour of the doors and windows of the house. The decking was beautifully made by local craftsmen and a "floating" bench seat was designed to prevent people from falling over its edges, while giving a lighter, less restraining feel than a standard balustrade.

The existing mixed hedge of x *Cupressocyparis leylandii* and fuchsia was reduced in height to open up the sea views. Planting on the upper level was dominated by evergreen foliage, including *Viburnum tinus*, cortaderia, cordyline and phormiums, plus *Fuchsia magellanica* 'Versicolor', *Lavandula* 'Vera', *Rosmarinus officinalis* 'Miss Jessop's' and *Perovskia atriplicifolia*. The lower "jungle" area had existing clumps of phormium, cordyline and purple-leaved cannas, kniphofias in profusion, *Eriobotrya japonica*, *Agapanthus* 'Purple Cloud', as well as drifts of Kaffir lilies (*Schizostylis coccinea*).

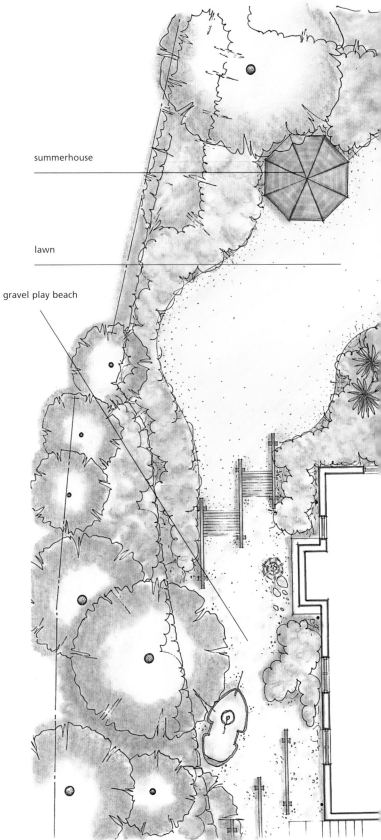

summerhouse

lawn

gravel play beach

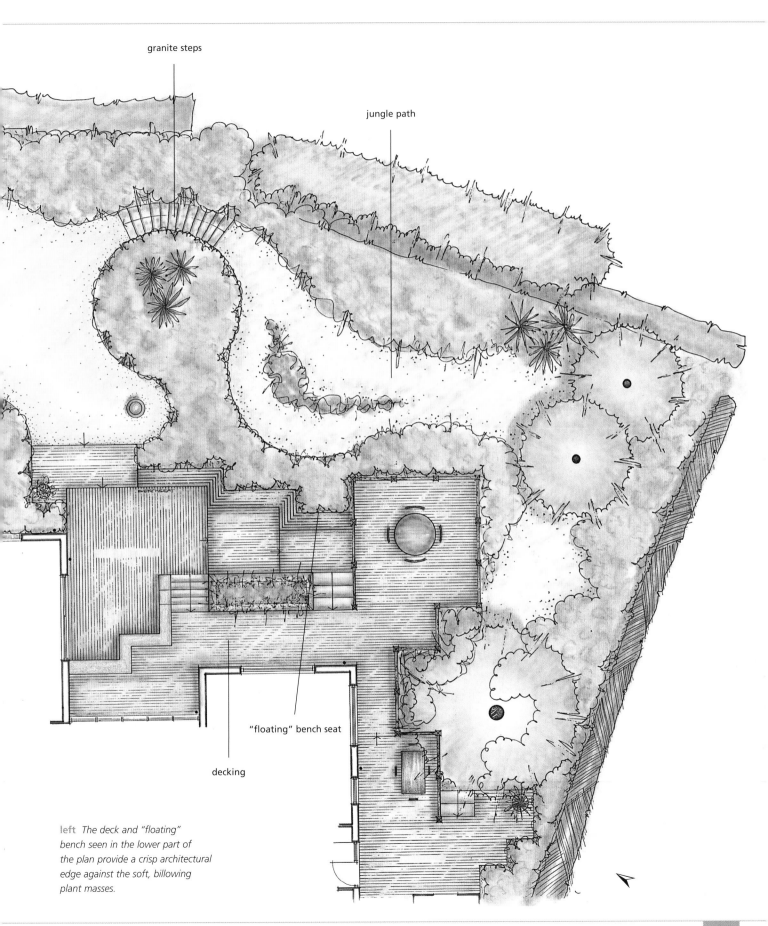

granite steps

jungle path

"floating" bench seat

decking

left *The deck and "floating" bench seen in the lower part of the plan provide a crisp architectural edge against the soft, billowing plant masses.*

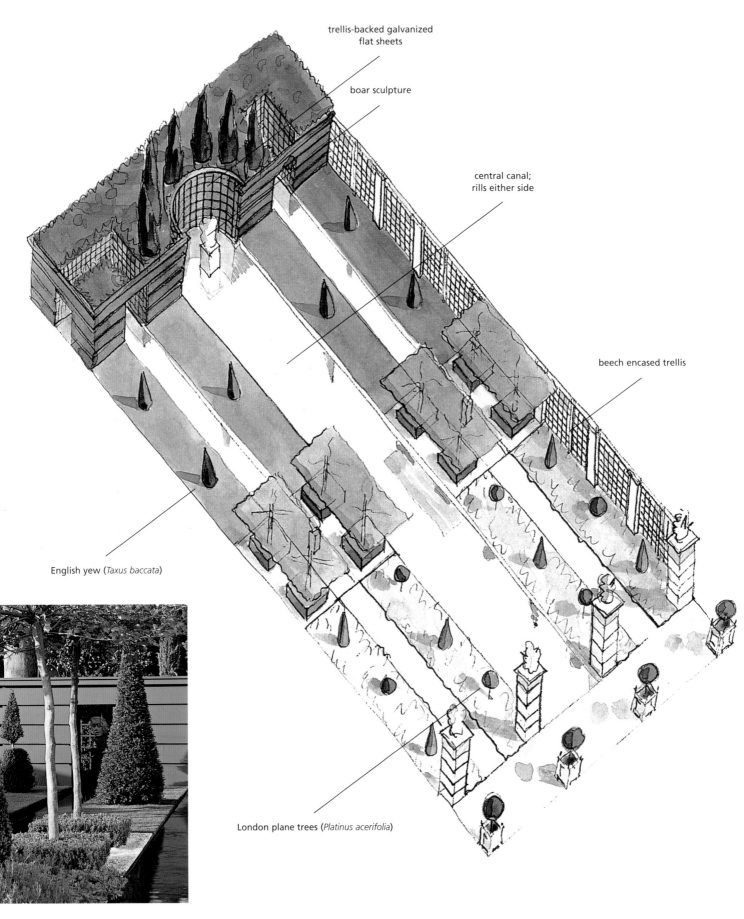

trellis-backed galvanized
flat sheets

boar sculpture

central canal;
rills either side

beech encased trellis

English yew (*Taxus baccata*)

London plane trees (*Platinus acerifolia*)

above and right *The axonometric drawing provides a clear three-dimensional image of the entire garden and its structural qualities.*

"Sculpture Garden"

George Carter Garden Design

dimensions: **26 x 11m (85 x36ft)**
soil: **good garden loam, neutral**
aspect: **n/a (show garden)**
key features: **piers with sculptures, galvanized steel screen**

As a show garden the brief came from the sponsors, Christie's Fine Art Auctioneers, who requested a garden to show off to advantage a number of contemporary pieces of sculpture as if in a collector's garden. The garden itself should also have a sculptural element created by the volumes and voids of the planting.

As a show garden it was designed to be viewed primarily from one viewpoint – however, this is precisely the principle behind the design of most enclosed town gardens. Consequently, the plan would work in reality with little modification.

The main features of the garden were the three canals which were constructed with black liners to increase the reflective quality of the water. In the foreground, four large rusticated piers supported four metal sculptures symbolic of different types of weather. Paths and terraces were constructed in Cotswold chipping gravel contained within timber boarding. At the southern edge of the site a galvanized steel and trellis screen had the effect of visually dissolving the boundary since it had a reflective surface.

The main structure planting consisted of a backdrop of English yew encased in trellis. In the middle distance, eight umbrella-trained London plane trees created an above-head height frame to the scene, and were underplanted with box cubes. In the foreground, four beds of grey and silver mixed herbaceous planting were accented with topiary specimens in box and *Phillyrea latifolia*. The majority of the structure planting was evergreen.

left *Reflective pools almost brim over, producing planting that seems to float on the surface of the water.*

above *A dramatic boar sculpture dominates the garden's central axis in which the reflective canal plays a pivotal role.*

"No Strings Attached"

Bonita Bulaitis

dimensions: **10 x 20m (33 x 66ft)**
soil: **moisture retentive but free draining**
aspect: **open, sunny**
key features: **raised square structure, polished wood bench**

This show garden was intended to explore the interplay of light and shade, contrast and illusion, creating a space to experience. Approaching the garden, a mass of linear grasses stood against the erect forms of grid-positioned fastigiate trees. A white, enclosed square structure set within the heart of the garden was already apparent. Upon entering the garden, the black stone gravel route widened and led the visitor towards this square, and a stream of red daylillies (*Hemerocallis*) began its journey through the space. The strong line of a polished wood bench penetrated into the square, and contrasted with adjacent textures.

Raised from the ground to create a light and floating effect, the structure revealed itself to be wound with string, the quality of which was lit up by sunlight. The density of the wrapping prevented a clear view through to the internal space, but on entering the visitor discovered mirrors mounted on steel rods to reflect light. Three mirrors hovered among the grass planting behind the bench. In sections, the strings were wound less closely to allow glimpses of the planting – the *Hemerocallis* is partially visible – and views beyond.

In addition to the stream of red *Hemerocallis*, the planting throughout relied on bold blocks of a limited number of specimens. These included the ornamental grasses *Deschampsia cespitosa* 'Goldtau', *Calamagrostis* x *acutiflora* 'Karl Foerster', *Miscanthus sinensis*, and *Molinia caerulea* 'Windspiel'. In addition, bold clumps of *Buxus sempervirens* were used for year-round structure.

left *This show garden, called "No Strings Attached", was created at the Jardins de Métis, in Quebec, Canada.*

red daylillies
(*Hemerocallis*)

mass grass planting

shallow "bo
with acry

right and far right *Two views of
this innovative show garden show
the exterior and interior of the
luminous white, enclosed square
structure. The garden's name comes
from the strings that are wound
round the inner structure.*

"coloured" polished
timber bench passes
under "string"

mass grass planting

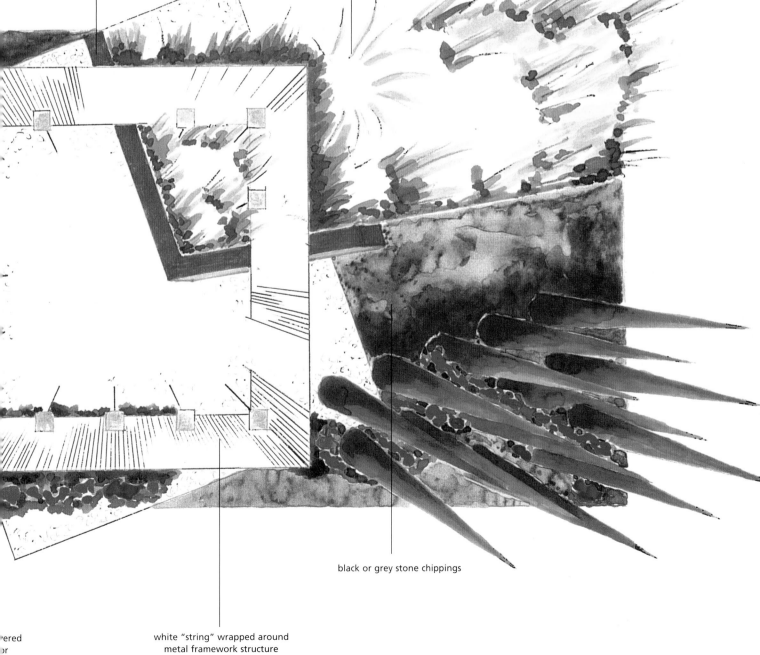

black or grey stone chippings

ered
or

white "string" wrapped around
metal framework structure

A Garden for Work and Pleasure

Andrew Wilson – Pockett Wilson Garden Design

dimensions: **10 x 8m (30 x 24ft) approx.**

soil: **neutral**

aspect: **n/a (show garden)**

key features: **terrace with "bed", screening wall**

The brief was to create a contemporary home office and garden – a space that could be used for both work and pleasure. The links between the interior and exterior spaces were important. The main constraints affecting the garden were its size, and the fact that it would have been viewed from three sides as an exhibition installation for the Chelsea Flower Show.

A small conservatory office space opened onto the garden, which had a main terrace, pool, and bed for lounging. Colours were muted to grey and grey-green shades in both hard and soft materials. A stainless steel free-form sculpture reflected into the pool.

Steel beams emerged from the suspended conservatory to frame views and surround a life-size figurative sculpture. A screening wall provided a frame for the garden against which planting was displayed. This was rendered and painted a pale grey-green, similar to the verdigris patina on oxidized copper, a neutral tone which provides an excellent foil for foliage textures.

Stainless steel was used as a detail to reflect light during the day and to be lit after dark, creating interesting reflections in the pool and shadows across the paving. The main paved terrace curved upwards at one end to create a "bed", which could be made up with cushions and mattresses on warmer evenings.

Planting schemes stuck to the same soft tones as the hard elements, combining grasses with perennials, such as verbascums and phormiums, and *Eucalyptus gunnii* for height and colour.

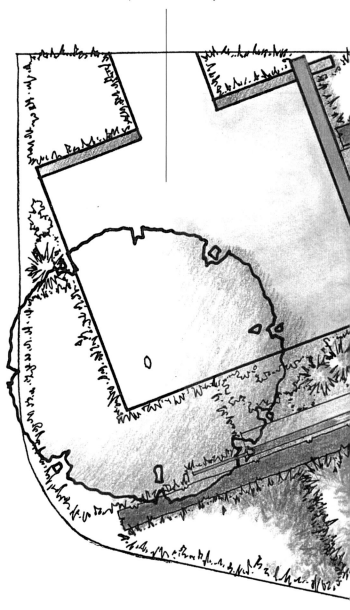

suspended conservatory

left *This perspective complements the garden plan by showing the scale of the various plants and key structures.*

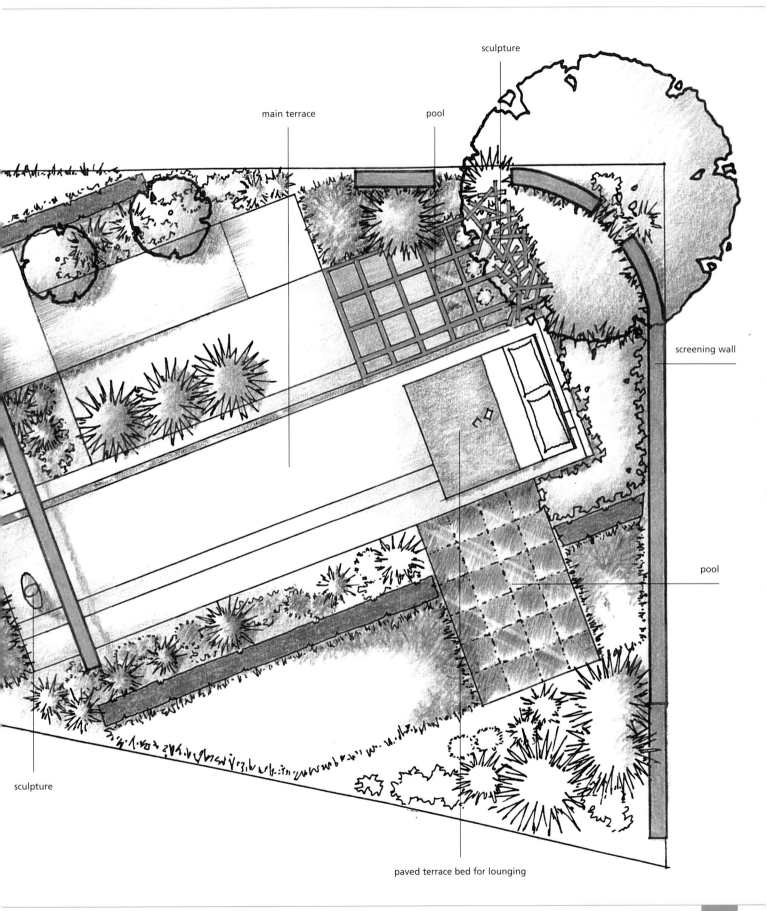

sculpture

main terrace

pool

screening wall

pool

sculpture

paved terrace bed for lounging

With the increasing trend for urban living a new kind of garden has developed. Often small in scale with enclosing boundaries and a lack of privacy, these gardens have become peaceful havens in our frantic towns and cities.

Historically, urban gardens borrowed from their country cousins, usually filled with scented plants and aiming to be green and even romantic. During the twentieth century, however, these gardens took on a new character that was smart, elegant, and theatrical. Lighting technology has been exploited in these restricted spaces to create dramatic backdrops, and roof gardens in particular have produced sensational links to the urban landscape.

With a completely man-made context almost anything goes in the urban garden, and hard materials have dominated. Contemporary garden designers have revelled in this architectural approach, creating sophisticated spaces decorated with fine materials, glass, water, and, often, vivid colour.

The celebrated American designer, Bernard Trainor, opens this section with a Californian town garden. The integrative American approach, relating house and garden together, can be seen in this elegant design that wraps around the house, creating variety and interest in a restricted and often awkward space.

Urban Gardens

Dry-Climate Garden

Bernard Trainor Design Associates

dimensions: **4876sq m (1 acre)**
soil: **clay**
aspect: **mostly full sun**
key features: **swimming pool, bocce court**

This garden was designed to reflect the owners' distinctive lifestyle. Combined with the unusual planting themes are several main features, such as a swimming pool, a bocce court, and curvaceous concrete walls. The contemporary outdoor dining courtyard showcased a large collection of edible plants, while the swimming pool garden boasted a Frank Morbillo sculpture, succulents, and tall ornamental grasses. The garden was transformed from a high maintenance, high-resource space to a specifically dry-climate garden that requires little supplemental water and no chemicals in its maintenance, and it provided a wonderful refuge from the busy streets of the Silicon Valley in Palo Alto, California.

Some plants from the old garden were retained, including yuccas, fig, oak, and pineapple guava. Water features, planting, and paving ideas were drawn from climate areas similar to this part of California, including South Africa, Australia, and the Mediterranean.

The owner wanted several distinct areas around the house. The outdoor dining courtyard was a natural extension of the kitchen. It featured a steel table on a concrete base, low concrete benches, a persimmon tree, and a large collection of edible plants. Besides this edible garden, a large pot fountain attracted hummingbirds, and introduced the soothing sound of trickling water. Behind the house was a charming covered outdoor room with upholstered benches, tables, artwork, and Indonesian influences.

The pool area was spacious and inviting. It featured succulents, tall ornamental grasses, and fragrant herbs, such as oregano, bronze fennel, hummingbird mint (*Agastache*), lemon balm, and lemon thyme.

curved concrete walls

bocce court

left *Succulents, herbs, and ornamental grasses soften the area around the swimming pool in this Californian garden.*

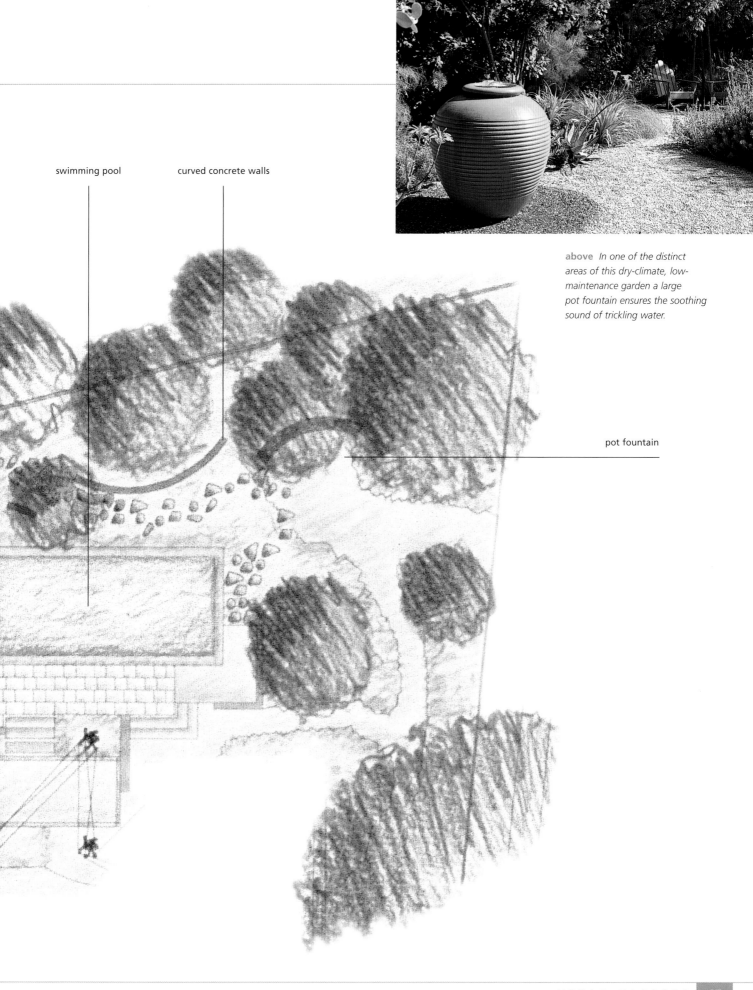

swimming pool　　　curved concrete walls

pot fountain

above *In one of the distinct areas of this dry-climate, low-maintenance garden a large pot fountain ensures the soothing sound of trickling water.*

Meditative Garden

Acres Wild

dimensions: **5.4 x 15.5m (18 x 51ft) including studio**
soil: **clay**
aspect: **southwest facing**
key features: **split level, oriental planting theme**

The brief was to create a cool, contemporary and meditative garden for a busy professional couple with a young child, providing access to, and a setting for, a garden studio. Practical problems included overlooking neighbours and a significant change of level.

To create a sense of urban calm, functional and flexible spaces were created on both levels for entertainment, play, and contemplation, enclosed within luxuriant and sculptural planting. A strong plan was essential as the garden could be seen from above, both from a first floor deck and from upper stories of the house. However, a strong elevation was equally important as the garden was also seen through full height and width glazed doors, and windows on the lower level. Light, airy verticals of birch and bamboo provided height and partial screening, while specimen

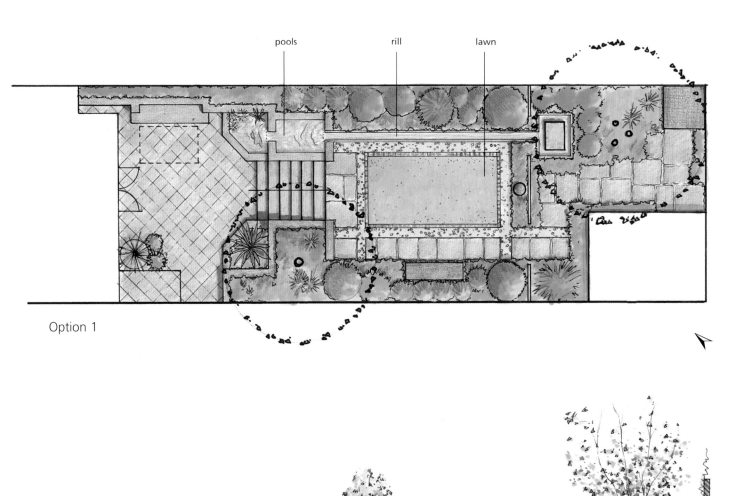

pools   rill   lawn

Option 1

above and right This plan and side elevation gradually evolved into the final garden as shown on the opposite page.

side elevation

plants and a basalt water feature provided focal points, with clipped box to provide a link between architecture, hard landscape, and plants.

The planting had a generally oriental theme, softening sculptural elements with grasses and perennials for movement and seasonal change. Dusky bronze shades were lifted with touches of bright green. Key plants included *Betula utilis* var. *jacquemontii*, *Acer palmatum* 'Bloodgood', *Phormium tenax* 'Purpureum', *Phyllostachys nigra*, *Astelia* 'Silver Spear', and *Buxus sempervirens* (cloud-pruned beneath the acer and clipped into box shapes to "support" the basalt cube). Groundcover between stepping stones and slate squares was provided by spreading *Soleirolia solerolii*.

Throughout, a limited range of colours and materials and a strong overall theme were used to unify this small space.

timber deck   steps   water feature   birch

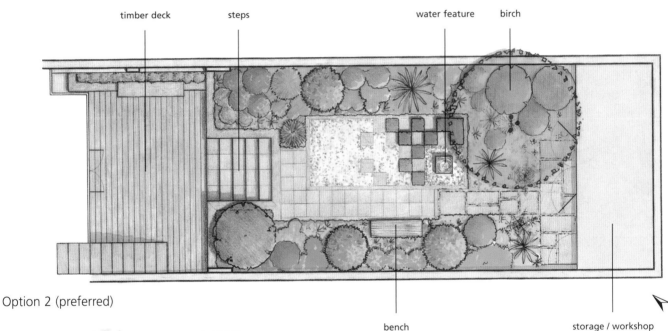

Option 2 (preferred)

bench   storage / workshop

left and above *This designer's drawing looks from the decking at the front of the garden (on the left of the plan) towards the back fence.*

top *Key planting included a variety of Japanese maple (Acer palmatum). This specimen is shown in its autumn colours.*

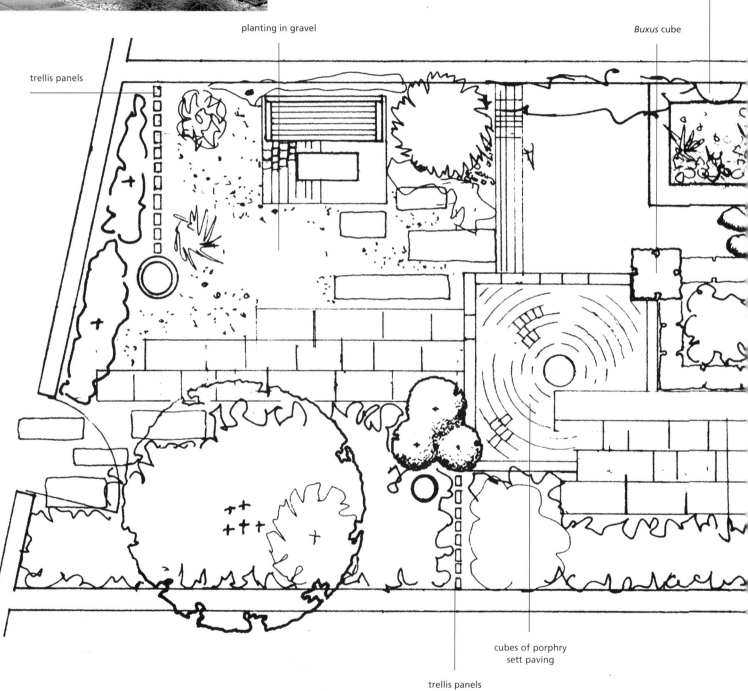

left *As this garden is by the sea it was necessary to select plants that could cope with salt air. For this reason the box hedging has now been replaced with santolina.*

water feature

planting in gravel

Buxus cube

trellis panels

cubes of porphry
sett paving

trellis panels

A Weekend Garden

Julie Toll

dimensions: **9 x 5m (30 x 16ft)**
soil: **well-drained sandy loam**
aspect: **south facing**
key features: **seaside planting, water feature**

This garden was intended as a low-maintenance garden for a single woman living in the house only at weekends. The design was to include space for entertaining, a water feature, and lighting.

Despite its town location, the garden is across the road from the sea and surrounded by walls so the salt air eddies around it. Consequently, plants had to be carefully selected to withstand these conditions. The aim was to provide plenty of soft planting in the beds and gravel areas to give seasonal colour, scent, and interest. Clipped box forms acted as accents, while bamboos, a santolina hedge, evergreen climbers, and multi-stemmed *Amelanchier spicata* provided the structure necessary to reinforce the hard landscaping.

Donegal quartzite paving was laid in linear bands running down the garden to increase the impression of length, ending randomly in water-washed pebbles and a central circle of porphyry setts to retain the desired sense of softness. Reclaimed granite kerbstones set in the pebbles acted as stepping stones to a garden bench in the small second room. Timber baton trellis panels, painted dark blue-green, also helped to delineate different spaces within the garden. A shelf and batons in the same design and colour are fixed on a high neighbouring wall as a means of minimizing its impact, with empty pots and other objects placed on the shelves.

An existing raised bed was converted into a reservoir for the wall-mounted snake design water feature. This was waterproofed, using a bituminous coating on the walls. Boulders softened the front edge and ran into the pebbles, while plants clothed the wall behind.

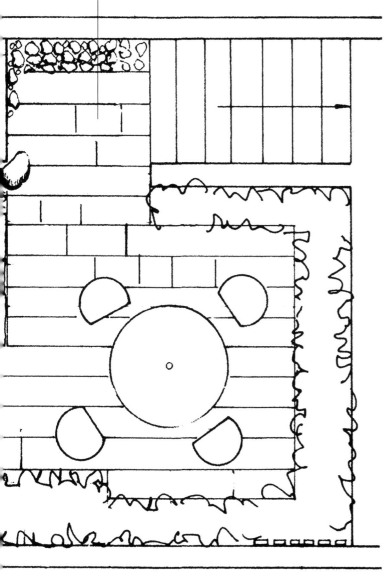

Donegal quartzite paving

right *Even in the most low-maintenance garden it is vital to include key features – here, a wall-mounted water feature.*

An Architectural Garden

Annie Guilfoyle, Creative Landscapes

dimensions: 14.5 x 11.5m (48 x 38ft)
soil: compacted clay with neutral pH
aspect: northeast facing
key features: curved walls, decking area, screening

The design for this garden was to be minimalist, bold, and contemporary, and it needed to work well with the alterations and new additions to the existing late Victorian house. The house had undergone extensive renovations but still kept its original Victorian features, although a "floating glass box" breakfast room extension with no visible support would greatly influence the garden design.

The owners entertained regularly and needed plenty of space for eating and socializing outside, but the garden also had to meet the needs of their two children and one cat. The owners love modern art and sculpture and wanted the garden to have a sculptural quality. The plants were to be simple and architectural. Relatively low maintenance and an irrigation system was requested. Screening from the neighbours was also a key issue.

Key features included a large curved rendered wall, which houses a water feature, and a decking area surrounded by water which echoes the glass box as it also appeared to float. This decking was made from pressure treated softwood, and the paving from replica York stone cut into lengths laid to echo the decking.

Evergreen screening was provided by a hedge of *Magnolia grandiflora*, with structural planting including *Buxus sempervirens*, *Elaeagnus* x *ebbingei*, *Cordyline australis*, *Phyllostachys nigra*, *Trachycarpus fortunei*, *Phormium tenax*, *Pseudosasa metake*, *Garrya elliptica*, *Fatsia japonica*, *Olea europaea*, and *Choisya ternata*. Other feature plants were *Dicksonia antarctica*, *Hydrangea quercifolia*, and *Amelanchier lamarckii*.

above *Stuctural planting in this garden included a serviceberry (Amelanchier lamarckii), a shrub or small tree with dramatic orange and red autumn colour.*

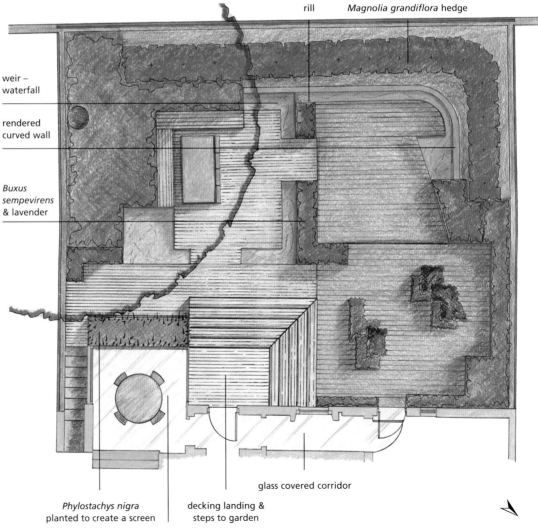

rill   *Magnolia grandiflora* hedge

weir – waterfall

rendered curved wall

Buxus sempevirens & lavender

glass covered corridor

Phylostachys nigra planted to create a screen

decking landing & steps to garden

"glass box" – breakfast room

Formal Lawn to Jungle Walk

Andrew Fisher Tomlin

dimensions: **15m x 14.5m (49ft x 48ft) plus existing terrace**
soil: **neutral loam**
aspect: **southeast facing**
key features: **central firepit, jungle walkway**

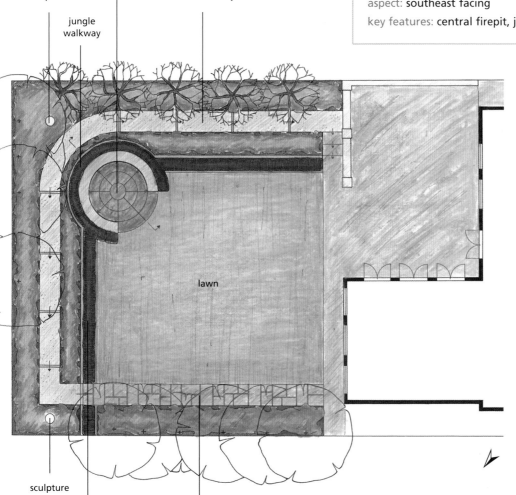

slate circle
with central fire pit

sculpture

jungle
walkway

secret walkway

lawn

sculpture

yew boundary   Indian sandstone path

above *One of the most popular plants in recent years for a "jungle" effect is the soft tree fern (Dicksonia antarctica), which can be grown outside in mild climates.*

The owners wanted a distinctive "green" garden with lots of foliage, both formal and "jungly", with strong structural elements within a low-maintenance plan.

The garden was positioned on a slope from the left-hand side of the house down to the right-hand bottom corner, so the ground had to be substantially built up to provide a level lawn which was surrounded by yew hedging. An unusual secret walkway was created around this raised level.

The new plan is dominated by a simple lawn with yew boundary, focussing on a slate circle incorporating a green oak seat with central firepit and circle of lights. In contrast to this controlled formality, there is a jungle walkway on the lower level.

There was considerable soil movement in the garden to accommodate the new levels in the design. Topsoil was bought in to infill, and the walling to the edge of the yew hedging took considerable time. The most important element was to raise the level to that of the existing terrace so that children could run straight out on to the lawn.

The planting emphasizes the different characters of the two different levels. In the jungle area, various tree ferns, bamboos, *Phormium purpurea*, and *Fatsia japonica* create the desired effect. The formal lawn is delineated by a hedge of clipped yew, *Taxus baccata*, while planting elsewhere is softer, including *Allium christophii*, *Anemone* 'Honorine Jobert', and *Crocosmia* 'Solfatare'.

Concrete Garden

Balston & Co

dimensions: **600sq m (1969sq ft)**
soil: **imported neutral topsoil**
aspect: **south facing**
key features: **circular lawn, concrete pergolas, canal**

The owners required a garden to empathize with a new, largely reinforced concrete house of bold modern design with remarkable interpenetration of internal and external space. The scheme was designed to extend this architecture to the boundaries, incorporating water and an interesting horticultural palette. The one real practical constraint was a strong slope from the north down to the south.

Key features included a circular lawn with curved borders and a large sculpture. In addition, there were pierced concrete walls, concrete pergolas, and a canal with stepped changes in level.

The house was framed on the street front with *Catalpa bignonioides* and a group of *Gingko biloba*. In between, dividing the garage area from the main entrance, is the rarer *Aesculus flava*. At the rear of the property the planting was dominated by an existing lime. New pears and apples picked up the old orchard feeling of this part of St Cloud, outer Paris. Closer to the house, in a key location was placed an *Acer platanoides* 'Drummondii'. Free-standing thuyas were proposed for the sides to give much needed privacy, and at the bottom of the site were a double rank of Chinese junipers. Around the circular lawn and on the upper terrace were mixed shrub and herbaceous borders. By the house, climbers contrasted with the precise lines of the beautifully executed concretework.

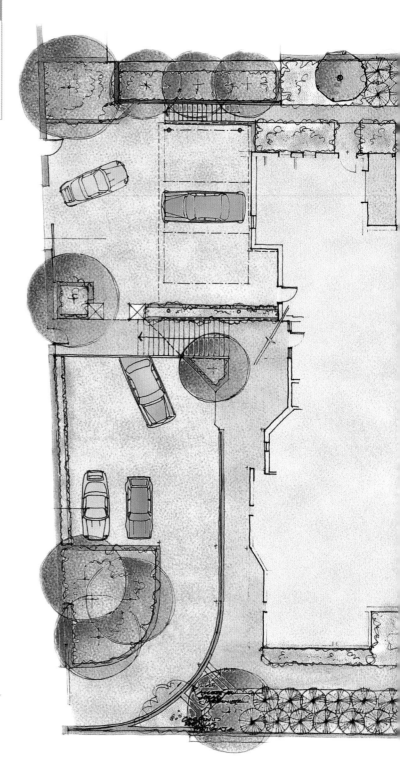

left *This axonometric provides a clear view of the complex level changes within the garden. The contrast between planting and structural elements can also be understood.*

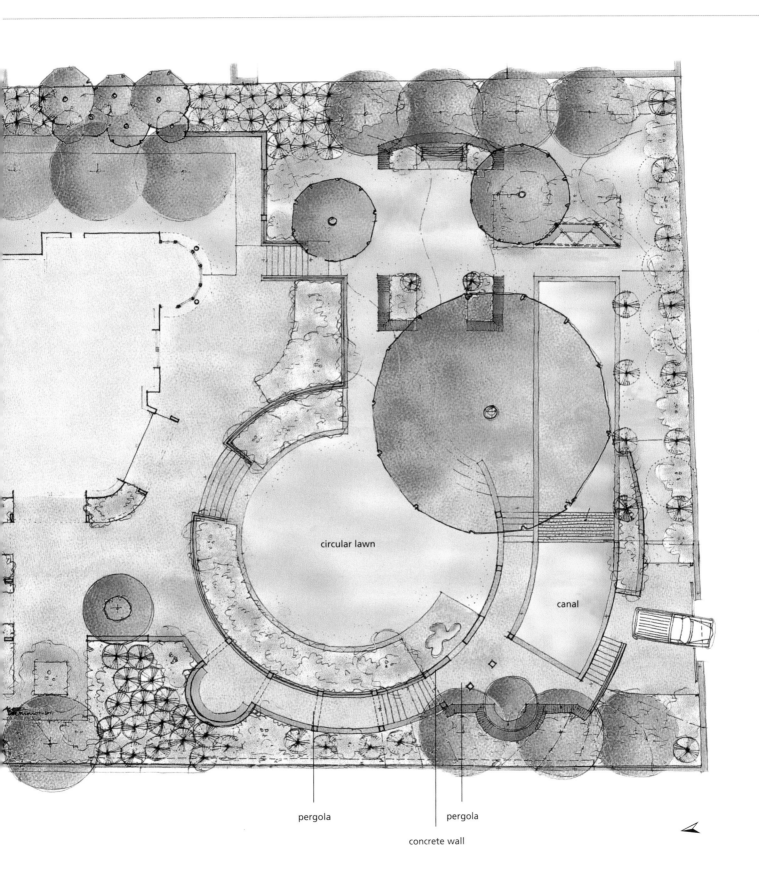

circular lawn

canal

pergola

pergola

concrete wall

Split-Level Garden

Youn-sun Chun

dimensions: **6 x 20m (20 x 70ft)**
soil: **clay over limestone**
aspect: **sunny to shady**
key features: **terrace, water feature with waterfall**

This city garden not only suffered from being overlooked but had the general urban problem of noise and pollution. The owner's brief was specific: privacy, containment, and simple but eclectic materials.

Practical issues were dealt with first. Pollution-tolerant plants such as bamboo and pines were selected to screen and provide an evergreen cocoon, with the foliage of the bamboo having an added bonus of blotting out intrusive sounds. The chosen species of bamboo and pine were also a perfect visual foil for the existing tree, a false acacia (*Robinia pseudoacacia*).

The position of the midday sun orientates the angles of the plan, creating an interesting pattern that shifts gently from side to side. A "seating and eating" terrace was placed in a sunny position with convenient access to the house. It had a functional, well-defined, olive-green slate surface, and the whole area was lit at night.

The progression through the garden from sun to shade followed a path past a water feature of burnished stainless steel trays that slightly overlapped to create a gentle fall of water. Even trickling sounds will help mask extraneous noise. Timber deck steps widened into platforms that were equally suitable for relaxation or secluded meditation.

Materials were chosen with contrasting textures – warm timber, sleek metal, firm slate – and they were brought together with a simple limestone chipping that forms a mulch for the planting. Lengths of recessed slim timber board ran through the chippings to reinforce the lines of the design.

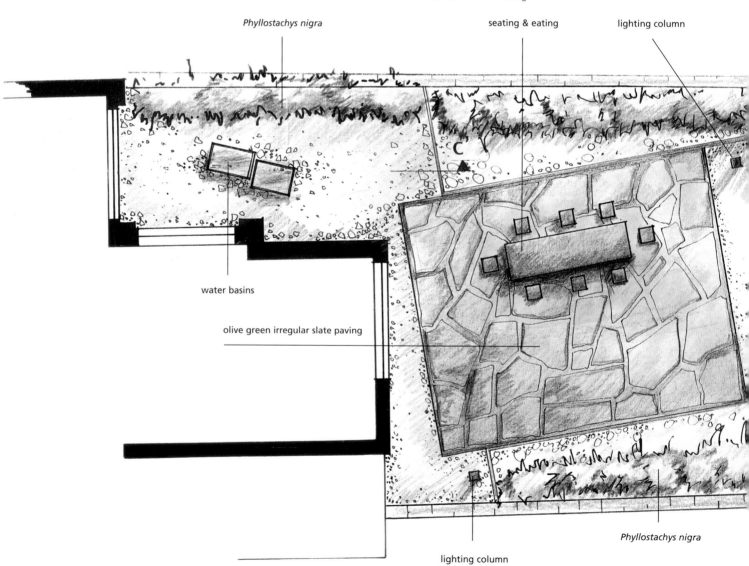

Phyllostachys nigra

seating & eating

lighting column

water basins

olive green irregular slate paving

Phyllostachys nigra

lighting column

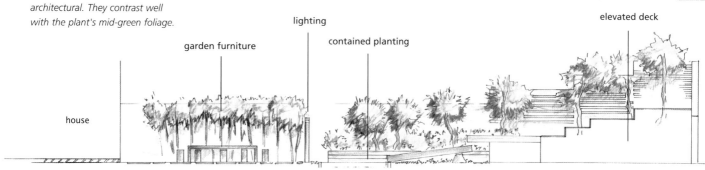

right *The Japanese red pine (Pinus densiflora) has interesting bark, cones and needles. The canopy provides a useful overhead screen.*

far right *Mature canes of the black- stemmed bamboo (Phyllostachys nigra) are tactile and architectural. They contrast well with the plant's mid-green foliage.*

lighting

garden furniture

contained planting

elevated deck

house

side elevation

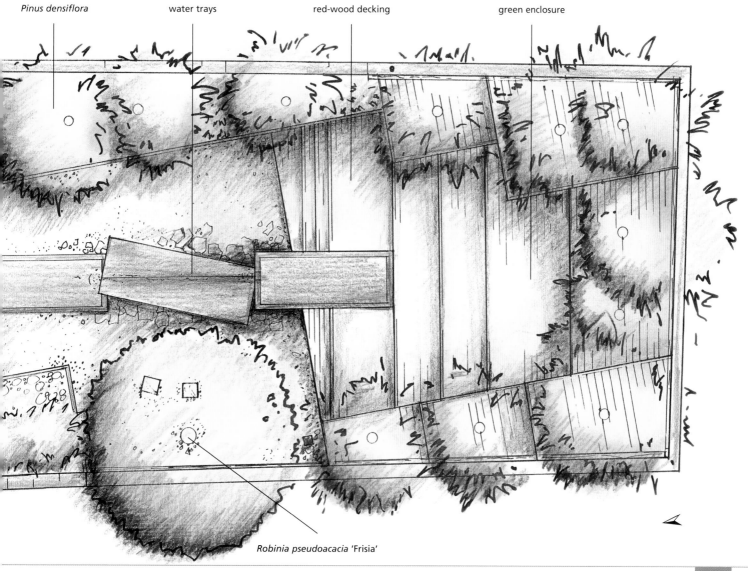

Pinus densiflora

water trays

red-wood decking

green enclosure

Robinia pseudoacacia 'Frisia'

A Party Garden

Paul Cooper

dimensions: **15 x 5m (49 x 16ft)**
soil: **alkali/neutral**
aspect: **south facing**
key features: **dance floor, projection screen, water curtain**

The brief was to create a garden for entertainment for young people. As a place to "party", this included a sprung dance floor and sliding projection screen. The garden backs on to a busy supermarket so some screening was important but the clients did not want to feel totally cut off from their town environment. However, noise from the supermarket traffic did need to be dealt with, and this was achieved by using sound-absorbing planting and several water features. The sound of cascading water, including a walk through a water curtain, was intended to serve as a distraction from the unwanted external noises.

Upper and lower pools were covered with steel grills so that they became integral to the garden, with the water curtain introducing a dynamic element. The sprung dance floor connected directly with the indoor living area, and footlights were inset down one side for added night-time drama. Sliding coloured screens could also be used to vary impact and drama levels. In addition to the sliding back-projection screen, a concealed underdeck fan introduced an element of humour with its unexpected "Marilyn Monroe effect" updraft. Two timber deck seating areas were linked with stepping-stone decking squares across grill-covered water. Storage space was built in wherever possible, to house cushions and other outdoor living paraphernalia.

Feature plants included *Elaeagnus* x *ebbingei*, an evergreen chosen for its sound-absorbing qualities, *Phyllostachys nigra*, and *Rubus thibetanus* 'Silver Fern'.

left *A view of the garden from the indoor living area shows one of two timber-deck seating areas and the sprung dance floor.*

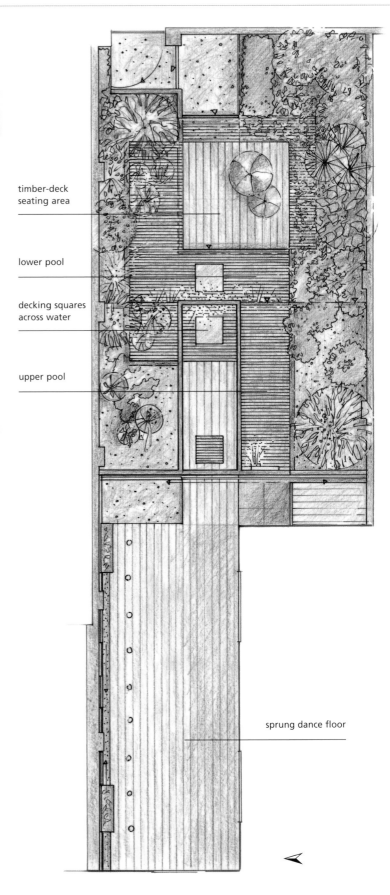

timber-deck seating area

lower pool

decking squares across water

upper pool

sprung dance floor

Wind Garden

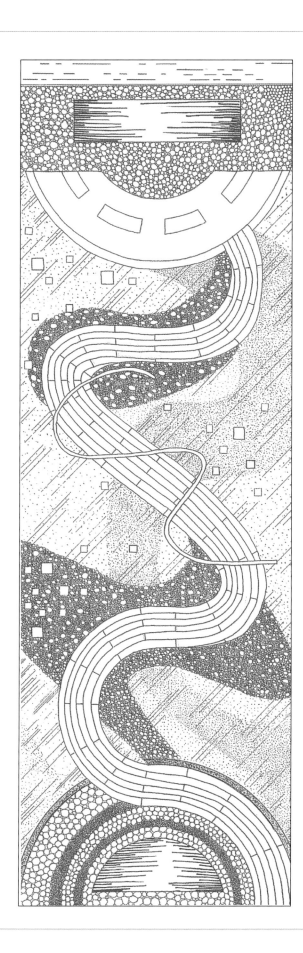

Benjamin Garcia Huidobro

dimensions: **10 x 30m (33ft x 99ft)**
soil: **ordinary**
aspect: **sheltered but sunny**
key features: **pergola, water feature**

The design of this garden was intended to create a sense of movement in a sterile area of a larger landscape. The source for inspiration came from nature, beds of ornamental grasses in a botanical garden, and art – specifically a Japanese sculpture. These influences are visible in the finalized design. The movement of wind, the sounds, and even the silence are the experiences the design should instil on a journey through the garden.

A limited palette of hard materials was chosen. An entrance path moved past the still, reflective welcome pool. The path was a gently undulating timber surface with a silvered finish that rises and drops over the length of the route like a suspended boardwalk. Pebbles in varying sizes and with muted tones were laid over the ground to form a river bed. Slim, angled pylons made a reference to the sea, and the slightest breeze made the flexible aluminium rods bend and wave like steel grasses. Wind chimes hang from a sinuous pergola that gently undulates across the path.

The garden's final resting place was quiet and undisturbed to suggest "the emptiness of wind". Beyond some seating the focus was held by the polished granite surface of the water feature, disturbed only by the gentlest movement of water over its surface – a place for contemplation. A vertical frosted glass panel alluded to some planting beyond.

right *Cobbles and setts can be used to create textured patterns in the garden. Their small unit size brings versatility to pattern making. The image shows pebbles laid in rectangles, while the plan shows pebbles laid in fluid curves.*

New Terrace for a High-Tech Home

David Stevens

dimensions: **15 x 20m (49 x 66ft) approx.**

soil: **light acid**

aspect: **west facing, full sun**

key features: **steel water column, contrasting paving**

This plan encompassed the area immediately adjoining the house and led to a main garden stretching away to the left. The whole property was being improved, and a new terrace was required to match the high-tech interior.

Two paving materials were selected – pale coloured Blanc de Bierge setts in uneven widths, and a crisp dark brown engineering brick – to give a dramatic colour contrast. The narrow strip at the side of the house, leading out from the kitchen, created a major visual problem and here setts were laid with expressed joints

between each course to produce a strong linear pattern. Midway along this side of the house a new full-height window was inserted, taking in views from both ground and first floor level. A bold panel of brick paving was suggested, leading to a simple pool with a stainless steel water column acting as a focal point and accent.

From here the terrace continued to the left, dropping down to a lower level between two wing walls. Here, the awkward return formed by the building was heavily planted with a specimen maple acting as a backdrop to an arrangement comprising a glazed bowl, boulders, loose cobbles, and groundcover planting.

At the end of the building a new floor-to-ceiling glass wall was proposed with broad steps leading to a generous paved area. Continuing this axis, additional steps led down to the main lawn and garden level. Turning across the terrace a long band of brick paving led both feet and eye to a statue which, since it could also be seen from the side garden, visually linked the two areas together.

left *Unite paving, such as brick, can be laid to exaggerate length or breadth in a garden, or to create visual element through pattern.*

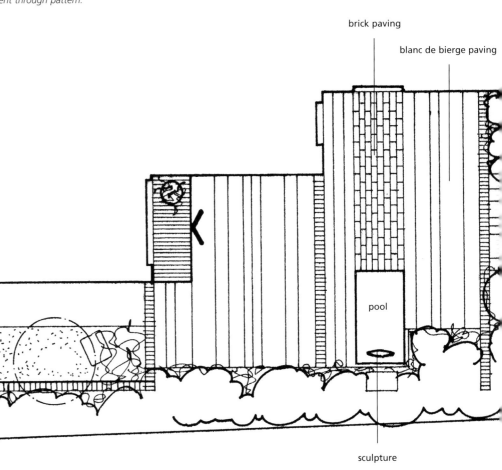

brick paving

blanc de bierge paving

pool

new planting

sculpture

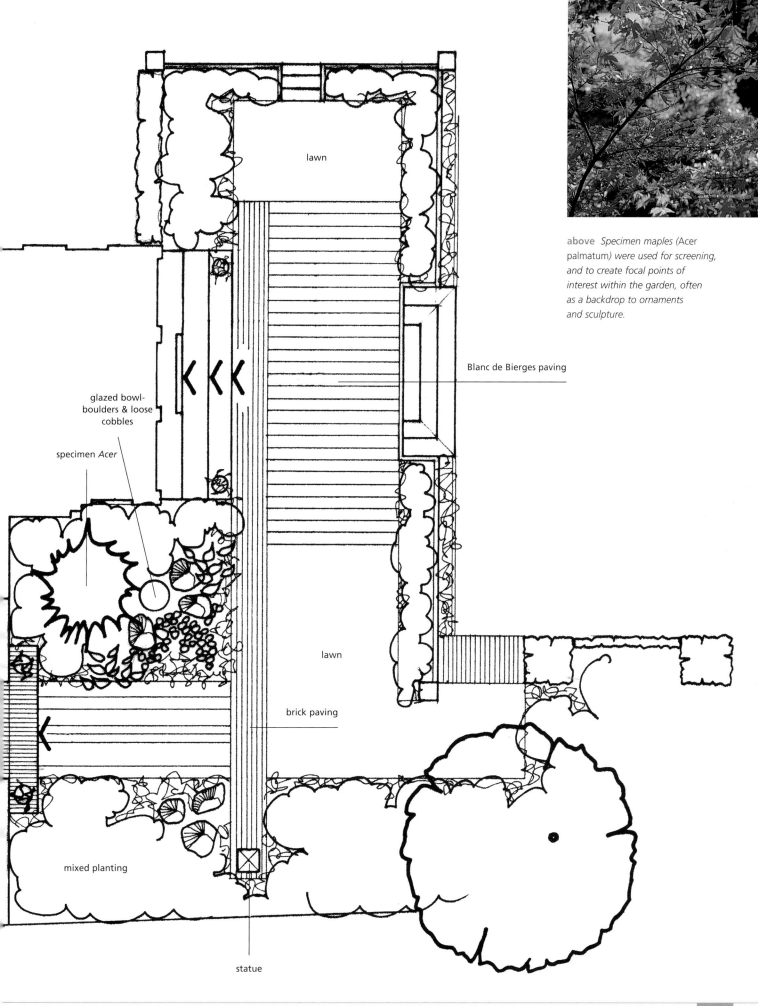

lawn

glazed bowl-
boulders & loose
cobbles

specimen *Acer*

Blanc de Bierges paving

above *Specimen maples (Acer palmatum) were used for screening, and to create focal points of interest within the garden, often as a backdrop to ornaments and sculpture.*

lawn

brick paving

mixed planting

statue

Mediterranean-Inspired Garden

Natalya Scott

dimensions: **10 x 22m (33 x 72ft)**

soil: **clay**

aspect: **east facing**

key features: **sloping site, terraces**

The client was originally from Sicily, and he wanted a garden with a Mediterranean feel to serve as a reminder of his homeland. In addition, he required a large space for entertaining, a water feature, and plenty of room to grow edible plants.

The garden sloped steeply towards the house and was quite overlooked to the north. There was one eucalyptus tree on the northern boundary which had attractive foliage and stature, but otherwise there was no vegetation worth retaining.

To maximize use of this sloping site, terraces were created in free-flowing shapes, which emanated from under a curving pergola running down one side of the garden to introduce an element of false perspective. To each terrace was designated a different function, with vegetables grown informally on the top level, a lawn on the second terrace, and a formal seating area and space for entertaining on the lowest level. Lavender hedges flanked each terrace and provided a reminder of the Mediterranean.

A water feature ran down the length of the garden, changing in character from one terrace to the next. So, on the lawn terrace, it formed a flowing organic stream with native planting and boulders around the edge. By contrast, within the seating area a raised pond was created for a more formal effect.

As a dominant feature of the garden, the pergola was carefully planted with a range of climbers, including *Clematis* 'Mrs N. Thompson', *C. armandii*, *Jasminum polyanthum*, and the vine *Vitis vinifera* 'Purpurea', to give another reminder of the Mediterranean.

above *An important feature – in this garden a pergola – needs a careful choice of planting.* Clematis armandii *is a vigorous evergreen with stunning scented flowers.*

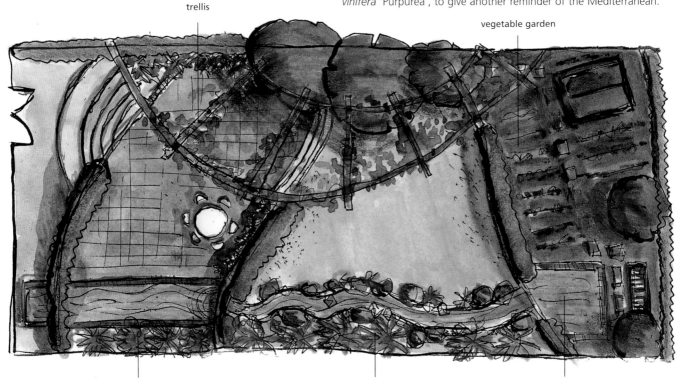

trellis

vegetable garden

Mediterranean garden

cottage garden

water garden

A Garden for Entertaining

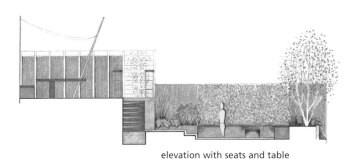

elevation with seats and table

James Aldridge

dimensions: **6.8m x 15m (22ft x 49ft)**
soil: **clay**
aspect: **southeast facing**
key features: **built-in seating**

left The elevation brings to life the dramatic level changes within this small garden. A tented canopy and cantilevered steps create exciting focal points, and planting gives privacy to the lower entertaining area.

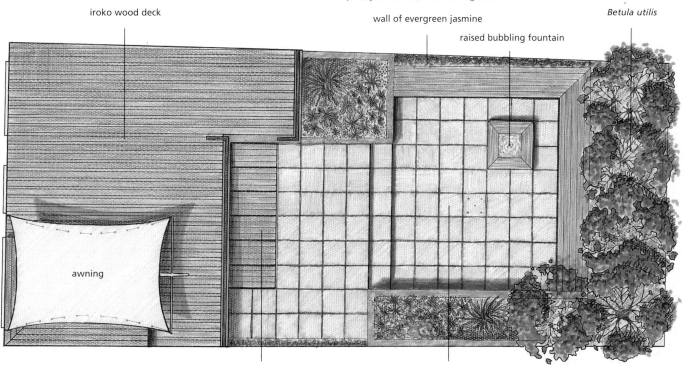

iroko wood deck

wall of evergreen jasmine

raised bubbling fountain

Betula utilis

awning

cantilevered steps

lower level

This garden was intended primarily as an outdoor living space. Low maintenance was a priority, and the owners were clear that they wanted a hard landscape solution with absolutely no grass. The awkwardly sloping site was to be rationalized into more gradual changes in level, and the owners specified a capacity to entertain six guests seated at a table, or up to twenty people for barbecues and other informal functions. A water feature and year-round interest were also important.

The plan divided the garden into three distinct levels. The uppermost of these was decked with Iroko wood, in boards laid to run away from the house. Built-in seats and a table were shaded by a sailcloth awning suspended on an aluminium mast that was integrated with the table. Aluminium railings with stainless steel cabling and an Iroko handrail enclosed the area and cantilevered steps, with a pool underneath, led down from it at right angles to conserve space on the next level.

The second and third levels were paved in Portland limestone and the lowest level had built-in seating on two sides, and a low table with a central pool that could be used for cooling wine.

The planting relied on a small number of stunning species randomly repeated throughout the planting. The mainstay were the row of multi-stemmed white Himalayan birches (*Betula utilis* var. *jacquemontii*), which provided a backdrop to the garden. Their brilliant white trunks would be enjoyable throughout the year.

Elevated Courtyard

John Kenny

dimensions: **8 x 8m (26 x 26ft)**
soil: **clay**
aspect: **south facing**
key features: **elevated courtyard, sunbathing deck**

The brief was to create an area for entertaining large evening parties and a daytime room for relaxing and outdoor cooking. Stylistically, the garden should reflect the modern, contemporary interior of the house, which belongs to a young working couple with no children.

Key features of the new garden included a Himlayan birch (*Betula utilis* var. *jacquemontii*) in the centre of a large, elevated courtyard. At night the white trunk of this tree was up-lit through a wrought iron tree grille set into the paving. On the end wall, a large mirror was used to make this small garden look bigger and reflect back the image of an ornate iron balcony at second floor level. On the lower level, a sunbathing deck was installed outside the basement sauna room.

Although the owners were initially nervous about loosing their existing lawn under an expanse of paving, the use of natural Indian sandstone was agreed to be both a practical and aesthetic success. Broad, shallow steps led up to this area, creating a sense of expansiveness and providing extra seating (for which seat cushions have been specially made) to cater for large parties. Small spot lights set into the side wall threw light across these steps at night, creating an attractive feature when viewed from the basement sauna.

In addition to the *Betula utilis* var. *jacquemontii*, a distinctive style of crop planting, within a measured grid, was used for an expanse of *Crocosmia* 'Lucifer'. Large-leaved *Hosta* 'Big Ears' softened wall bases and large fronds of a shield fern (*Polystichum*) were used in shady areas. Many culinary and aromatic herbs were grown in pots placed on both wall shelves and the steps to the basement deck.

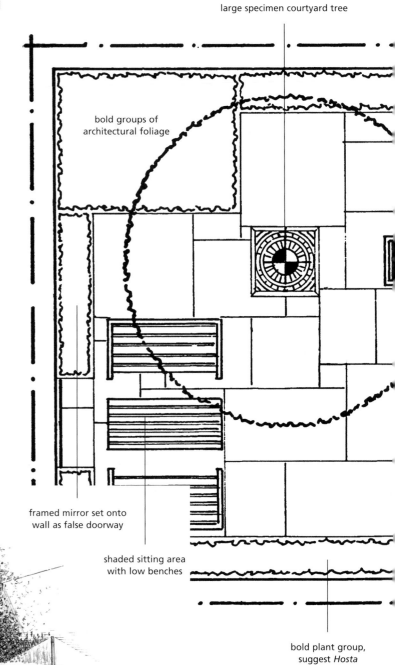

large specimen courtyard tree

bold groups of architectural foliage

framed mirror set onto wall as false doorway

shaded sitting area with low benches

bold plant group, suggest *Hosta*

right *As well as the architectural planting of trees and shrubs, strong design statements can be made with perennial plants – which in this garden include an expanse of the fiery Crocosmia 'Lucifer'.*

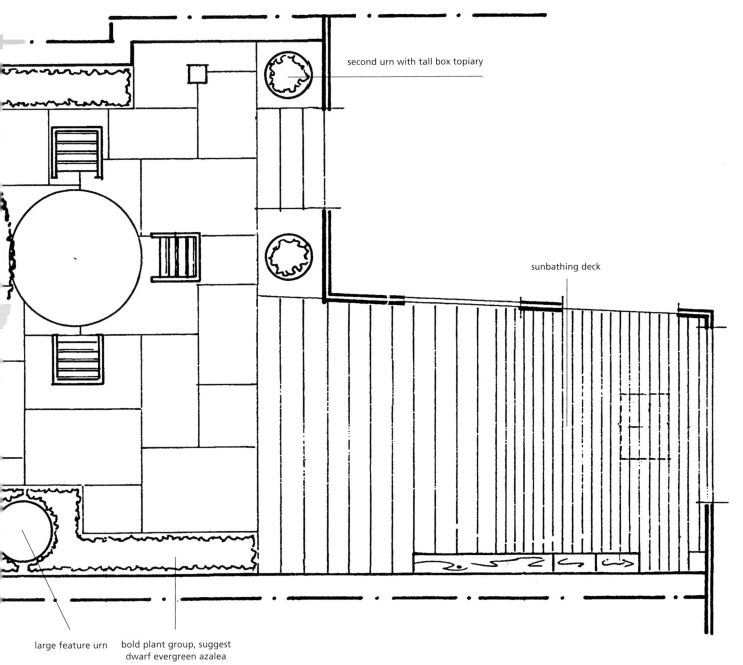

second urn with tall box topiary

sunbathing deck

large feature urn

bold plant group, suggest dwarf evergreen azalea

Country Park-Style Garden

Elizabeth Banks – Elizabeth Banks Associates

dimensions: **36.5 x 26.5m (125 x 115ft)**
soil: **imported loam**
aspect: **north facing**
key features: **sculpture, terrace, specimen trees**

The brief was to design an informal landscape with the feeling of a country park while creating privacy from surrounding tall buildings. The design had to take into account the historic features of the house and garden, the lifestyle of the owner, and the demands of his three dogs. The design took inspiration from the forms and geometry of the architect Edwin Lutyens.

As the garden is surrounded by tall buildings on all sides, as well as being north facing, the light levels are low. The new garden levels meant that it sloped away from the terrace to north end of the garden but the existing level around the mulberry tree had to be retained.

It was decided that an existing sculpture of Sir Thomas More should remain, together with the addition of a new sculpture, and that the existing York stone should be relaid randomly to create a broad terrace. This terrace included ample space for a seating area for twelve people. The courtyard featured a hidden fountain inset in cobbles in York stone paving.

The owner's interest in unusual species inspired a selection of mature specimen trees and rare conifers. The existing mature mulberry tree (*Morus nigra*) was cloud-pruned to create a focal point in the lawn. Dense shrub planting with an under-storey of herbaceous plants and bulbs frames the existing statue and screens the storage shed.

below *This perspective of the top right corner of the garden shows how the planting encloses the space, and the York stone creates an informal quality.*

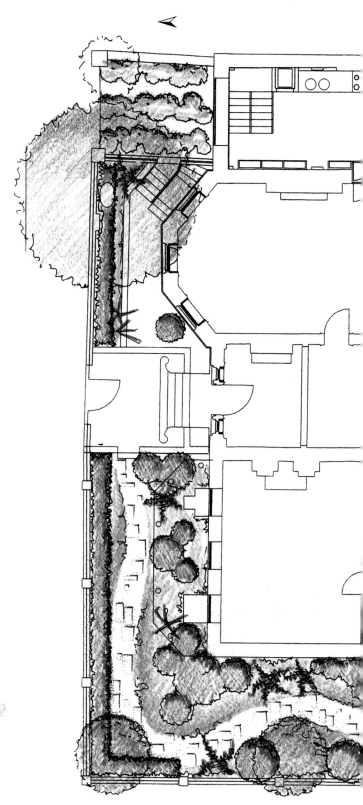

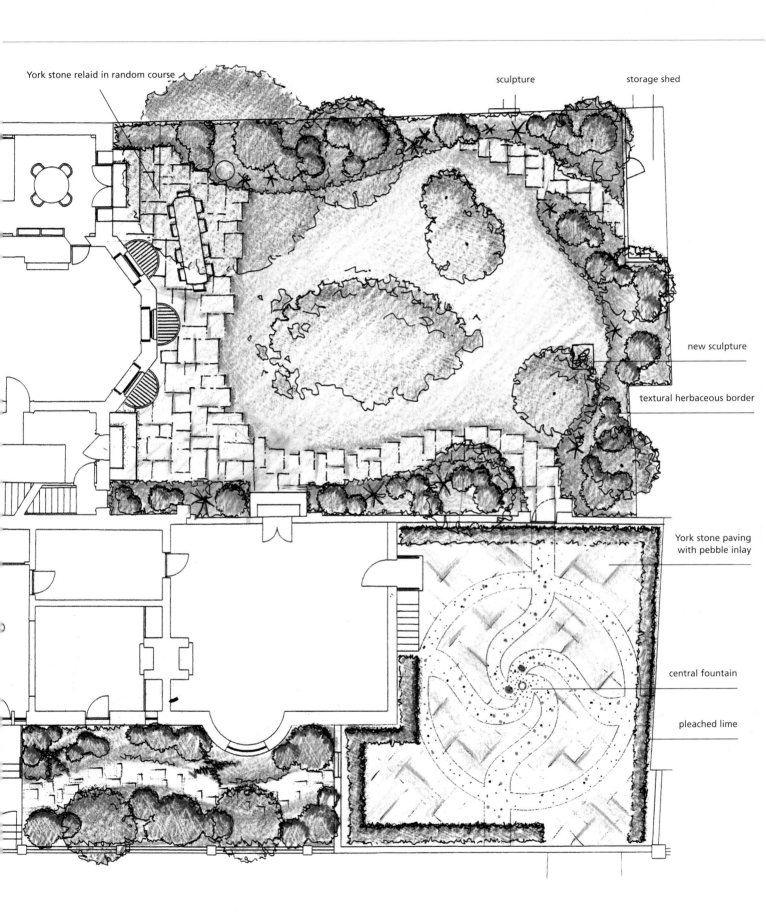

York stone relaid in random course

sculpture

storage shed

new sculpture

textural herbaceous border

York stone paving with pebble inlay

central fountain

pleached lime

A Garden for Entertaining and Play

Sarah Layton at Allium Gardens Ltd

dimensions: 30 x 14m (98 x 46ft), narrowing to 5m (16ft)
soil: heavy clay soil
aspect: west (back garden) and east facing (front garden)
key features: deck steps, built-in bench, playhouse

The owners have two young children and wanted to make the most of an awkwardly shaped site to create a garden that could be used all year round and incorporate a playhouse. Their Edwardian house was decorated in contemporary style, and the client wanted the rear garden to echo this and provide an attractive year-round focal point from the windows of the frequently used west-facing sitting room. In contrast, the front and side gardens were to enhance the period feel of this beautiful red brick house.

In order to deal with significant level changes in the rear garden, a series of deck steps were created with retaining walls acting as raised beds around the edges and providing useful additional seating. A dining area with built-in bench was contained within the lower retaining wall, making good use of available space. The patio close to the house was paved with buff coloured limestone in which fossils can be seen, and the play area at the back had a floor of bark chippings in which woodland plants are growing. A shed was customized with attractive gable boards and window boxes to create a play house.

The front garden has the same limestone paving, this time laid in a random pattern for a more period feel. The original walls were topped with a dainty picket fence, and a gate opened on to a front path laid in a basket weave pattern of reclaimed London stock brick.

The planting was designed to give strong year-round interest, incorporating specimens with strong architectural forms.

left *The planting in this garden, designed to have year-round interest, included the Himalayan birch (*Betula utilis *var.* jacquemontii*), whose brilliant white bark makes a strong statement in winter.*

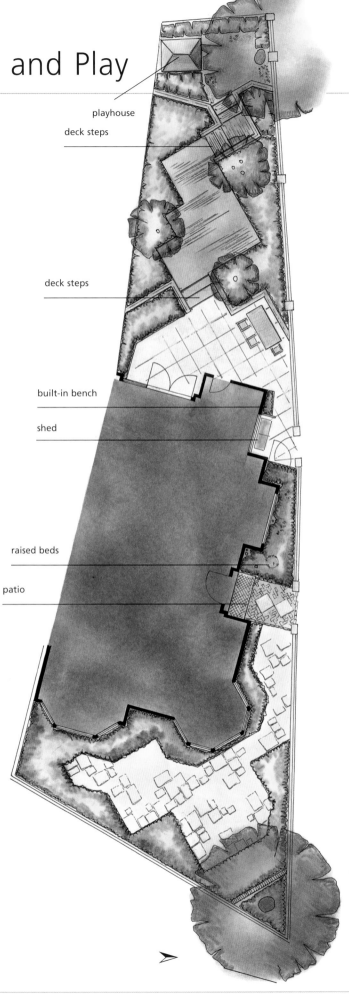

playhouse

deck steps

deck steps

built-in bench

shed

raised beds

patio

Two Courtyards

Olin Partnership – Dennis McGlade – Principle

dimensions: **7350m sq (24,114ft sq)**
soil: **slightly acid**
aspect: **partial sun or full sun; a few areas in full shade**
key features: **intimate courtyard, open courtyard**

right *The main borders in this campus design are articulated with structural plants, such as* Cornus alternifolia *'Argentea', the layered branches of which create a strong horizontal emphasis.*

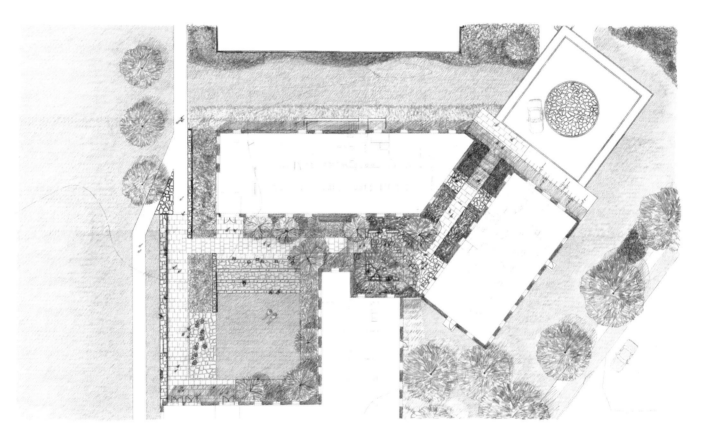

The brief was to assist the architect in selecting a site for a new dormitory on this Pennsylvania college campus, siting the buildings, and designing an outdoor environment which was comfortable and pleasing to the students while meeting the requirements of the Scott Arboretum, an institution that shares the site.

The design included two courtyards, one an intimate, quiet place between the two buildings, and the other a more open space facing out on to large lawns. The smaller courtyard sat at the end of a more "urban" corridor between the buildings. It was paved with a local irregular fieldstone with planted joints, and had benches, a barbeque, and shade-tolerant plantings. The larger courtyard consisted of a square lawn panel with broad stone steps

that people could sit on as well as a stone terrace. Both the stone terrace and the steps were made of the same local fieldstone with joints planted with sun-loving and drought-tolerant plants.

The arboretum was keen to use more unusual plantings, which inspired innovation on the planting design. So, for example, *Acorus gramineus*, *Euphorbia amygdaloides*, and *Hypericum calycinum* were used in place of more common groundcovers. A number of interesting trees were incorporated, including *Cladrastris lutea* 'Sweetshade', *Gymnocladus dioica*, *Liquidambar styraciflua*, *Liriodendron tulipifera*, and several choice magnolias. Seeking the expertise of local professional horticultural gardens and arboreta is always a wonderful way to enrich planting designs.

African-Inspired Garden

Stephen Woodhams

dimensions: **19 x 5m (62 x 16ft) approx.**

soil: **n/a**

aspect: **east facing**

key features: **deck, water feature, glass balustrade**

The owner of this roof garden wanted to create an African landscape in the City of London. His home has an African-inspired interior design and he wanted the outdoor space to co-ordinate with the interior. Another consideration for the design was the exposure to wind that is often found on a roof garden.

Iroko decking inset with three square panels made of three different woods in a herringbone pattern formed the groundwork for this garden. A palette of powder coated cream and chocolate colours were used throughout to represent animal stripes, such as in the cream, beige, and chocolate concrete pots. A glass balustrade was chosen so that it would not interrupt the view and to protect the plants.

At the core of the design were ten steel African shields and lead sculptures resembling African wood carvings. These were used in a still pool of water, framed with a dramatic backdrop of broad leaved bamboos. A dining area opposite the pool consisted of a zinc-wrapped table with railway sleeper benches on either side, and at each end Zulu king and queen thronal chairs made of oak carved logs with brushed stainless steel backs.

Plantings, which were all planted in containers, included *Arundinaria* 'Meteque', succulents, *Phormium* 'Platt's Black', *Astelia chathamica*, *Pennisetum villosum*, white *Agapanthus*, *Carex buchananii*, *Festuca glauca*, and *Stipa gigantea*.

left *The need to plant in containers on roof gardens, due to problems of weight, allows the designer to experiment. Here, clean inverted cones provide an architectural quality.*

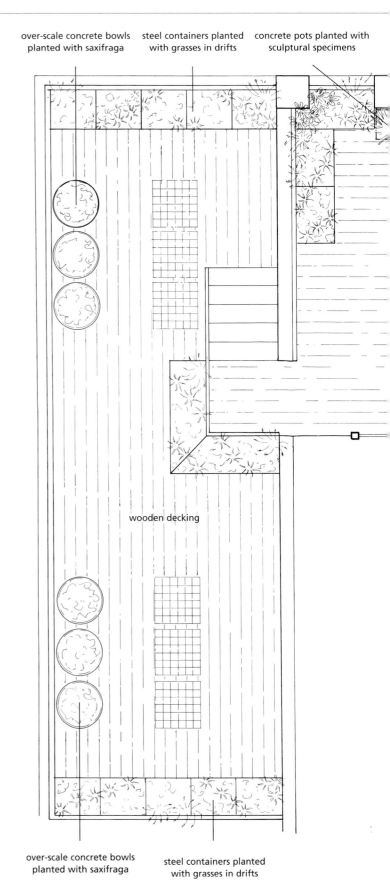

over-scale concrete bowls planted with saxifraga

steel containers planted with grasses in drifts

concrete pots planted with sculptural specimens

wooden decking

over-scale concrete bowls planted with saxifraga

steel containers planted with grasses in drifts

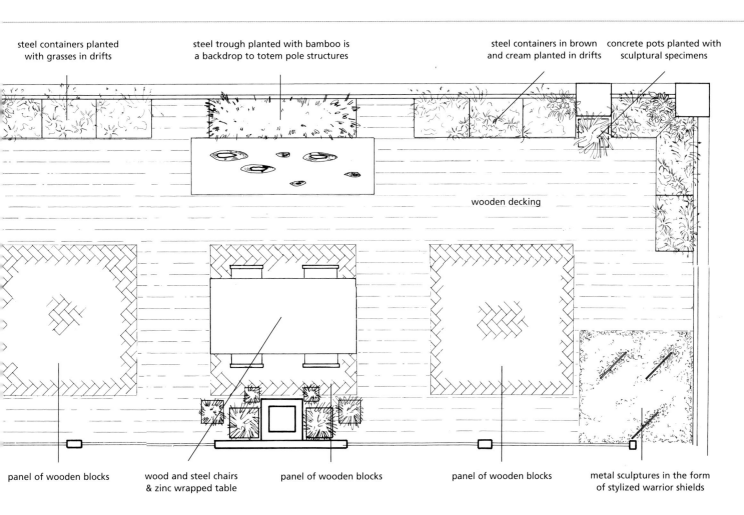

steel containers planted
with grasses in drifts

steel trough planted with bamboo is
a backdrop to totem pole structures

steel containers in brown
and cream planted in drifts

concrete pots planted with
sculptural specimens

wooden decking

panel of wooden blocks

wood and steel chairs
& zinc wrapped table

panel of wooden blocks

panel of wooden blocks

metal sculptures in the form
of stylized warrior shields

right *In this area of the garden
African shields and lead sculptures
make a dramatic backdrop to the
dining area.*

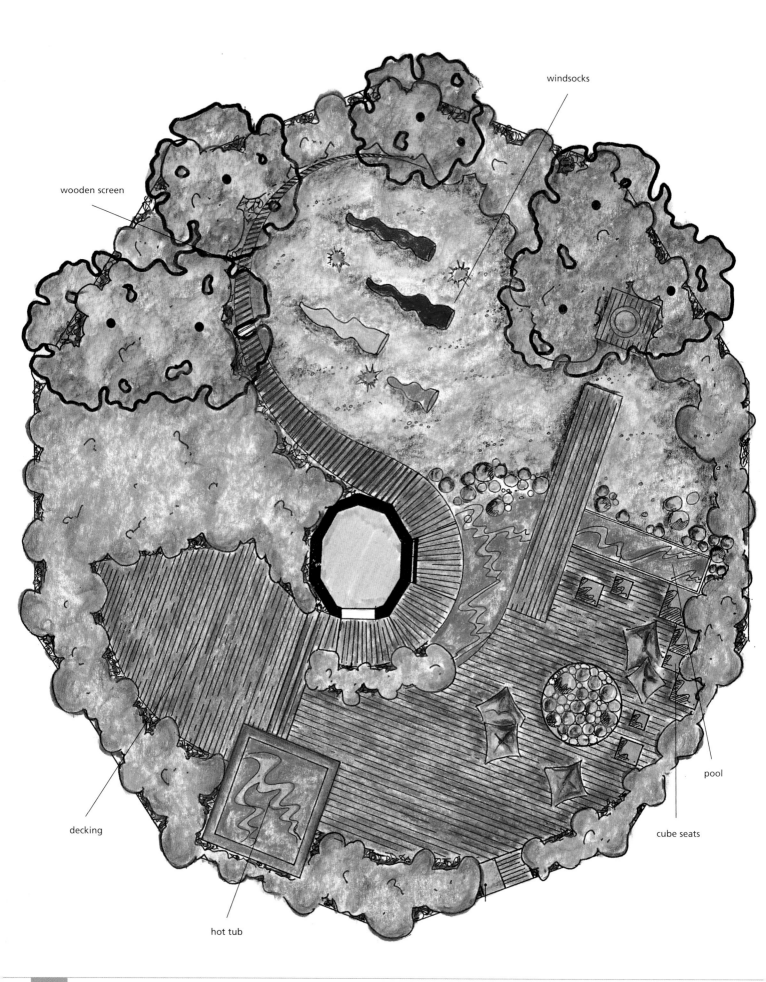

windsocks

wooden screen

pool

cube seats

decking

hot tub

Roof Terrace

The client was a young bachelor working in the City of London, who wanted a modern roof garden with a real "wow" factor. Using the garden at night and for entertaining were both important, as was making the most of the incredible views of London.

Inspired by the proximity of the River Thames, which curves around the building below, the designer included a large area of gravel, cobbles, and boulders to create a beach effect. The waterside feel was enhanced by plenty of tall grasses that sway in the wind, and the inclusion of decking and a pool of water that reflected the sky.

As a humorous acknowledgment of the windy location, the designer created three windsocks on permanently rigid frames. The brightly coloured material was also an easy way of injecting colour into the often grey London skyline.

A wooden slatted screen provided a backdrop and also filtered the wind to create a more sheltered part of the garden. An existing hot tub was incorporated, and a camp fire created using a mains gas powered flambeaux surrounded by sculptural oak cube seats. There was also plenty of room to accommodate a table and chairs.

As with most roof gardens load-bearing was an issue, so the bulk of the weight was distributed around the edge of the terrace, and a special light-weight planting medium used. The plant selection was dictated by the demands of this windy, exposed site. The evergreen framework included phormium, rosemary, *Pittosporum tobira*, escallonia, lavender, and *Agave americana*, while Himalayan birch (*Betula utilis* var. *jacquemontii*) added height. Suitably hardy flowering perennials included *Kniphofia* 'Torchbearer', *Verbena bonariensis*, *Achillea* 'Terracotta', and *Rudbeckia* var. *sullivanti* 'Goldsturm'.

Andy Sturgeon Garden Design

dimensions: **14.5m (48ft) across approx.**
soil: **peat-based potting compost and perlite to limit weight**
aspect: **open, sunny**
key features: **decking, pool, windsocks, screen, cube seats**

left *Among the basic planting framework for this garden the designer used lavender – the compact variety shown here is* Lavandula angustifolia *'Hidcote'.*

left *This section of the roof terrace shows the area of decking where the designer has created a camp fire and placed sculptural cube seats of oak.*

"A City Space"

Mark Anthony Walker Associates

dimensions: **10.5 x 14m (34 x 46ft)**
soil: **neutral**
aspect: **n/a (show garden)**
key features: **central seating area, water canals**

above *As a contrast in colour and form, an antique limestone well head was used as a focal point at the end of the water canal, framed by the pleached limes..*

right *The dynamic angles of this urban garden have been emphasized by clipped box (Buxus) hedges within which much looser planting can be contained.*

This garden was designed to bring dramatic impact to a relatively small, tightly enclosed urban space. Although in fact a show garden, the design explored solutions to the common problems of high enclosing brick walls and partial to heavy shade.

The concept set out to contrast old with new. So the uninspiring brick wall to the rear of the garden was clad in dark blue glazed bricks while a second lower brick boundary wall to one side was replaced with a rammed earth wall. The remaining open sides (where viewers stood) implied an unseen glazed wall with vista and entrances to the garden, adding to the illusion of a courtyard space.

Contrasting with the strong colour of the walls, black Indian limestone was used to form terrace steps, pool coping, and a large central seating area. Long canals of still and moving water divided the space, gave movement, and provided reflective surfaces. A large antique stone wellhead was sited at one end of the canal.

The central tree planting was arranged in a formal grid of eight tall fastigiate oaks with clear stems. The layout was designed to maximize views, minimize shade, and create added perspective and depth. The rows of pleached limes to the rear also had clear stems, to reveal the blue-glazed wall beyond. For contrast, trees with more natural forms were located within the "neighbouring" garden.

The planting concentrated on dark-green shade-loving species, including acanthus, hellebores, and ferns, massed in bold swathes. Against this backdrop, intense patches of colour, such as the deep red climbing roses trained up the glazed wall, enlivened the palette.

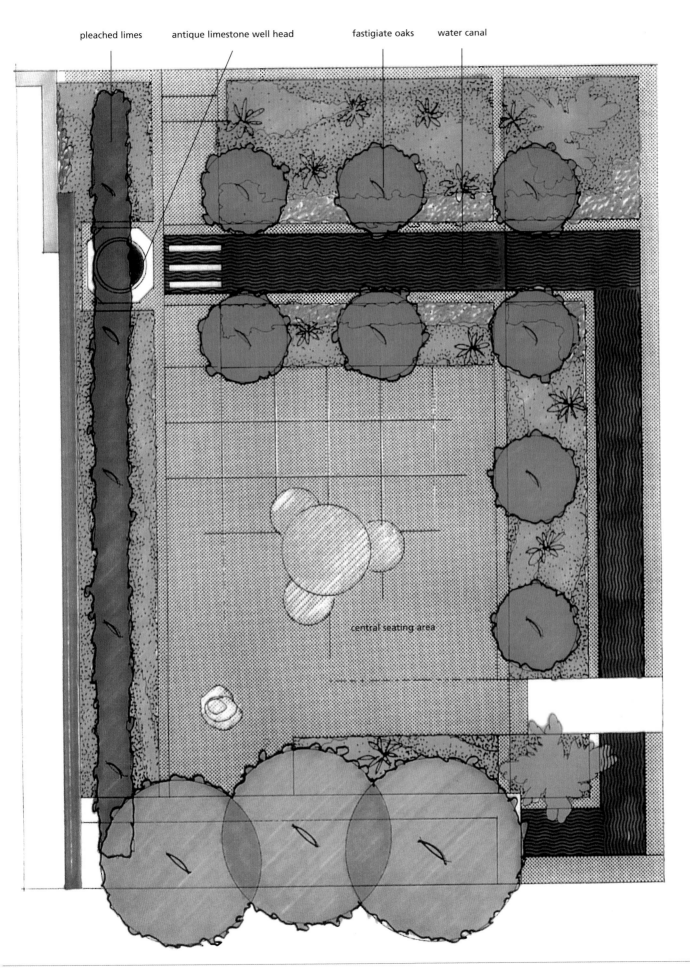

pleached limes   antique limestone well head   fastigiate oaks   water canal

central seating area

A Contemporary Courtyard

Jill Billington

dimensions: **3 x 4m (20 x 30ft)**

soil: **neutral loam over clay**

aspect: **shady**

key features: **trellis, lighting, water feature**

The garden is a small yard surrounded by high walls, with little sun except for at midday in summer. The owner requested an outdoor space for sitting and entertaining that was also low maintenance.

This contemporary design aimed to reduce the depressing effect of the courtyard. High trellis, set at an angle, created a more interesting area. The trellis was made of square lattice, which relieved the "heaviness" of the space, and introduced a lighter feeling of airiness while also implying hidden spaces. In the first half of the courtyard the trellis was open, revealing the shade plants behind. But in the second part the trellis was backed by mirrors to reflect as much sunlight as possible. The plants behind were suited to shade.

The courtyard was paved in cream Cotswold reconstituted stone. Lighting was important, and there were six tall slim lights designed to avoid glare. The client also wanted a water feature and this echoed the form of the lights. It comprised three triangular columns in the pebble-strewn ground. Planting pockets were included among the stones, allowing the feature to be integrated with the rest of the planting. The lines of the design were emphasized by dwarf box hedges that neatly enclosed the plants and reaffirmed the simplicity of the design. Most of the plants were shade tolerators and offered year-round interest with seasonal colour. Climbers softened the walling.

right The lines of this garden were emphasized by planting dwarf box hedges (*Buxus sempervirens*); shown here is low box hedging.

trellis

dwarf box hedges

water feature

trellis

A Vertical Garden

Balmori Associates

dimensions: 855sq m (2804sq ft)
soil: n/a
aspect: southeast facing
key features: vertical garden, moss wall

This townhouse has a limited amount of space and the client wanted to maximize the quantity of landscape surfaces. Consequently, roof and wall surfaces were utilized in addition to the ground plane, and ultimately shaped the experience of the gardens.

To achieve this innovative effect, a number of ecological technologies were incorporated, including a sedum carpet on the roof, and state-of-the-art systems for lightweight planting on the terraces. The vertical "gardens" were covered with climbing ivy that grew in dimensioned metal screens, and vines and climbing plants colonized frameworks to wrap the house in gardens. In addition, there was a "Moss Wall", based on lightweight plastic mesh technology, that was stitched to a drainage mat, filled with moss and clipped to the wall. A reflecting pool presented views of this moss feature which could be viewed from various points in the garden. There was even a lawn for entertaining on the second floor terrace.

This garden graphically illustrates the point that landscape should incorporate all dimensions, and innovative technologies encourage the use of plants outside their natural context to create unexpected spaces. So, although the planting here concentrated on relatively common elements such as bamboo, turf, moss, river birch, grasses, and ivy, the finished result were very far from ordinary.

above A photo-montage of the garden shows how effective the tapestry of mosses, planted into a plastic mesh, can be. The space becomes a gallery for the display of plants.

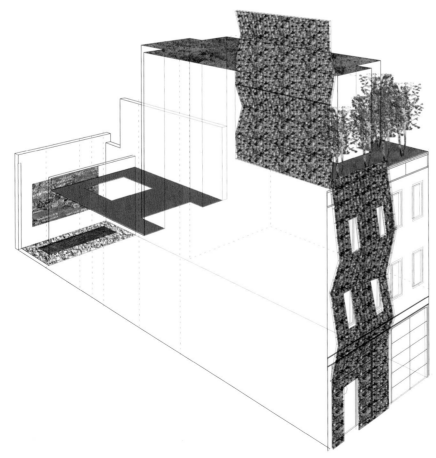

Penthouse Garden

del Buono-Gazerwitz Landscape Architecture

dimensions: **215sq m (705sq ft)**
soil: **n/a**
aspect: **sunny and exposed**
key features: **decking, zinc and timber planters**

The client, a property developer, wanted preliminary schemes for the private gardens of four luxury penthouses, originally planned for the top two floors of a tall 1940s building in London. The client was anxious to make the most of the amazing, 360 degree, views over the whole city of London, but it was necessary to make allowance for the hostile exposed conditions which would be found on the roof of any tall building.

The development of the final designs was shaped by the usual constraints which apply to all roof garden projects, specifically the need to build a garden over the structure of an existing roof which could not be altered, working over and above its structure and within its load capacity. Two different options were developed, with Option 1 taking a more formal approach to the space, while Option 2 incorporated curving lines which became particularly evident at the points where different hard surfacing materials met. The same materials were proposed for both options. So expanses of limestone paving were broken by bands of timber, complemented by adjacent expanses of timber decking. The planting was contained within zinc or timber faced planters.

Option 1

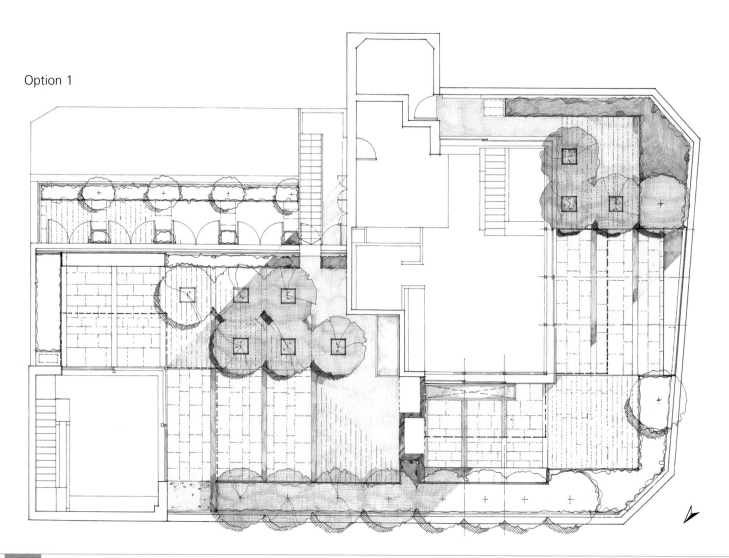

Option 2

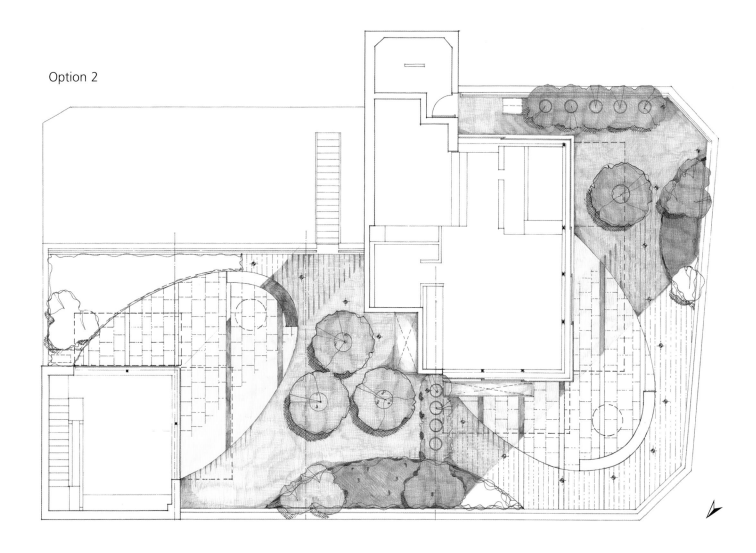

left and above *Two different options were prepared for this client, with option 1 based on harmonious rectangles, and option 2 on curves, contrasted dynamically with rectangles.*

above and right *All the planting in this penthouse garden was contained within zinc or timber faced planters. The galvanised metal and blue wooden containers shown here might be equally effective.*

Garden in an Awkward Space

Jan King

dimensions: **184sq m (602sq ft)**
soil: **poor**
aspect: **south facing, partly shaded**
key features: **decking, pool with jet fountains**

The clients wanted a secluded, private garden with space for outdoor eating and entertaining, and incorporating a water feature. Although the garden is south facing, an old factory wall shaded the west side of the upper garden. There was a good birch tree in one corner of the lower garden but a yew was removed. The newly designed house was built of brick, oak, and stainless steel, and these materials were to be repeated in the garden.

Thanks to the old factory wall, the upper garden is the most secluded area. This is where the family eats and entertains out of doors. Decking provided a continuous, warm surface, with steps wide and deep enough to sit on. Large terracotta pots against the north wall of the extension formed a feature seen from the hallway.

The design incorporated a deck that looked out over a lawn edged with concrete paving slabs, at the far end of which is a pool with two jet fountains. A tall, stainless steel obelisk stood behind the pool, between two slim junipers. Gravel was suggested for other hard surfaces in the lower garden. From the larger gravelled area under the birch tree, a seat looked across the lawn to a row of aluminium planters. Further up the garden the planting was bisected by narrow gravel paths, each with a large terracotta urn at its apex.

In order to unite the house and garden, two grids were used on which the plan was drawn. One was based on the south-facing window of the sitting room; the other was based on the extension jutting out at an angle to the main building.

left By using an existing factory wall to enclose the area on one side, the designer created a secluded upper garden where the clients could eat out and entertain.

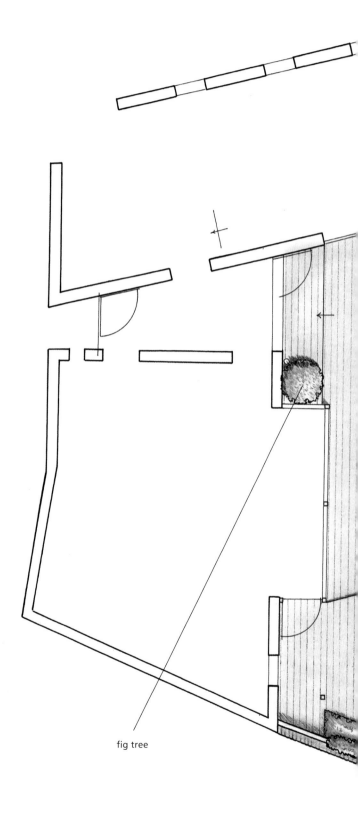

fig tree

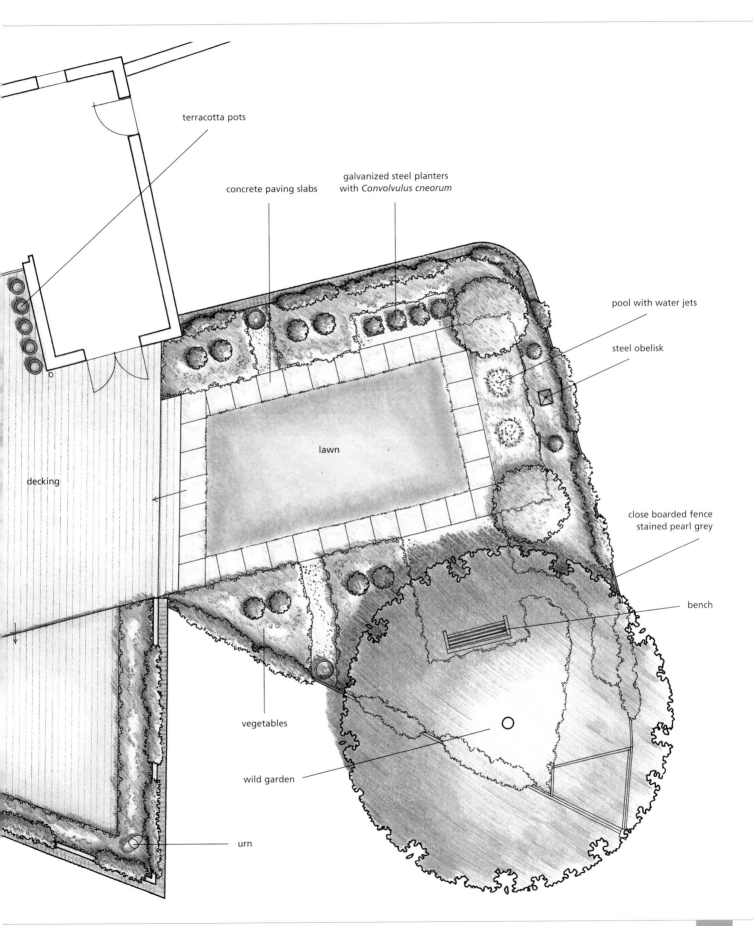

terracotta pots

concrete paving slabs

galvanized steel planters
with *Convolvulus cneorum*

pool with water jets

steel obelisk

lawn

decking

close boarded fence
stained pearl grey

bench

vegetables

wild garden

urn

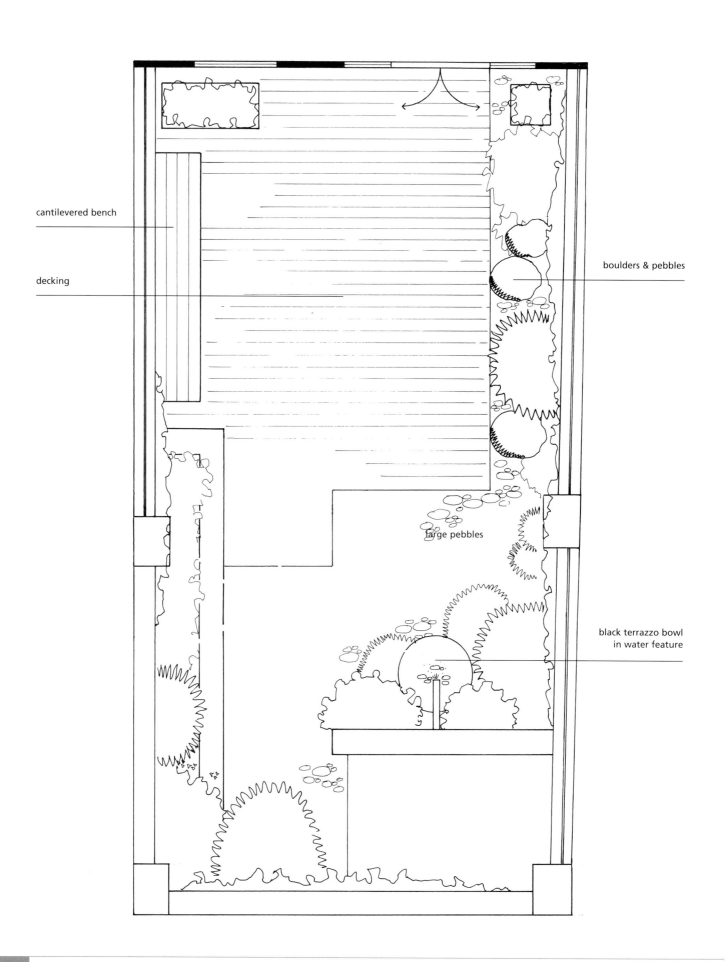

cantilevered bench

decking

boulders & pebbles

large pebbles

black terrazzo bowl
in water feature

Compact Courtyard

Catherine Heatherington Designs

dimensions: **4.1 x 7.5m (13 x 25ft)**
soil: **clay**
aspect: **southwest facing**
key features: **decking, cantilevered bench**

The owner requested a contemporary style, low-maintenance courtyard garden for entertaining. The view of the garden as seen from the house was an important element, and space was required for the storage of bicycles.

The existing site was flat, fairly overlooked, and formed part of a terrace of small cottages in what is now a built-up city area. All existing fencing was to be replaced with new walls.

Given the restricted size of the site, a simple geometric design evolved, which generally works better than curves in a small space. Approximately half the garden was decked to provide plenty of space for entertaining. The bench down one wall was cantilevered, rather than floor standing, to avoid interrupting the transverse sweep of this deck, thus contributing to the illusion of space. New rendered walls provided a calm backdrop against which were set simple geometric beds. Beyond the deck, boulders and pebbles created a softer look, with informal planting areas and a black terrazzo bowl brimming with water from a stainless steel pipe. This water feature was spotlit to create a dramatic feature after dark.

Sticking to the same principles of simplicity which dictated the design of the hard landscape, the variety of different plants used throughout was kept to a minimum. Key elements of the scheme included the evergreens *Pseudosasa japonica*, *Hebe topiaria*, *Phormium tenax* 'Dazzler', *Stipa tenuissima*, and *Trachelospermum jasminoides*. In addition, *Rhus typhina* 'Dissecta', *Heuchera* 'Pewter Moon', and *Sedum* 'Autumn Joy' helped to create a subtly changing effect through the year. *Rosa* 'Mme Alfred Carriere' and *R.* 'Ghislaine de Féligonde' added summer colour and fragrance.

left *Among the architectural plants used in this planting schemes was the striking, tall (1m/3ft high) bulb* Allium *'Purple Sensation'.*

below *The elevation shows the informal planting area and black terrazzo bowl into which water drips from a stainless steel pipe.*

A Garden of Rooms

Joe Swift

dimensions: **24 x 6m (79 x 20ft)**
soil: **neutral clay**
aspect: **north facing**
key features: **coloured concrete, pergola of yachting wires**

This is the designer's own garden, and evolved over the years from a place to relax and entertain friends to a low-maintenance garden suitable for a young family. As a keen gardener, at every stage of the design, he was careful to keep plenty of border space in which to indulge his love of plants.

Although part of the garden was originally laid to grass, this area was often in deep shade and consequently would get very soggy in wet weather and take ages to dry out. So, the lawn was removed to make the garden more practical for a young family.

With the new design the long garden was divided into three distinct rooms, each covered with a different hard surfacing material. The sections were linked together by the planting, and also by shallow steps that introduced additional interest to a once-flat site.

The first room had a concrete surface coloured with a steel-blue pigment. The concrete had been poured right up to one of the side walls so that the children could kick a ball up against it. From here the path passed under a pergola constructed from yachting wires into the second room. This area consisted of two large tanalized deck areas with a large wooden table (made from sanded scaffold planks), which was perfect for entertaining. The last room, at the end of the garden, was an area for sitting and relaxing. Lush planting surrounded a brick circle in this, the sunniest spot in the garden.

coloured concrete

pergola

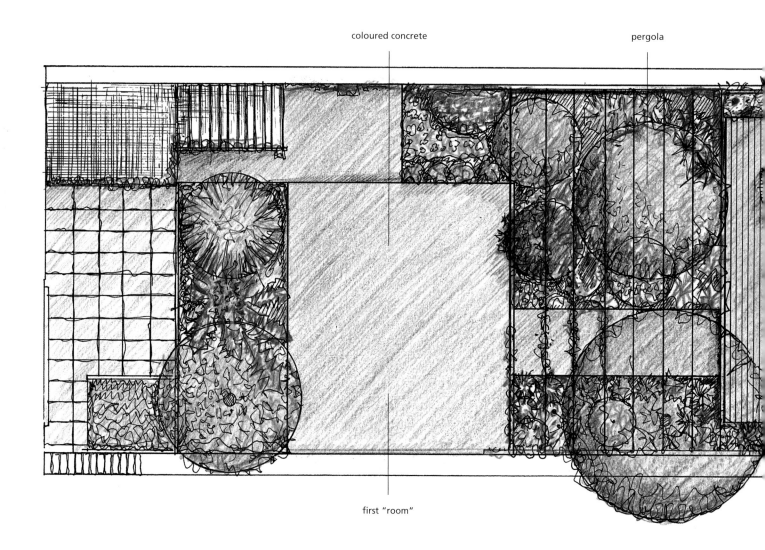

first "room"

The planting scheme throughout was dense and eclectic. It included sculptural items such as banana (*Ensete*) and *Agave americana*, several types of bamboo, a large ceanothus, *Acer palmatum* 'Sango-kaku', and grasses, including *Helictotrichon sempervirens*. Wisteria and golden hop were trained along the eight steel cables which formed the pergola between the first and second garden areas. These cables were set high across the width of the garden, to provide height and structure without interrupting the view.

right *The central garden room of a raised area with a large table is surrounded by lush, textured planting.*

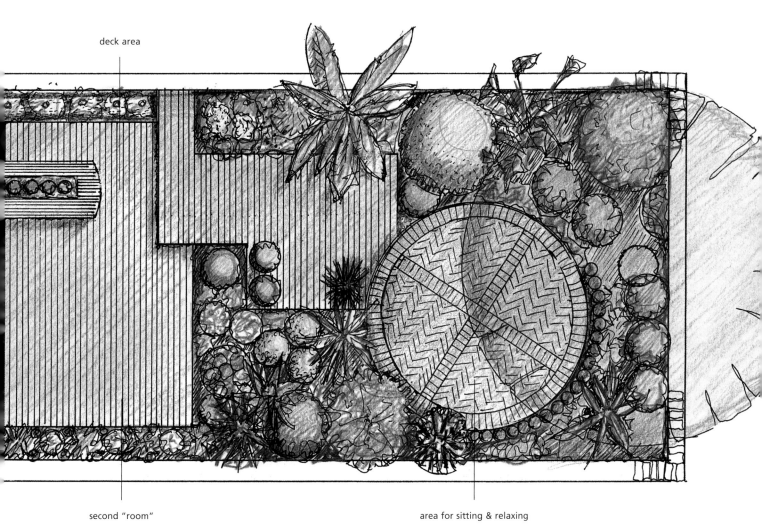

deck area

second "room"

area for sitting & relaxing

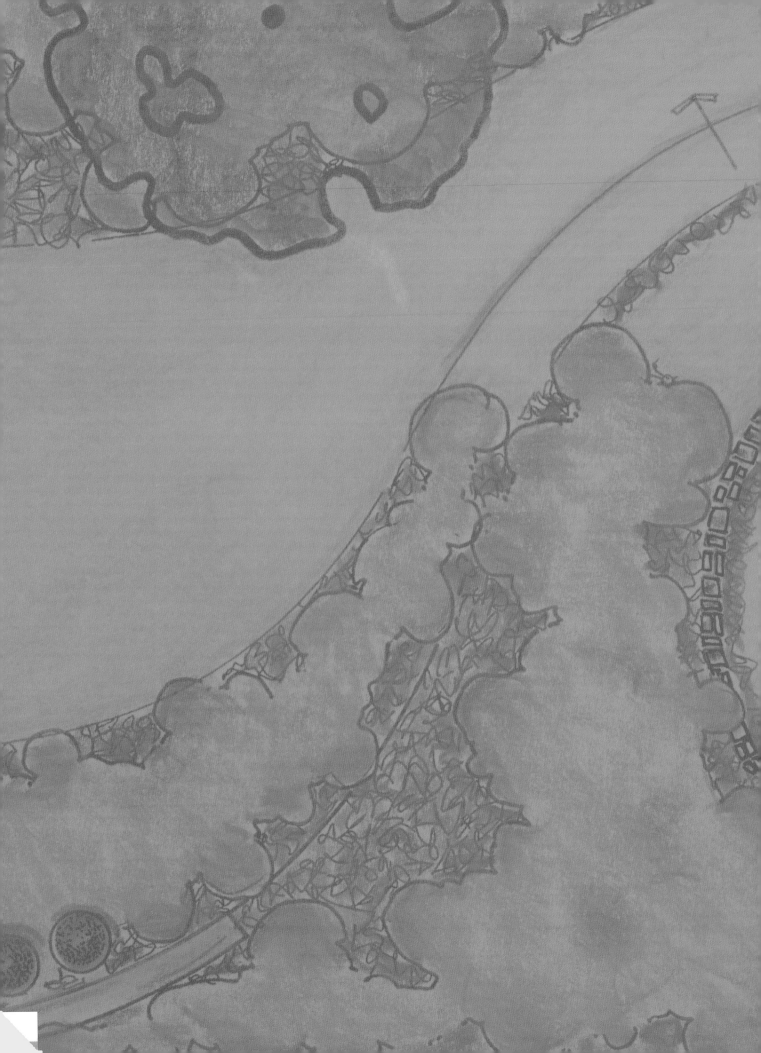

Informality lends a relaxed approach to garden making. Historically, gardens have tended towards formality, particularly in the geometry of layout. The English landscape style changed this approach but still retained a sense of grandeur in its scale.

With the advent of Modernism in the twentieth century patterns of symmetry were replaced by asymmetric layouts, creating a new sense of balance and order, often inspired by Japanese philosophy.

Designers on America's West coast embraced this approach, reflecting a new and leisured way of life. In what became known as the room outside, people began to use their gardens for relaxation, outdoor dining, and for play, activities that related to a more informal way of life.

The restrictive corset of axial design with symmetrical repetition gave way to organic shapes, spirals, diagonals, and interlocking rectangles. In the informal garden, pathways meander, lawns sweep, and borders vary in depth and shape to provide surprise, variety, and drama. Planting too is organized in informal groups or interlocking blocks of different heights and textures, moving away from the controlled layering of herbaceous borders.

Elizabeth Banks, whose work opens this chapter, shows how the informal approach to garden design can produce exciting results. This garden loses its confining trapezoidal shape in a combination of circles and curves that distract the eye away from the boundaries.

Informal Gardens

A Garden of Circles

Elizabeth Banks Associates

dimensions: 15 x 17m (49 x 56ft) at widest points
soil: improved clay, imported loam in new areas
aspect: southwest facing
key features: split levels, decking, circular shapes

The owner requested an open space for the family as well as a stylish setting for entertaining. The design needed to amalgamate three disjointed spaces comprising the existing garden, an adjacent sunken area that was previously disused, and a new area created by decking over a single storey building.

The design responded to the challenging topography, using changes in level to articulate the space. Since the levels within the garden varied by up to 1.35 m (4 ft), several level changes needed to be catered for with stairs. The strong graphic motif of the circle was used throughout the design in varying scales and ways, from layouts to details. Rendered walls, changes in planting, and hard materials were used to make each space distinct.

The area close to the house contained a large, calming pool of water, dining area, and a small amount of decking. The second area contained a series of decks which span the single storey building beneath to provide a space for entertaining and games. A small area towards the end of the deck was intended for secluded sunbathing or for observing the street life below. Finally, in the shady, formerly disused, sunken space at the end of the garden, ferns and raw materials created a lush, heavily planted garden to walk through or to be admired from the other areas.

Trees specified for this plan included an existing plane tree, plus multi-stemmed birches, palms, pines, and Italian cypresses. Other planting included bamboos, ferns, and grasses.

Cupressus
sempervirens

Betula

water feature

palm

left *Among the trees specified for this garden were Italian cypresses* (Cupressus sempervirens) *– chosen for their elegant, columnar quality, and vertical emphasis.*

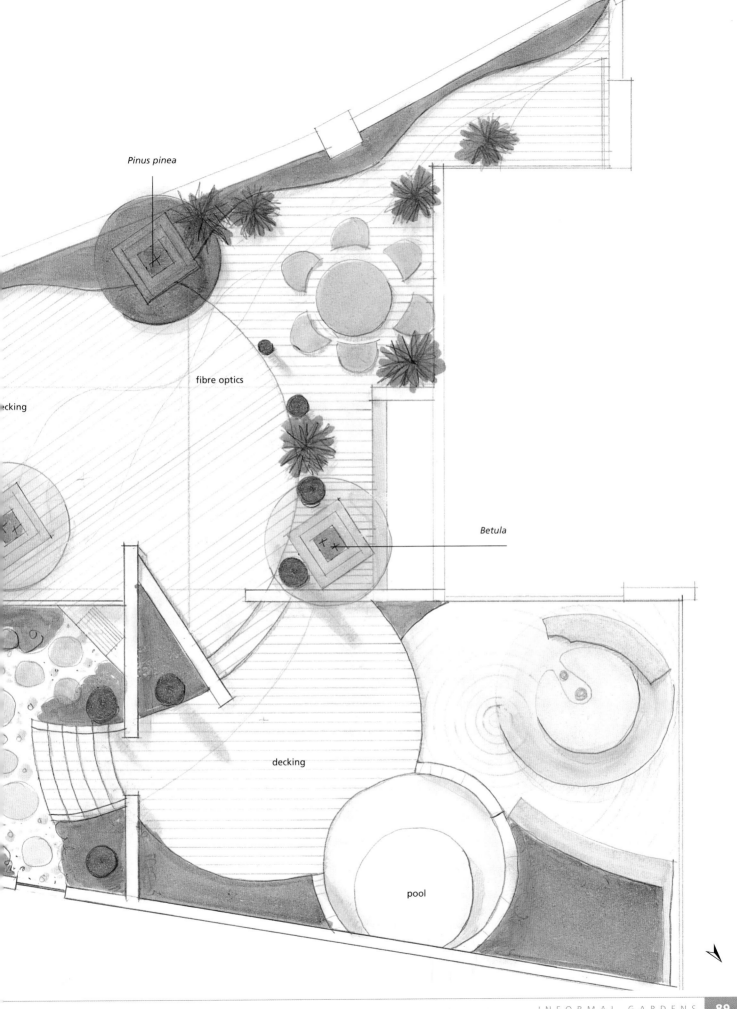

Pinus pinea

fibre optics

cking

Betula

decking

decking

pool

Secret Garden

Jill Billington

dimensions: **6 x 9m (20 x 30ft)**
soil: **loam over clay**
aspect: **west facing**
key features: **decking, large rocks for seating**

The design alluded to past garden style with a lawn surrounded by flowering shrubs. The spaces were handled in a simple and contemporary manner, with plenty of provision for flowers. Initially the problem was that the rectangular space was overlooked from the back, thickly filled with mature shrubs, and reached from the house by two small sets of steps. The levels were simplified by creating one step that stretched across the site, and also provided a "platform" for plants in containers. The second step down to garden level was further from the house and followed the line of the deck. And there was a very low step down on to the lawn from the second deck area. Here, too, a similar raised "platform" offered a place for container plants but provided seating as well.

Decking was used to maintain ventilation for the old house and offer warm footing for summer days. There was an inviting and enclosed seating space extending out into the garden. Privacy from houses at the far end of the garden was achieved by "louvered" timbers. These were attached to a base and, like louvered blinds, could be moved to follow the sun. The plants behind could be glimpsed through the posts and fragrances filter through. Large flat-topped rocks that doubled as seats for parties and for children to climb on added a rural feeling to the garden.

The owners wanted a lawn and this, wrapped around the garden out of sight of the house, made the space appear larger than it was. This hidden space behind the seating area was also a secret area for children. A storage shed was also required but preferably not visible, so a stand of bamboo hid it.

left *In order to hide an unsightly storage shed the designer planted a stand of tall bamboos – the species growing here is the black bamboo, Phyllostachys nigra.*

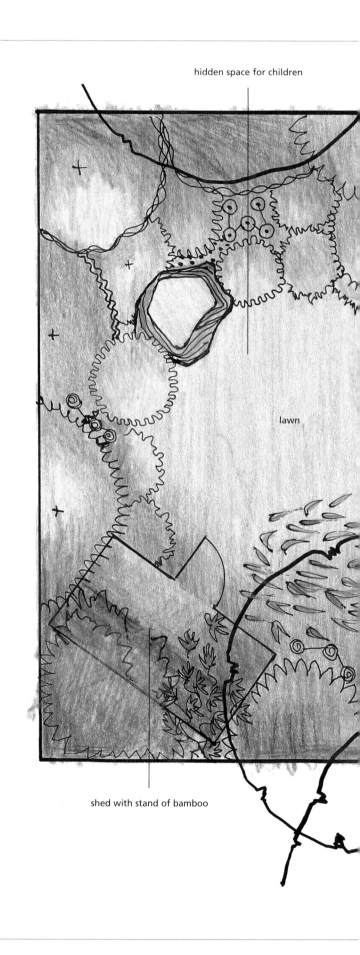

hidden space for children

lawn

shed with stand of bamboo

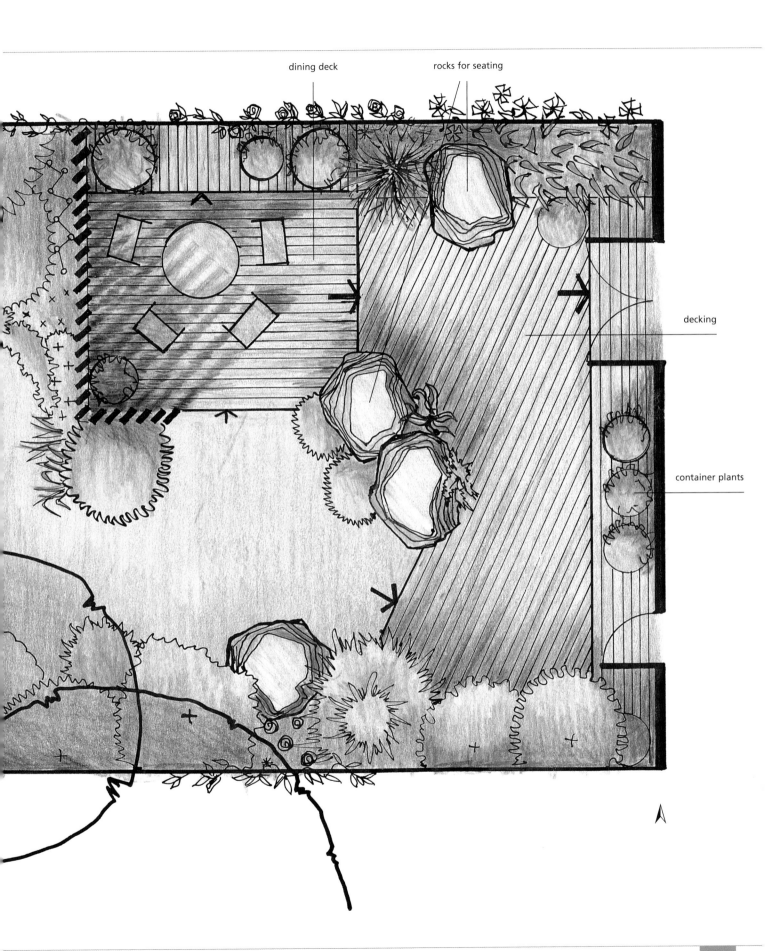

dining deck

rocks for seating

decking

container plants

"Land of Contrasts"

Dene Hohwieler

dimensions: **10 x 12m (33 x 39ft)**

soil: **neutral**

aspect: **designed to be open, south facing**

key features: **antipodean planting, boardwalk**

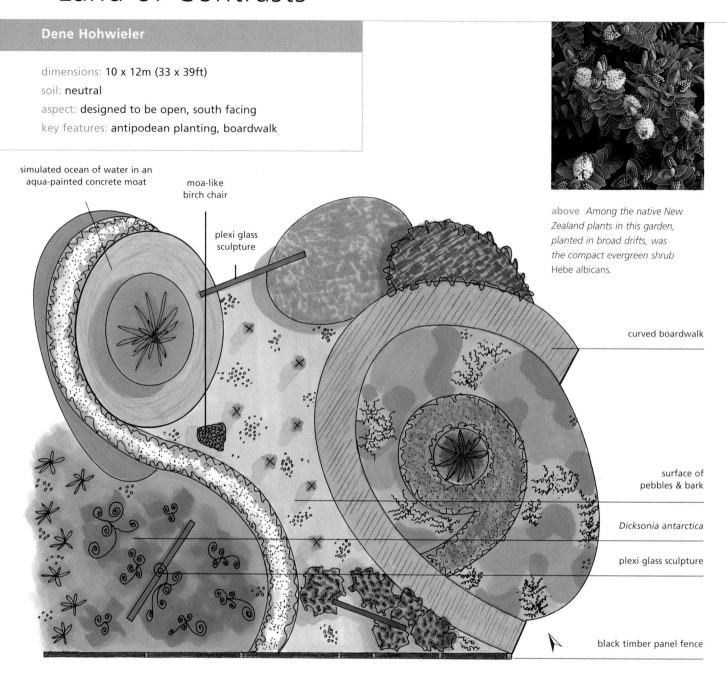

simulated ocean of water in an aqua-painted concrete moat

moa-like birch chair

plexi glass sculpture

curved boardwalk

surface of pebbles & bark

Dicksonia antarctica

plexi glass sculpture

black timber panel fence

above *Among the native New Zealand plants in this garden, planted in broad drifts, was the compact evergreen shrub Hebe albicans.*

This design was a college project to create a show garden for the RHS Hampton Court Flower Show with an open brief. The garden was titled "Land of Contrasts", and set out to create an open but lush setting, incorporating New Zealand native species and other antipodean plants.

Bold massed planting was the main focus of this garden with hard landscaping playing a secondary role, although three large plexiglass sculptures featured highly in the scheme. In addition, a curving boardwalk made from hardwood timber provided a means of access into the centre of the garden, and other hard surfaces were covered with smooth grey beach pebbles. The planting set inside the boardwalk rose gradually on natural mounds of earth,

upon which moss-like plants and grasses were planted in a bumpy, mounded fashion. From here, the swathe of lilac agapanthus was raised slightly further, creating a swirling surround for phormiums on a high mount.

On the other side of the garden, the pre-formed moat of aqua-painted concrete encircled an island mound. This mound was formed from clay-based soil secured in a chicken-wire form, covered by turf matting, and supported a container-grown cordyline at its apex. The plexiglass sculptures were secured in the ground by metal rods. The boldness of these sculptures enhances the light and colours of the garden. Elsewhere, an oversized birch chair complemented a stand of surreal toothed lancewoods (*Pseudopanax ferox*).

Space-Age Garden

Andrew Fisher Tomlin

The owners had already re-developed the house interior in a contemporary style. Now they wanted something similarly striking for the outdoor space that would be low maintenance but provide good structure and year round interest, with views from the house.

The key feature of this design was a series of three activity pods, based on 1950s furnishing fabric patterns, loosely allocated to play, sun, and entertaining. Ideally, curved areas of paving should be cut from natural stone, which gives the best edge. However, when working to a limited budget, a reasonable finish can be achieved using simple concrete slabs, although riven paving does not work in this context. In this garden, the soft outline of the paving was echoed in the curving lines of an exposed gravel path. In addition, lighting was integrated into the scheme for night-time viewing.

In order to create a strong structural planting scheme, the palette was limited to a few plants with year round interest. This included a stand of seven *Betula utilis* var. *jacquemontii*, low hedges,

dimensions: **12.5 x 12.5m (41 x 41ft)**
soil: **clay with neutral, loamy soil**
aspect: **west facing**
key features: **1950s-style "pods"**

and balls of clipped box, and a selection of ferns and ornamental grasses. In addition, lavender, perovskia, and rosemary all introduced shades of steely silver and soft purple, together with wonderful fragrance. Climbers included *Clematis armandii* and *Jasminum officinale*, and the herbaceous planting brought together such reliable performers as *Alchemilla mollis*, *Anemone* 'Honorine Jobert', *Crocosmia* 'Solfatare', and *Ligularia* 'The Rocket'. In addition, large quantities of a limited range of bulbs were planted, including *Galanthus nivalis* and *Narcissus* 'Pheasant's Eye'.

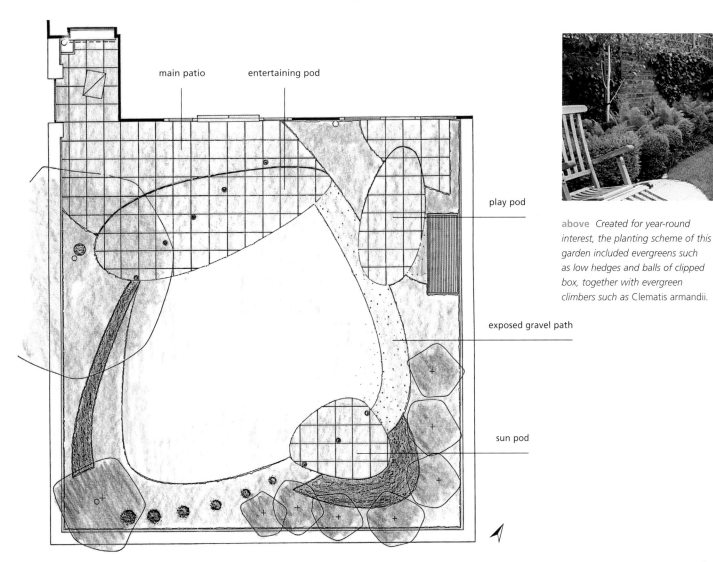

main patio

entertaining pod

play pod

exposed gravel path

sun pod

above *Created for year-round interest, the planting scheme of this garden included evergreens such as low hedges and balls of clipped box, together with evergreen climbers such as* Clematis armandii.

A Garden with Outlooks

Michael Day

dimensions: **10 x 15m (33 x 49ft) approx.**

soil: **alkaline**

aspect: **southeast facing**

key features: **slope from house down to boundary wall**

The owners wanted a low-maintenance garden that provided good outlooks from the house, and integrated the garden with the downland landscape beyond. They were keen to incorporate timber, especially sleepers, and climbing plants, and also requested a pond and a small seating area sited to catch the evening sunshine.

The site was dominated by a high boundary wall which, in the lower part of the garden, hid views of the landscape beyond. In addition, an oil tank on a concrete base was visible from all points in the garden and needed to be screened.

Existing concrete pavers were replaced with reconstituted stone slabs and shingle, the colour of which was chosen to compliment the paving but contrast with the house brick. From the terrace,

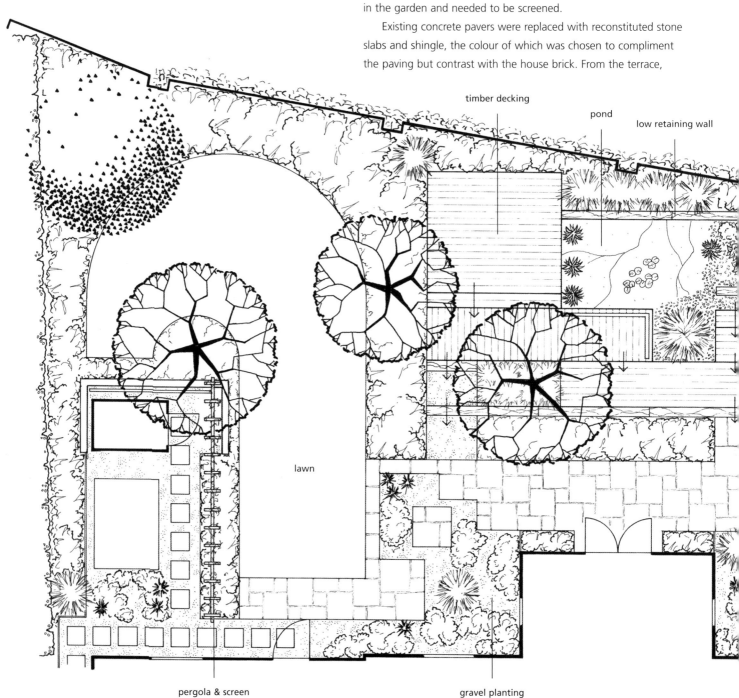

timber decking

pond

low retaining wall

lawn

pergola & screen

gravel planting

reclaimed railway sleepers form steps down the garden and provide a material contrast to the timber decking. The changing levels were enhanced by alternating the direction of the decking boards from one level to the next, and handrails were made high enough to lean on and wide enough to rest a glass on.

In the lower garden, a new pond became the focus of interest, distracting the eye from the high boundary wall. On three sides the pond was constructed using concrete block walls but the fourth side was a beach area to encourage wildlife.

The oil tank and a new storage shed have been screened using planed, ornamental fence panels with a pergola above providing another support for the clients' much-loved climbers.

above *The photograph shows the changing levels of decking and the handrails, made high enough to lean on and look at the pool below.*

below *The axonometric shows more clearly the pond in the lower garden, with a beach area on one side to encourage wild life.*

planting in pebble beach

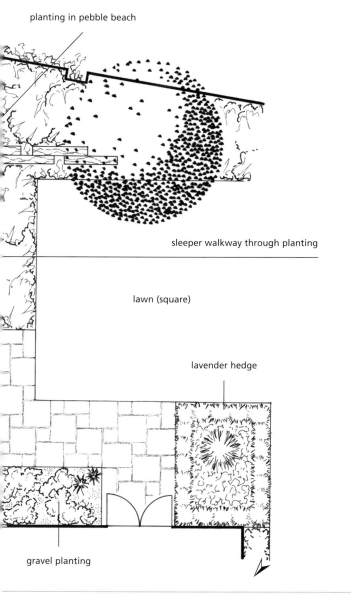

sleeper walkway through planting

lawn (square)

lavender hedge

gravel planting

Spiral Garden

Andy Sturgeon Garden Design

dimensions: **9 x 5.5m (30 x 18ft)**
soil: **sandy loam, very slightly acid**
aspect: **southeast facing**
key features: **spiral paving, water feature**

The owners wanted an outdoor room beyond their conservatory, continuing some design features (be it planting or colour) from inside to outside, and a water feature appropriate for a young child.

To offset the squareness of the site curves were introduced that swung out in an organic shape from the house. By spiralling the paving the eye was led into the garden, helping to create a sense of space. Introducing changes in level further enhanced this impression.

Boundaries between inside and out were blurred by raising the paving up almost level with the floor inside, and using light paving

and wall finishes to echo the bright decor of the kitchen. The colour of the kitchen units were also picked up in some of the planting.

The area immediately outside the doors catches the morning sun while the main seating area is in sun and shade at different times of day. The curved wall around this seating area now served as occasional seating for entertaining, as did the steps in the paving.

Rendered walls added height and, along with the water feature, provided a focal point that distracted from the imposing flank wall of the neighbouring house. Bamboo behind the walls would eventually grow up and act as a foil to the walls themselves. A bespoke bike store was built into the back of the walls and totally disguised by them, and a child's swing was also tucked away in this hidden area.

The planting consisted of an evergreen framework of shrubs with seasonal colour provided by flowering perennials and grasses that would be left standing in the winter. Height and structure were provided by a maple (*Acer griseum*), small *Sorbus*, and black bamboos.

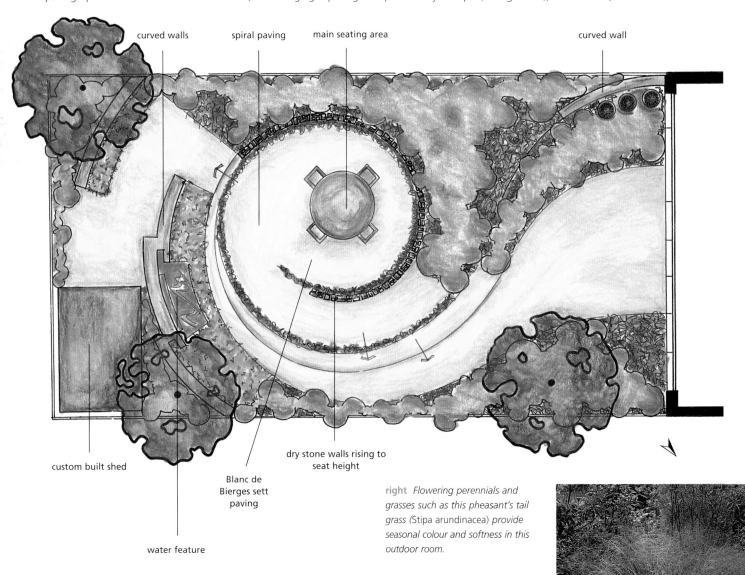

curved walls   spiral paving   main seating area   curved wall

custom built shed

dry stone walls rising to seat height

Blanc de Bierges sett paving

water feature

right Flowering perennials and grasses such as this pheasant's tail grass (*Stipa arundinacea*) *provide seasonal colour and softness in this outdoor room.*

A Garden for Wheels

Nigel Fuller

dimensions: **13.5 x 12m (44 x 39ft)**
soil: **neutral**
aspect: **northeast facing**
key features: **wheel-chair friendly, pergola**

The instructions was to create a contemporary courtyard for the owner's disabled wife. Consequently, the garden needed to be low maintenance and wheelchair friendly. Space was to be provided for large pots, and a sheltered, shady seating area was required.

This was a new site, and therefore presented a blank canvas; however, access was somewhat limited and the design had to consider this problem. The ground was covered with large paving stones, and the plantings set back to allow room to manoeuvre the wheelchair. A pergola provided a shady area.

The final design was quite simple, and involved landscaping the garden at a 45-degree angle to the house. However, this created an appearance of spaciousness, and the owner consequently felt he had far more garden than before.

above *The sweeping lines of the paving area gives a sense of spaciousness to this contemporary courtyard garden, while the pergola provides shade.*

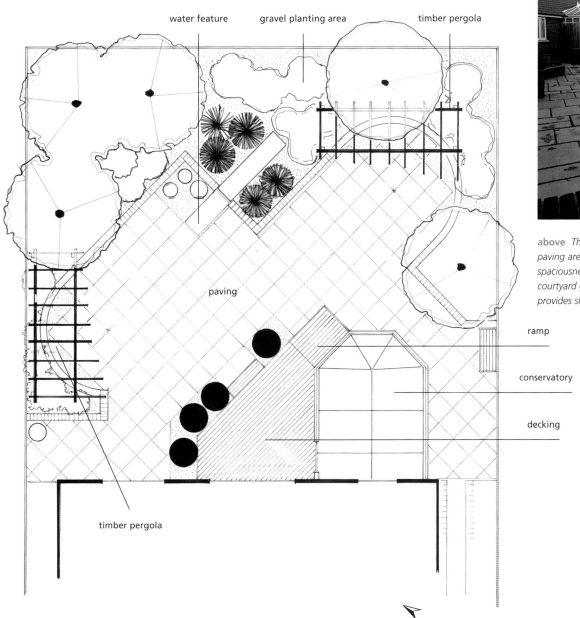

water feature   gravel planting area   timber pergola

paving

ramp

conservatory

decking

timber pergola

Bird's Eye-View Garden

Alex Johnson

dimensions: **10 x 8m (33 x 26ft)**
soil: **alkaline clay**
aspect: **northeast facing**
key features: **curving steps**

The owners requested a contemporary garden, without grass, which would make the most of the small space and complement the modern house. The view from the upper floors of the house were very important, making a strong ground pattern a priority, particularly in winter and spring, and at night.

Apart from some paving and a first floor balcony, the garden was virgin territory, but sited in an area of mature gardens with significant trees nearby. The garden was overlooked by neighbouring properties, and the boundary at the end of the garden consisted of a tall chain-link fence which needed to be disguised. Some sense of privacy was required.

A generous terrace provided plenty of space for a table and chairs. From here, dramatically curving steps swept up and away from the house. This created a bold pattern when viewed from the upper floors of the house and, by changing levels within the garden, helped to make a small space seem larger.

Sticking to a limited plant palette gave the space a greater integrity than if a large number of different specimens had been thrown together. The colour palette was equally subdued, with an evergreen backdrop of *Choisya ternata*, *Corokia cotoneaster*, *Hebe rakaiensis*, *Callistemon pallidus*, *Ceanothus* 'Blue Mound', and *Carpenteria californica*. Against this canvas, a few carefully chosen perennials introduced seasonal interest, including *Crocosmia masoniorum*, *Kniphofia galpinii*, and *Anemone blanda*, together with the ornamental grasses *Stipa pinnata* and *Festuca* 'Elijah Blue'.

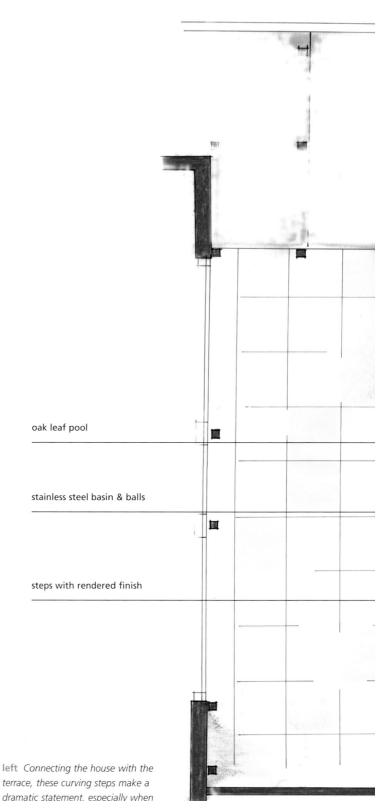

oak leaf pool

stainless steel basin & balls

steps with rendered finish

left *Connecting the house with the terrace, these curving steps make a dramatic statement, especially when seen from above.*

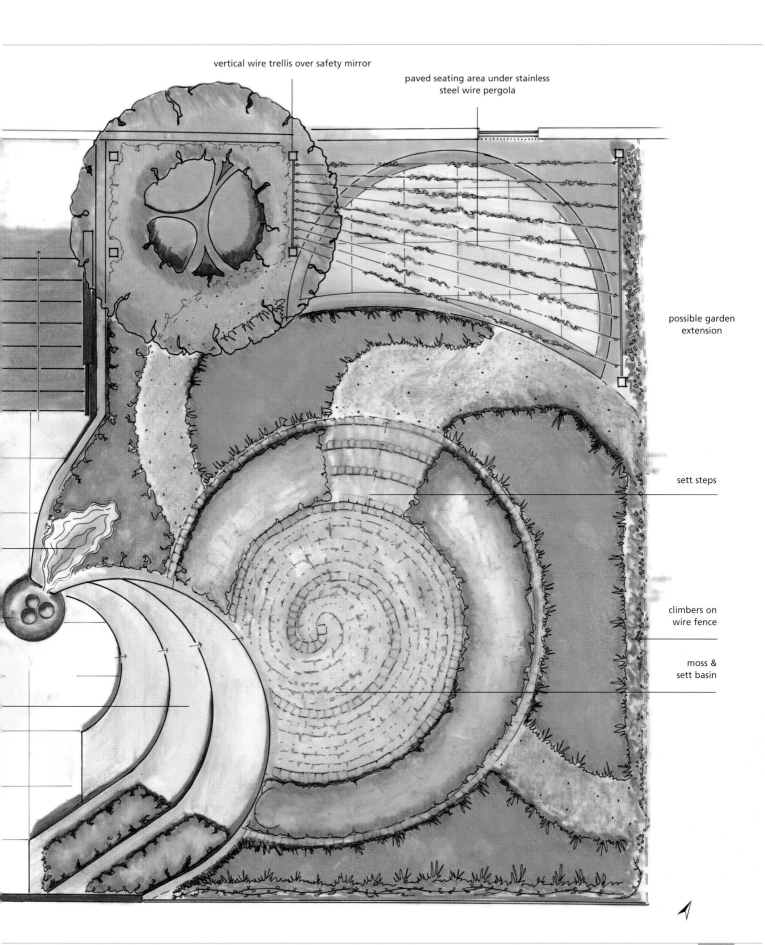

vertical wire trellis over safety mirror

paved seating area under stainless
steel wire pergola

possible garden
extension

sett steps

climbers on
wire fence

moss &
sett basin

A Sub-Tropical Garden

John Moreland

dimensions: **65m x 25m (213ft x 82ft)**

soil: **neutral to acid**

aspect: **sheltered, but exposed to easterly winds**

key features: **terraces, pool, fountain, hidden areas**

The existing walled garden within this estate in Cornwall, southwest England, had lain empty for years, and the owners wanted a sub-tropical garden to be enjoyed by hotel guests and the general public.

The site runs from east to west with a fall of about a 1m (3ft) down to the western corner. This slope was exploited by terracing throughout, with a central seating area, wide terraces, and steps leading down to a lavender-edged pool and fountain. The overall design curved sinuously to create open spaces leading to hidden areas which provided an element of mystery and surprise.

The overall intention was to create a sub-tropical feeling garden, typical of this part of Cornwall. There was also a desire to give an immediate sense of time and maturity, and to this end a framework of large cordylines was planted. In addition to these cordylines, the planting included phormium varieties, bamboo, *Pittosporum tobira*, and an olive tree.

To evoke the hot scents of the Mediterranean region, the design incorporated plants such as cistus, lavender, and rosemary that give off essential oils. Escallonia, lavender, and box were used as hedging, most notably in the serpentine hot border where box (*Buxus sempervirens*) was clipped at an angle to ensure growth at the base of the hedge. This border had a basic structure of flowering shrubs at the rear, and alternating purple and variegated cordylines, with an increasing variety of climbers including clematis and passion flower.

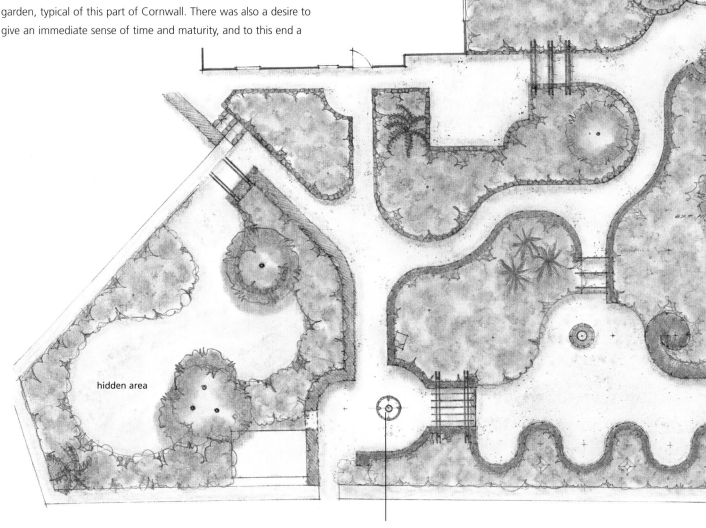

hidden area

fountain

right *The comon box (*Buxus sempervirens) *surrounding each of the cordylines has been clipped at an angle to ensure growth at the base of the hedge, a contrast to the explosive forms above.*

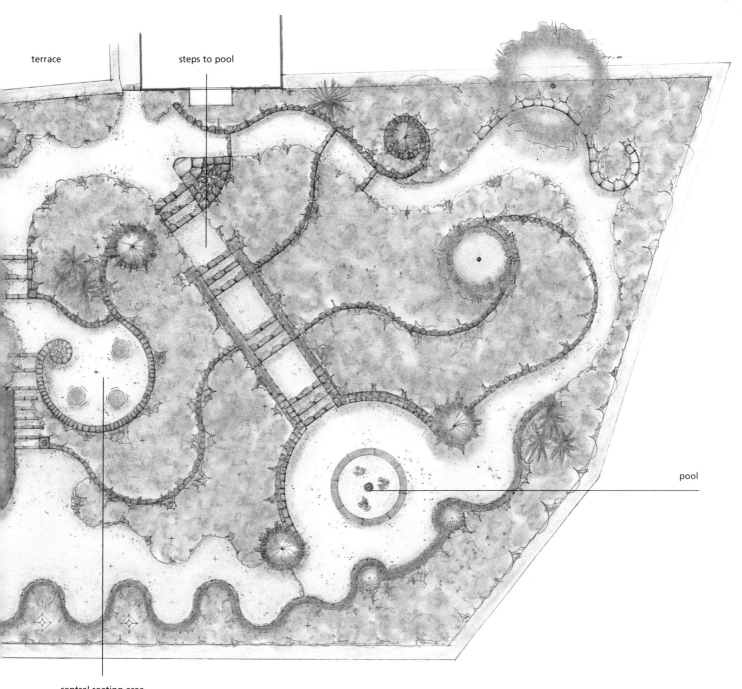

terrace

steps to pool

pool

central seating area

Garden in an "Ampitheatre"

Ryl Nowell

dimensions: **17 x 19m (56 x 62ft)**
soil: **clay**
aspect: **north facing**
key features: **steep slope, curving ramp, pergola**

above *In this garden a wooden pergola and seat, similar to that shown above, provided a well-concealed space and views beyond the boundary.*

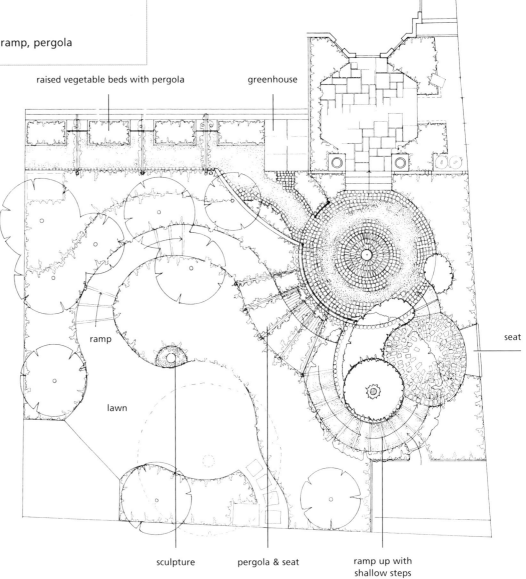

raised vegetable beds with pergola

greenhouse

ramp

lawn

seat

sculpture

pergola & seat

ramp up with shallow steps

The client wished to create a garden on what appeared to be an impossible slope, and to link the house with its rather remote plot. There was a need to provide privacy, especially from a neighbouring house overlooking the site, create a place for a greenhouse and vegetable garden, and provide an entertaining area near the house.

Major slopes on two planes created an amphitheatre with little level ground, rendering the space virtually unusable. The aim was to gain the maximum advantage of a relatively large London garden by utilizing slopes and extending flatter areas wherever possible.

To this end, a swirling, shallow ramp was created to take the longest route from upper to lower level. The existing flat enclosure near the house was enlarged to provide space for a table and chairs, using an angular design to echo the house, with retaining walls built of yellow London stock bricks to match the house.

A relatively flat area on top of the bank was extended by means of a substantial retaining wall. Its circular design extended the formality of the upper terrace at a lower level and provided a focal point from the house. Part way down the slope, and backing against the retaining wall of this stone circle, a seat was tucked under a pergola supported by the wall above, providing a well-concealed space with views beyond the boundary. At the bottom of the slope, a lawn and informal beds provided a contrast to the hard elements of the upper levels, and the planting scheme concentrated on fragrant plants to increase the sensual pleasure of this space.

Swiss Garden

Anthony Paul

dimensions: **60 x 35m (197 x 115ft)**
soil: **alluvial glacial silt**
aspect: **south facing**
key features: **long, sloping site**

The owners wanted a garden design which would sit naturally around the house but also meld into the surrounding countryside and made the most of the spectacular views. While the views are wonderful, the site is exposed and treeless. However, the owner wanted to keep the planting low so that it would not block the views. There were also large glacial boulders still in the site and these were incorporated into the design.

Decks were extended from the house, dropping down in a cascade of levels to sit within bold drifts of planting.

above *An overview of this garden shows how the low planting and water feature blend seamlessly with the surrounding countryide.*

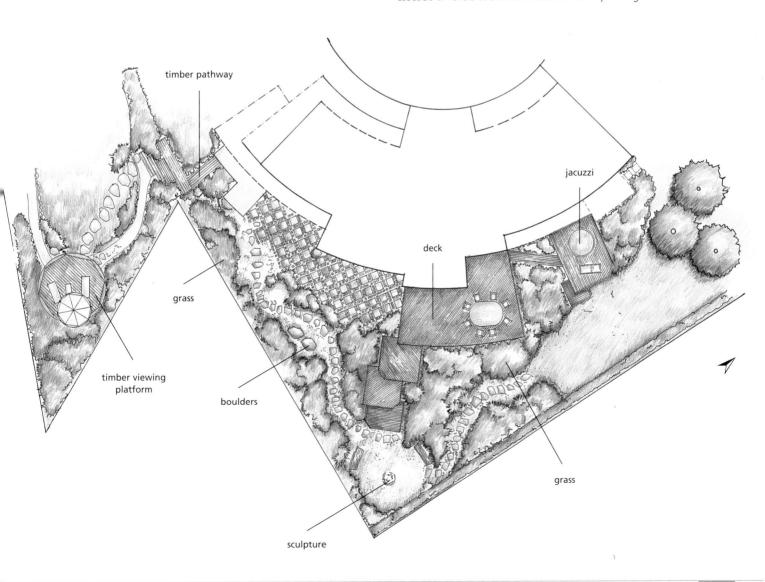

timber pathway

jacuzzi

deck

grass

grass

timber viewing platform

boulders

sculpture

"Inward"-Looking Garden

Keith Pullan

dimensions: **17 x 12m (56 x 39ft)**
soil: **well drained silty loam, slightly alkaline**
aspect: **south facing, sheltered**
key features: **central water feature, pergola**

The owner requested an informal garden with a strong, clear structure. A low-maintenance, low-cost solution was required, removing the existing lawn but re-using the concrete slabs laid around the house and patio areas. Boundary fences were to be renewed, since the owner was prepared to sacrifice existing views to create a more enclosed, private garden.

The main focus of the plan was a central circular water feature with a curved pergola forming a spiral into the centre. Railway sleepers set in gravel accentuated this spiral design. A timber arch from the patio area echoed the pergola and provided a further directional emphasis down the length of the garden towards a pair of bench seats in an enclosed section at the end of the garden. This followed the general principle that the layout for an enclosed, "inward"-looking garden should have strong structural lines which concentrate interest within the garden and dense planting to soften boundaries and take away their dominance.

Washed gravel was laid in favour of grass, in a thin layer over compacted unwashed binding gravel and hoggin, to form an attractive, firm, and, above all, low-maintenance surface. The existing concrete paving slabs were re-layed with alternate courses of small brick setts to match the house brickwork. This is a good example of how existing materials, though quite unattractive on their own, can be successfully re-used if combined with a contrasting material and set out with a more interesting design.

The planting was designed to provide sensual interest throughout the year. This is typified by the planting scheme of the central curved bed, where *Rosmarinus officinalis* 'Miss Jessopp's Upright', *Perovskia atriplicifolia* 'Blue Spire', and *Artemisia* 'Powis Castle', combined with structural *Phormium* 'Sundowner', and a clipped ball of *Buxus sempervirens* to define each end.

above *Two attractive types of low-maintenance surfaces are washed gravel and alternating courses of brick setts.*

below *The elevation gives a clear impression of the central water feature surrounded by a curved wooden pergola.*

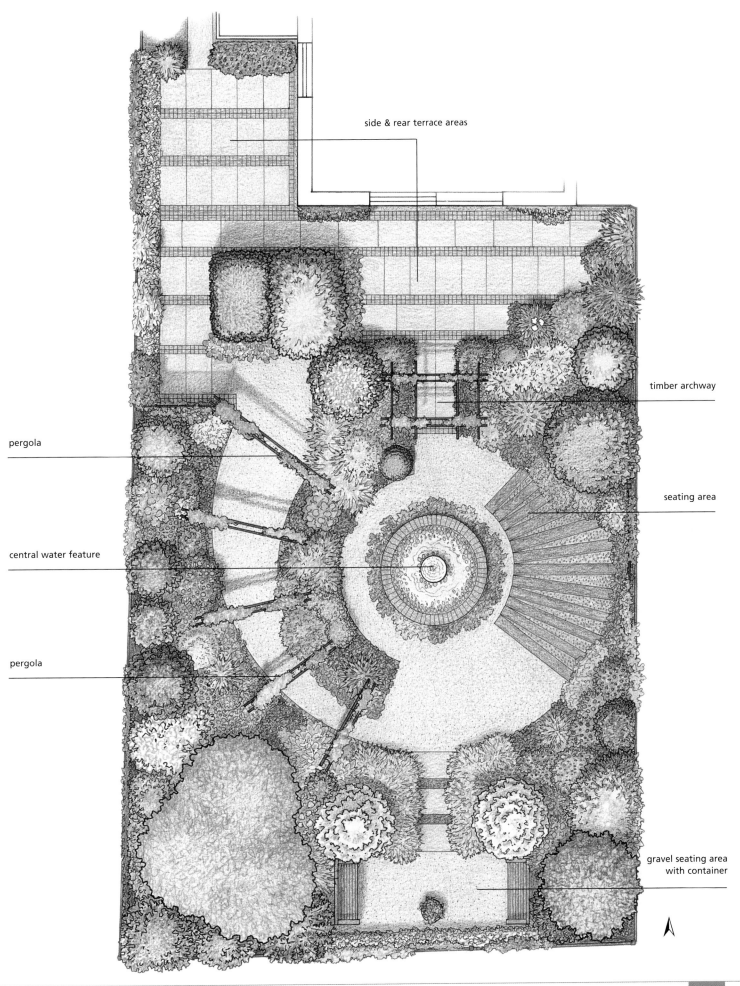

side & rear terrace areas

timber archway

pergola

seating area

central water feature

pergola

gravel seating area
with container

Connecting Lawns

James Aldridge

dimensions: 13.5 x 40m (44 x 131ft)

soil: clay

aspect: south facing

key features: **long, sloping site**

right *The multi-stemmed Himalayan birch (*Betula utilis *var.* jacquemontii*) is a good medium-sized tree for any garden; in winter its attractive white bark compensates for its lost foliage.*

The owners of the garden had no particular suggestions in mind, so the design was free of limitations. The main constraint was a long, sloping site.

All parts of the garden were based on a grid of the house and were conceived as a series of carefully proportioned spaces. There was a split-level terrace that can be accessed from the house. This led down to the garden, where there was a series of lawn spaces connected by floating deck bridges. A raised brick terrace sat to the centre of the lawn near the house and was the same size as the main terrace and in line with it.

The planting consisted of a series of broken hornbeam hedges (*Carpinus betulus*) across the garden. These will grow to a medium height. The trees were multi-stemmed Himalayan birches (*Betula utilis* var. *jacquemontii*). The rest of the planting was a series of mixed evergreens, clipped into different size spheres, including box, yew, and holly. The remainder of the garden was laid as lawn.

Radiating Garden

David Stevens

dimensions: **5.5 x 13m (18 x 43ft)**
soil: **slightly acid**
aspect: **east facing**
key features: **decking, water feature**

left *Among the most attractive of informal paths are stepping stones – the path shown here is made of natural stone.*

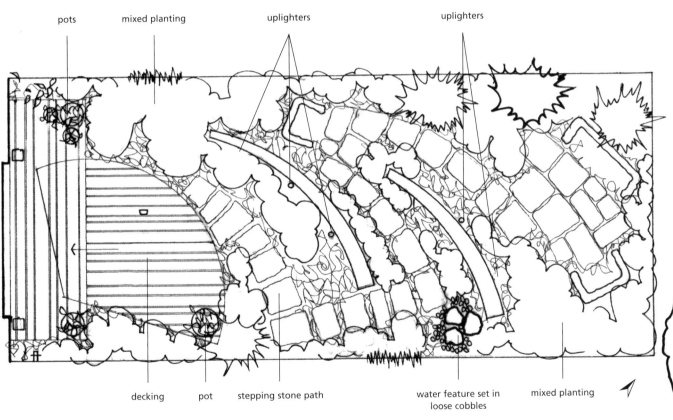

pots   mixed planting   uplighters   uplighters

decking   pot   stepping stone path   water feature set in loose cobbles   mixed planting

This tiny urban yard in South London had nothing of any merit, apart from a view to a wooded railway embankment. The brief was for an ultra-contemporary living space that radiated out from the modern conservatory built onto the rear of the building.

Leading out from the glass sliding doors was a two-tone deck with boards laid both across and away from the house. The boards nearest to the house were painted blue, linking with the interior colour scheme; those further away, yellow. The colour of the radius of the further section continued into that nearer the house, setting up an interesting and challenging visual dialogue.

From here the garden was progressively softer to link with the wooded landscape outside the garden. Stepping stone paths in natural stone zig-zagged between two walls – one painted yellow, the other blue – to extend the theme of the deck into the garden. These walls were uplit with grazing lights from ground level and were wider at one end than the other.

Just over half way up the garden three standing stones of unequal height provided a focal point, the lowest boulder being drilled so that water bubbles up and flows down the surface. Another light was set between these so that at night the feature glowed and stood out in relief against the surrounding planting.

Planting for this garden was very soft to counterbalance the overall architectural pattern and also to blend with the borrowed landscape of the embankment beyond.

A Bold, Geometric Garden

Acres Wild

dimensions: **60sq m (197sq ft)**
soil: **heavy clay**
aspect: **south facing, exposed**
key features: **stream, waterfalls**

The owners wanted a garden to complement their bold new house, softened with full, luxuriant planting with both flower and foliage interest. It had to provide shelter, and reduce the impact of wind and traffic noise, while retaining a view of the South Downs in southern England. They also wanted a large terrace for entertaining, a retreat, water – both reflecting and moving – and an area to exercise dogs.

The bold, geometric design was inspired by northern European house architecture and Kandinsky paintings. A large semi-circular reflecting pond that complemented the strong geometry of the house enclosed a large entertaining terrace. Actually two ponds – one fed by stream, the other aerated by a boulder fountain – the waterfalls in the stream, and a fountain helped offset traffic noise. An earth ridge along the boundary planted with tough wind-tolerant trees and shrubs provided shelter and enclosure. A variety of routes around the garden will stand up to the wear and tear of dogs.

A variety of background and sheltering plants were used including hawthorn, willow, viburnum, hydrangea, and dogwood. Feature plants include *Catalpa bignonioides* 'Aurea', *Pennisetum alopecuroides*, *Hosta sieboldiana* 'Elegans', and *Euphorbia characias* subsp. *wulfenni*. Among the blocks of tough, colourful perennials were *Euphorbia griffithii* 'Fireglow', *Echinacea purpurea*, *Ligularia dentata* 'Desdemona', and *Rudbeckia* var. *sullivantii fulgida* 'Goldsturm'. Alchemilla, bergenia, and ajuga were used for groundcover, and *Pontederia cordata*, *Scirpus zebrinus*, and *Sagittaria sagittifolia* were planted around the pond.

above *The semi-circular reflecting pond is softened by the drifts of pickerel weed (*Pontederia cordata*), Japanese arrowhead (*Sagittaria sagittifolia*), and* Scirpus zebrinus *planted nearby.*

right *A wider view of the garden, looking across the decks and pools to the elegant sweep of the lawn and planting masses beyond.*

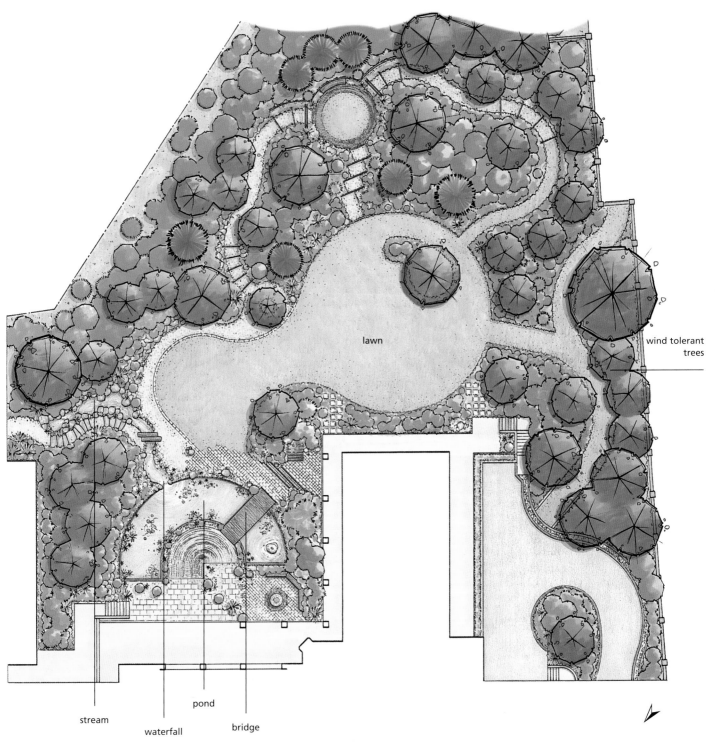

right *A wooden bridge crosses the semi-circular pond on one side, while the boulder fountain can be seen in the background.*

wind tolerant
trees

lawn

stream

waterfall

pond

bridge

Corridor Garden

Cleve West

dimensions: **30 x 4m (98 x 13ft)**
soil: **loamy, neutral**
aspect: **north facing**
key features: **bamboo grove, pond**

The owners wanted to transform a very narrow garden into separate spaces to loose the "corridor" effect. They also wanted a minimum use of flower or colour, so the garden had to rely on foliage and different shades of green to provide interest. Water spanning the length of the garden was another essential component requested by the owners.

Simplicity was the key element for this garden. A diagonally arranged bamboo grove and pond provided drama but also created movement across the garden to give an illusion of width. Divisions formed by bamboo, screens, and raised beds also helped to divert attention away from the garden's narrowness. Plants were chosen specifically for their interesting foliage and shades such as *Miscanthus sinensis* 'Gracillimus' and *Phyllostachys nigra*. All the trees are multi-stemmed birches (*Betula pendula*).

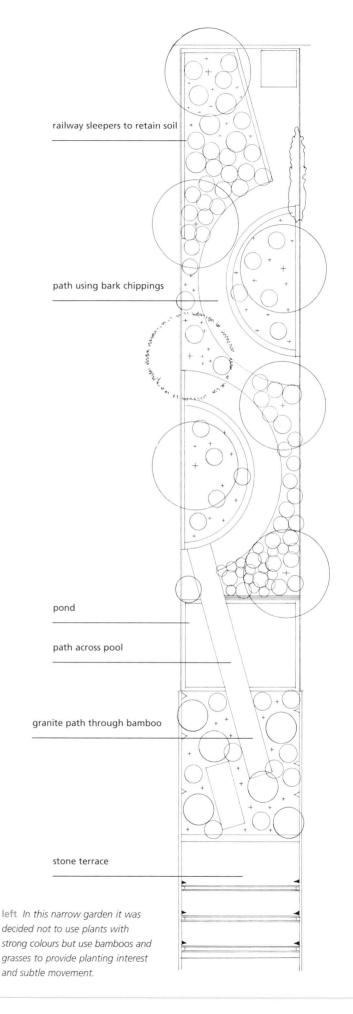

railway sleepers to retain soil

path using bark chippings

pond

path across pool

granite path through bamboo

stone terrace

left *In this narrow garden it was decided not to use plants with strong colours but use bamboos and grasses to provide planting interest and subtle movement.*

Garden for Sunbathing

Jane Follis Garden Design

dimensions: **7sq m (23sq ft)**
soil: **silty clay loam, neutral**
aspect: **northwest facing**
key features: **roof decking**

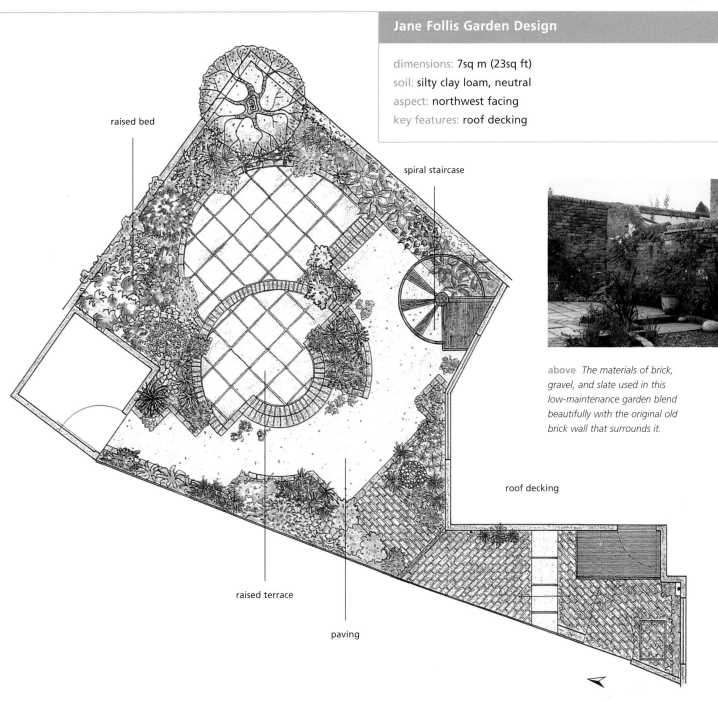

raised bed

spiral staircase

roof decking

raised terrace

paving

above *The materials of brick, gravel, and slate used in this low-maintenance garden blend beautifully with the original old brick wall that surrounds it.*

The owner wanted a low-maintenance garden where she could sunbathe at all times of the day. The cottage is situated in a conservation area and included a beautiful old brick wall, so every effort was made to use materials in keeping with the surroundings.

For maximum sunlight a spiral staircase was designed and built so that the owner could use the flat roof over the kitchen. This was covered in decking and surrounded with iron railings to match the staircase for both safety and aesthetics. There was minimum access to the garden, which meant that the components had to be assembled in the garden, including the staircase.

The staircase actually inspired the design and by using small terracotta tiles, mixed with brick to match the wall, the spiral look was reflected in the paving. There was a slight slope to the garden so to add extra interest there is one step up on to the paved area. A large piece of slate the owner had "saved" from her last house was incorporated near the steps.

A raised terrace was built with one step up from a gravel area, and it included raised beds. The owner had given instructions to include only purple, blue, white, and grey plants, and this colour theme comprised the planting.

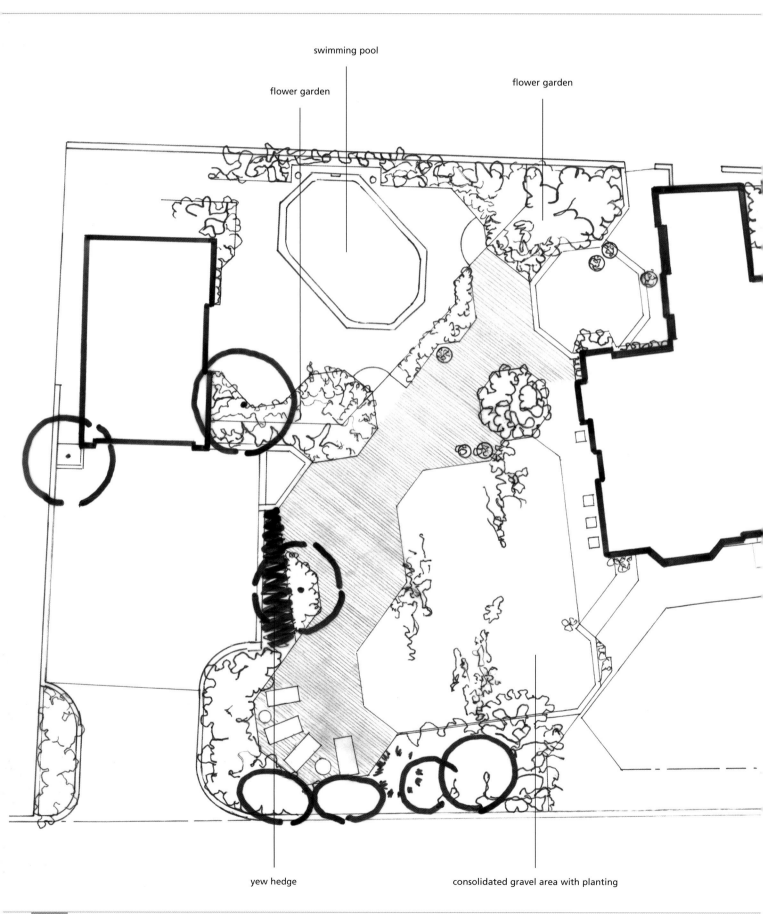

swimming pool

flower garden

flower garden

yew hedge

consolidated gravel area with planting

Seaside Garden

John Brookes

dimensions: **30 x 22m (98 x72ft)**
soil: **alkaline, sandy**
aspect: **north facing, sea wind**
key features: **seaside plantings**

The concept of this garden was as a place for children to play, and for family and friends to use in summer. The owners are not gardeners, although the wife was prepared to try, so easy maintenance was a consideration. There is a road beneath the garden wall so there is little privacy in the house, and the owners would not allow the wall to be raised because the house is located near a harbour and the view from the home is superb. While the owners were prepared for a certain loss of privacy, they also wanted a secluded corner which could not be seen and which would catch the sun. The garage would eventually double as a sort of pool house, with planting at the rear of it.

Among the features in the garden were a terrace in old York stone, a viewing platform, brushed concrete play area, a tree house in a cherry tree, and a swimming pool. A simple fence was chosen for the perimeter, trees in tubs were positioned near the house, and a boat on bricks to cover a manhole provided a nautical feel.

The top entrance of the garden was designed with gravel and pebbles to simulate the harbour over the wall at low tide, which has native rushes and grasses growing in the salty mud. This was "copied" in the garden but with more decorative grasses, low growing pinks, and sun roses. All plantings have to survive a salt-laden winter wind coming up into the harbour and the garden. Among those chosen were hydrangeas, rosemary, firethorns, roses, viburnums, yews, senecio, hebes, elaeagnus, and escallonia.

right *Among the key plantings in this garden was a cherry tree with a treehouse. Cherries – such as the Prunus incisa 'Oshidori' seen here – make excellent specimen trees.*

cherry tree &
tree house

concrete play area

terrace in old York stone

boat on brick covering manhole

viewing platform

Industrial Garden

Andrew Wilson – Pockett Wilson Garden Design

dimensions: **0.4 hectare (1 acre) approx.**
soil: **slightly acid**
aspect: **south/southwest facing**
key features: **screen walls, pool**

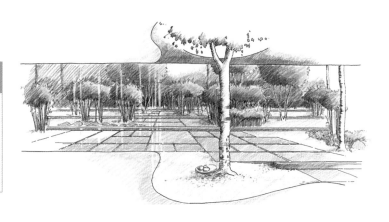

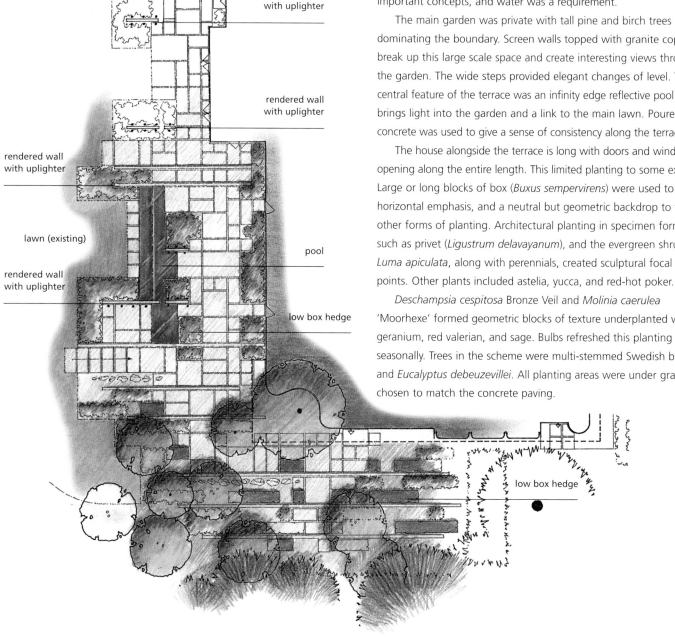

rendered wall with uplighter

rendered wall with uplighter

rendered wall with uplighter

lawn (existing)

pool

rendered wall with uplighter

low box hedge

low box hedge

The owners wanted a large paved area for entertaining and to provide a link between the house and garden. They asked for a slightly industrial quality in the design, something progressive to relate to a new extension to the house. Peace and tranquillity were important concepts, and water was a requirement.

The main garden was private with tall pine and birch trees dominating the boundary. Screen walls topped with granite coping break up this large scale space and create interesting views through the garden. The wide steps provided elegant changes of level. The central feature of the terrace was an infinity edge reflective pool that brings light into the garden and a link to the main lawn. Poured concrete was used to give a sense of consistency along the terrace.

The house alongside the terrace is long with doors and windows opening along the entire length. This limited planting to some extent. Large or long blocks of box (*Buxus sempervirens*) were used to give horizontal emphasis, and a neutral but geometric backdrop to the other forms of planting. Architectural planting in specimen form such as privet (*Ligustrum delavayanum*), and the evergreen shrub *Luma apiculata*, along with perennials, created sculptural focal points. Other plants included astelia, yucca, and red-hot poker.

Deschampsia cespitosa Bronze Veil and *Molinia caerulea* 'Moorhexe' formed geometric blocks of texture underplanted with geranium, red valerian, and sage. Bulbs refreshed this planting seasonally. Trees in the scheme were multi-stemmed Swedish birch and *Eucalyptus debeuzevillei*. All planting areas were under gravel, chosen to match the concrete paving.

Spanish Garden

Bernard Trainor Design Associates

dimensions: **2134sq m (7000sq ft)**

soil: **sandy loam**

aspect: **sunny front garden/sun and shade rear garden**

key features: **enclosed entrance courtyard, water bowl**

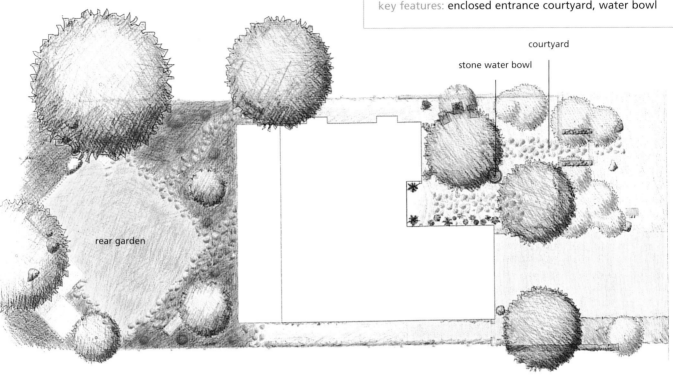

courtyard

stone water bowl

rear garden

The owners wanted livable front and rear gardens for the family with a Spanish theme to marry the architecture of the house. The gardens themselves were typical compact city gardens. One aspect of the design was to make these tight spaces appear larger than they are in reality.

By creating slightly different themes in garden rooms, the garden users will have a wide variety of experiences from day to day and season to season. Two distinctly different micro-climates separated the front and rear garden. Each garden section, while small, was brimming with interesting design details, including unique containers, garden walls, custom gates, and a sumptuous carved stone water bowl.

The design explored ways of making the gardens multi-dimensional in their use in order that a single garden element can function for both adults and children in a variety of ways. An example of this was the water bowl that created an exciting visual element for adults and for children, as well as relaxing sounds. Intended to be touched, this was carefully planned in both its scale and placement.

The front garden, basically an enclosed entrance courtyard, contained manzanitas, madrones, and succulents, while the rear garden had a lush and leafy appearance, predominantly planted with tall ornamental grasses and herbs, nestled beneath a California buckeye tree (*Aesculus californica*).

left *A key feature is the water bowl; this has been carefully placed for maximim enjoyment by both adults and children.*

far left *Planted with a chestnut tree and ornamental grasses and herbs, the rear garden has an informal, relaxing feel.*

Walled Garden

dimensions: **40 x 29m (131 x 95ft) including house**
soil: **sandy clay loam, slightly acid**
aspect: **rear garden, sunny/front and sides, shady**
key features: **reflecting pool, woodland garden**

The owner wanted the garden to reflect the period character of the house in a clean and uncluttered way with a minimum of maintenance. Her style inside her home is elegant and sophisticated, and she wished to keep to this in both colour schemes and layout, while also incorporating the traditional hard landscaping style and materials found in the house. The garden was surrounded by high walls and was very inward looking, relating to the architecture of the house. Most of the front garden was overshadowed by a large copper beech tree, creating an opportunity to develop a woodland flora.

The main landscaping features included a formal canal-shaped reflecting pool with a fountain, a bench seat, and lighting next to a random rectangular stone paved dining area with a small herb garden. There was also a deep bed vegetable and fruit garden. A stone wall with a gate enhanced the feeling of separate rooms within the garden. Stone steps up to the front door with box balls in planters created a more formal entrance. Low-level lighting throughout the garden lights pathways, created an atmospheric mood, and gave a sense of security at night.

The unavoidable maintenance needs of the lawns were reduced by edging them with paving stone at the right height. The gravel paths were also edged to give a neat finish and keep the gravel, lawn, and borders separate. Planting was dense to reduce the need for weeding, and the plant species used were chosen to suit the conditions, and were ones that thrive with minimal attention.

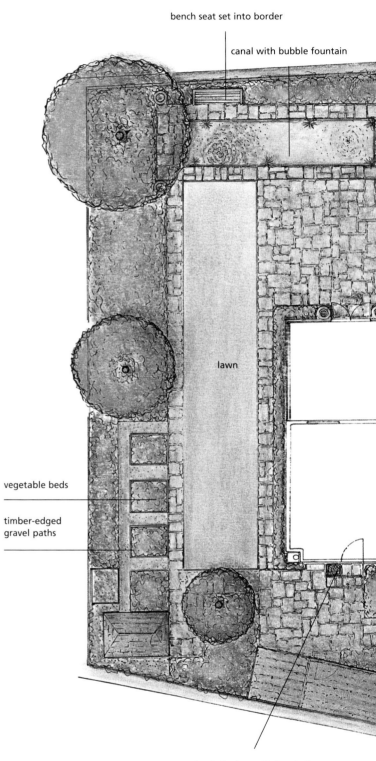

bench seat set into border

canal with bubble fountain

lawn

vegetable beds

timber-edged gravel paths

lead planters with box balls either side of steps

left *In order to reduce the maintenance of the lawns the designer has edged them with paving stones.*

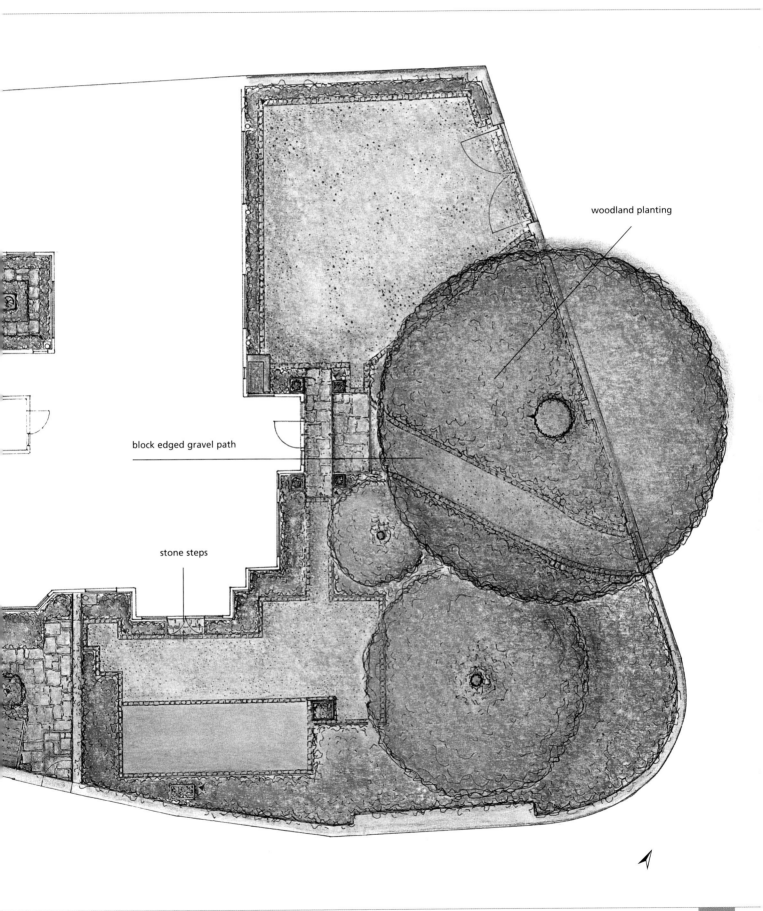

woodland planting

block edged gravel path

stone steps

Triangular Roof Garden

Joe Swift/Sam Joyce – The Plant Room

dimensions: 6 x 4.5 x 4m (20 x 15 x 13ft)
soil: n/a
aspect: southeast facing
key features: perspex screen, steel water feature

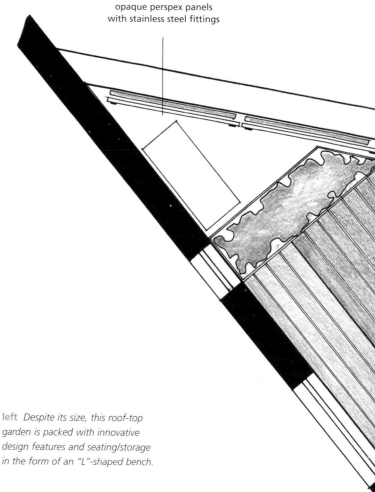

opaque perspex panels
with stainless steel fittings

left *Despite its size, this roof-top garden is packed with innovative design features and seating/storage in the form of an "L"-shaped bench.*

The owner of a roof-top garden wanted a low-maintenance, modern space for entertaining, with a simple water feature and some storage. An air conditioning unit and a tall metal flue belonging to the café below needed to be screened as they dominated the existing small triangular terrace. The wall facing the building had four large windows overlooking the terrace and the owner's bedroom, and these also needed to be screened but without cutting the light to the windows. The existing terrace used wooden diamond trellis panels to disguise the windows and flue, however this only added to the problem of the space looking cramped and busy.

When attempting to screen unsightly areas it is important to keep lines clean and bold, thereby keeping the interest in the garden so that the eye does not wander. An opaque screen of perspex was mounted on to the wall with stainless steel fittings and lit behind with blue halogen tube bulbs to create an ideal screen for the day (not blocking the neighbour's light), and an

interesting lighting feature at night.

A simple steel water feature was mounted onto a painted marine plyboard wall that helped to hide the flue. An "L"-shaped bench makes the most of the available space by providing ample seating and under-bench storage. The original shop-bought decking squares were replaced with hardwood decking, and the long, clean lines of the planks helped to make the overall space feel a lot bigger and more spacious.

Weight is always an issue when designing a roof-top garden. All the planting was in lightweight galvanized steel containers that had been lined with builders plastic. Broken-up polystyrene was used in the bottom of the planters to create drainage, and a specially mixed container compost with added slow-release fertilizer and water-retaining gel was added on top of the polystyrene. The containers were planted with the black bamboo *Phyllostachys nigra*, the perennial *Acanthus mollis*, Japanese mock orange (*Pittosporum tobira*), and New Zealand flax (*Phormium tenax*).

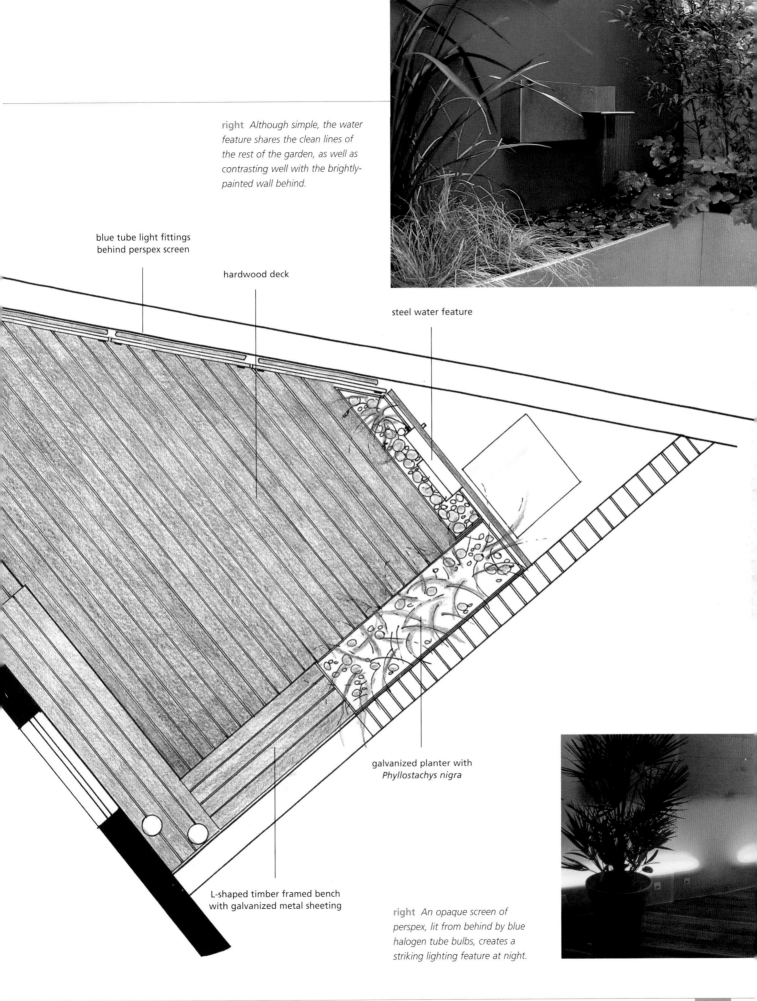

right *Although simple, the water feature shares the clean lines of the rest of the garden, as well as contrasting well with the brightly-painted wall behind.*

blue tube light fittings
behind perspex screen

hardwood deck

steel water feature

galvanized planter with
Phyllostachys nigra

L-shaped timber framed bench
with galvanized metal sheeting

right *An opaque screen of perspex, lit from behind by blue halogen tube bulbs, creates a striking lighting feature at night.*

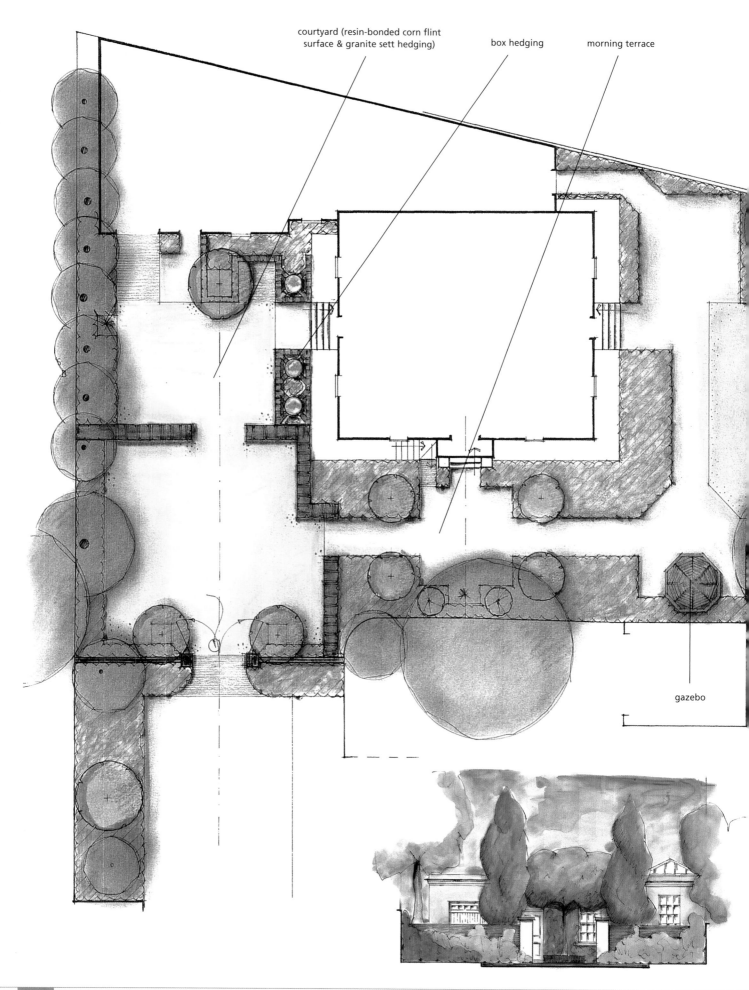

courtyard (resin-bonded corn flint surface & granite sett hedging)

box hedging

morning terrace

gazebo

Family Garden

Mark Lutyens

dimensions: **75 x 20m (246 x 66ft)**
soil: **clay**
aspect: **open and sunny**
key features: **summerhouse, courtyard**

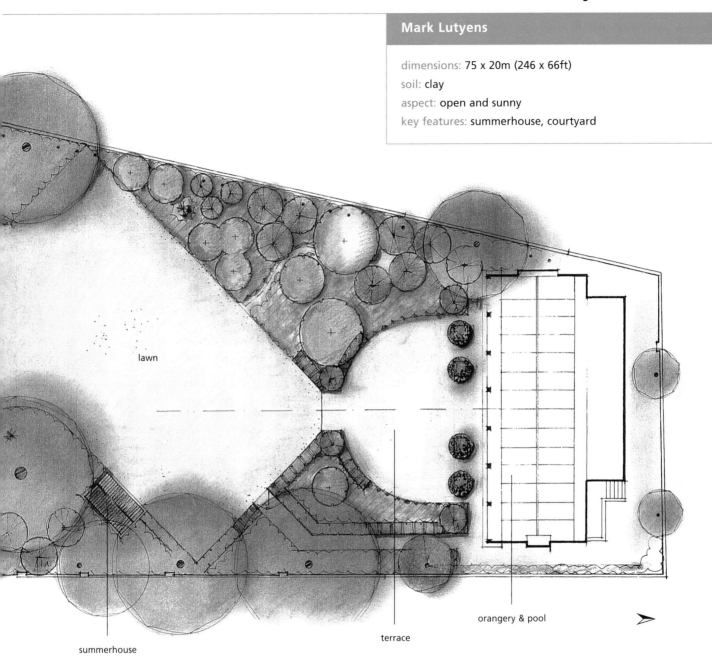

lawn

summerhouse

terrace

orangery & pool

The owners were very open to any design suggestions, as long as it consisted of a generously planted family garden. The house itself is big, with a newly constructed indoor pool disguised as an orangery and a few existing trees. The proportion of building to garden is high, and access for cars and people was a major consideration. Although the garden is open and sunny, the house casts a shadow over the centre of the garden. The design process was like putting together a jigsaw puzzle, organizing all that is required within the framework of what is already there to best effect.

This is a garden that was big enough to have a series of areas with their own planting character. A series of spaces were first designed, framed with beautiful planting. Yew, box, and beech hedges provided perennial structure, together with some strategically placed evergreen trees such as holly, holme oak, strawberry tree, and pencil cypress. The courtyard where cars are parked was formal and evergreen. The approach to the front door and around the house was structured but pretty with lots of colour and scents, while the main garden was more shrubby and robust – and football proof. The terrace at the end of the garden outside the pool, the sunniest place in the garden, had a more Mediterranean feel, with olive trees and rock rose among other planting.

Also included in this garden was a summerhouse as a refuge for the children – in every garden with children there should be a place where they can do their own thing.

Herbaceous Garden

Pickard Garden & Landscape Design

dimensions: **16 x 16m (52 x 52ft) average**
soil: **medium loam, slightly acid**
aspect: **south facing**
key features: **long, sloping site**

The owners wanted an area to entertain family and larger groups of friends. Most of the family wanted to sit in the sun but the father, who wanted a built-in barbeque, likes to cook in the shade. The owners also wanted a greenhouse in a classic style with a contemporary twist. The existing mature boundaries were lovely, walled on two sides, and with mature hedges on the other two.

The new gardens had to reflect the owners' taste in contemporary art, while not looking out of place with their Victorian house. This coming together of styles was achieved by using traditional good-quality materials such as oak timber and York stone but giving them a subtle contemporary twist. The whole was held together by a matrix planting of herbaceous perennials.

The garden was designed using geometric rules to form squares, rectangles, and spirals. Part of the mature yew hedge that enclosed one of the entrances was cut into a flowing curving arch that reflected in elevation the plan pattern of the pathways. The main seating area was centered in the space to catch the sun from early morning to sundown. The circular bench also acted as a retaining wall for the upper level of garden. Lush, textural planting in rich colours softened the garden's structure.

The garden is now a relaxing haven from the rigours of life. A variety of herbaceous plants, along with shrubs, climbers, bulbs, and perennials, created a soft, natural look, forming a cross between a traditional herbaceous border and a wildflower meadow.

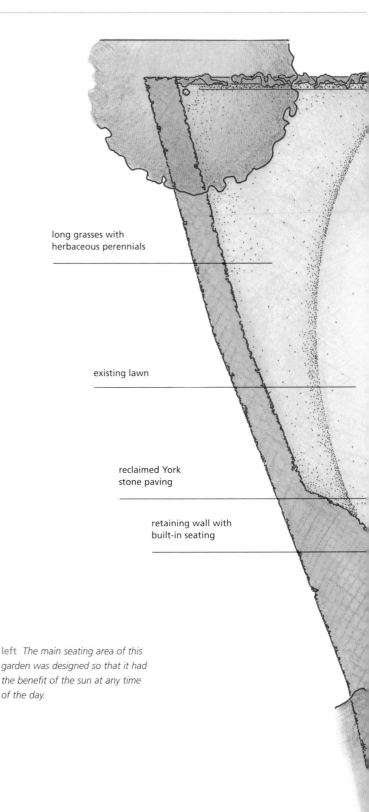

long grasses with
herbaceous perennials

existing lawn

reclaimed York
stone paving

retaining wall with
built-in seating

left *The main seating area of this garden was designed so that it had the benefit of the sun at any time of the day.*

mixed planting

culinary herbs

greenhouse

proposed lawn

mixed planting

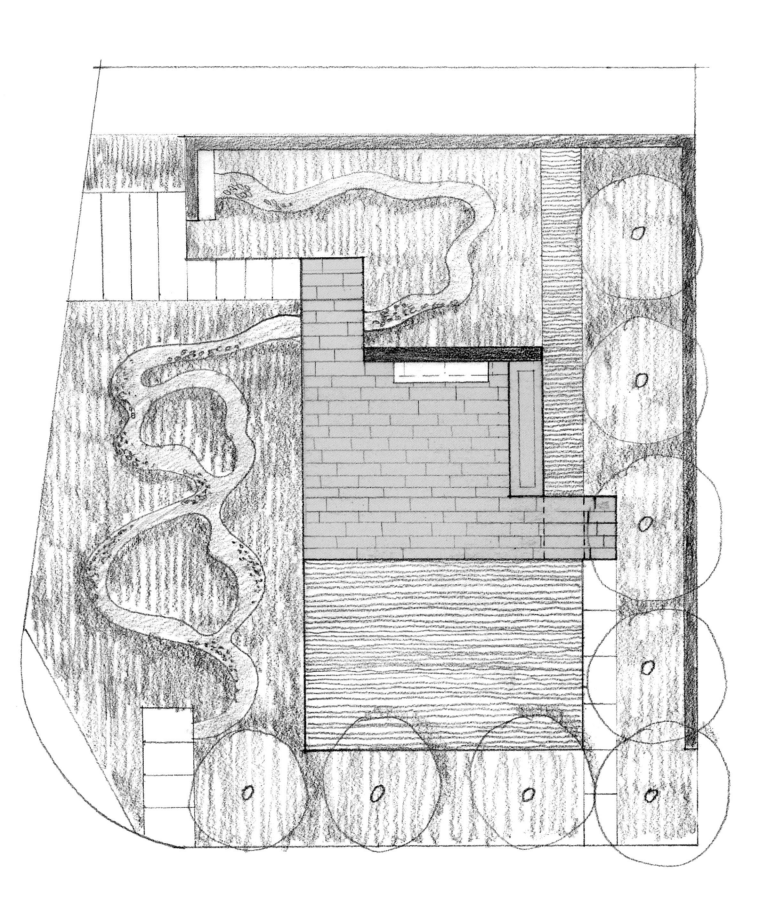

Renaissance Garden

Tom Stuart Smith

dimensions: **15 x 15m (49 x 49ft)**
soil: **moisture retentive (show garden)**
aspect: **open and sunny**
key features: **sandstone terrace, water trough, pool**

The design draws inspiration from sources as diverse as Mies Van der Rohe's Barcelona Pavilion, the American prairie, the Renaissance garden of Villa Lante, and the contemporary use of concrete by architects such as Tadao Ando and David Chipperfield.

The garden contrasted a minimal architectural aesthetic with an abundance of a wild meadow planting. The built elements comprised an enclosing in situ concrete wall and a central terrace made from soft red sandstone. The terrace was a single piece of furniture, like a large sofa near the middle of the space, reached by two planks of contrasting hard limestone paving. The central terrace included a water trough that can used as a champagne or wine chiller. Water spills from the trough out into the adjacent rill and from there into the pool in front of the terrace. The inspiration for this detail was the dining table at Villa Lante, perhaps the supreme masterpiece of Italian Renaissance gardening.

The garden was enclosed by two rows of massive pollarded limes. These trees are over 50 years old and have been regularly pollarded every other year. There are no shrubs in the garden. The herbaceous planting created an effect somewhere between a fen and a prairie. About 40 percent of the plants were tall grasses. The remainder were tall flowing plants, including meadow rue, *Anchusa*, masterwort, geraniums, mulleins, and columbine, planted in drifts through the grass to achieve a broad, thigh-high naturalism.

above The central terrace comprises a single monolithic wall and bench in soft sandstone, reached by two flat bridges of limestone, floating over reflective pools.

above The aerial perspective gives a clear overview of the garden's design, including the two rows of pollarded lime trees.

right An abundance of wild meadow planting, including grasses and drifts of tall perennials, softens the impact of the garden.

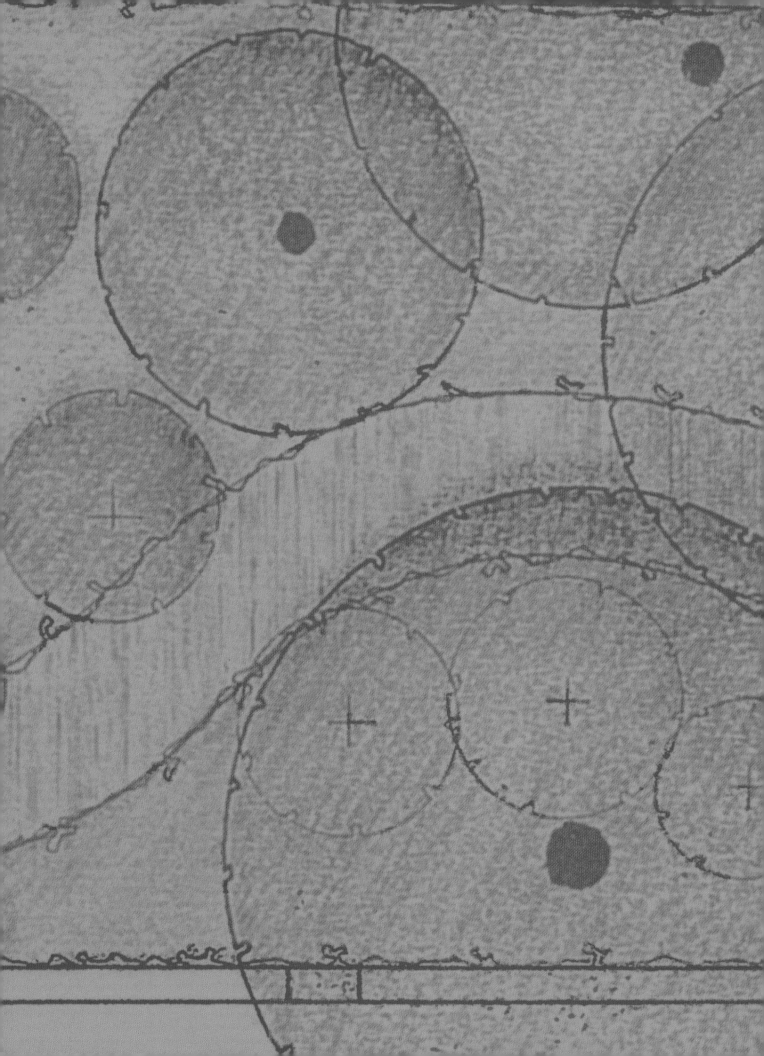

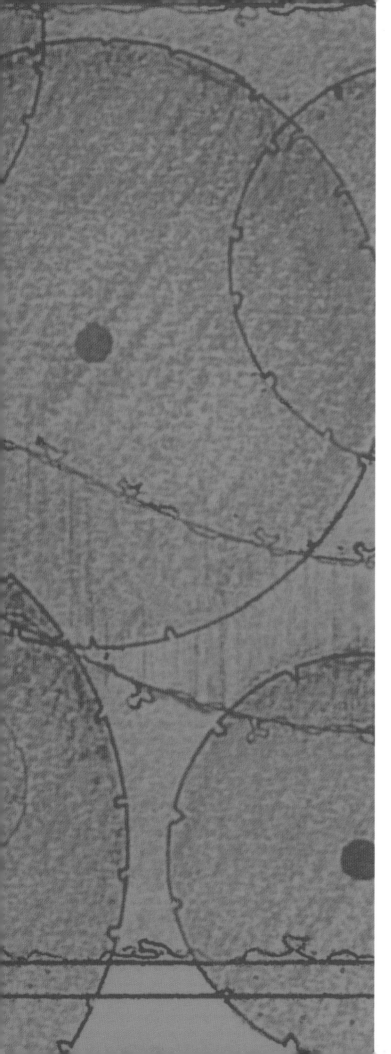

For many people, particularly urban dwellers, garden space can be extremely limited, both physically and psychologically. The design of the small garden, despite its restricted size, can prove complex and challenging.

Scale and simplicity are both key issues in that complex designs can create an over elaborate result, and a junk shop characteristic that can be claustrophobic. Planting and ornamentation are also often down-sized on the basis that more can be crammed in.

The most successful gardens use plants that would be at home in larger gardens, lending shade, bold textures, and drama. The key factor here is that there would be fewer of them, creating the added value of usable space.

The need for privacy is also an important consideration, with overlooking and observation from above proving key concerns for small garden owners. Pergolas, climbing plants, and trees can resolve these issues with the resulting shade disguising boundaries or true size.

It is also important to keep the palette of plants and hard materials simple and restricted, use lighting for dramatic impact, and view the garden as an extension of the interior rather than a separate entity.

The small gardens created by John Brookes that open this section show restraint and simplicity as key qualities. The rectangular geometry is well proportioned and bold, with architectural blocks of planting articulating the space.

Small Gardens

French Summer Garden

John Brookes

dimensions: **8.5 x 9.5m (28 x 31ft)**
soil: **n/a**
aspect: **mostly shaded**
key features: **pool with fountain**

Option 1

above *Grown in a container, one of the key plants in the garden was the scented evergreen climber Trachelospermum jasminoides.*

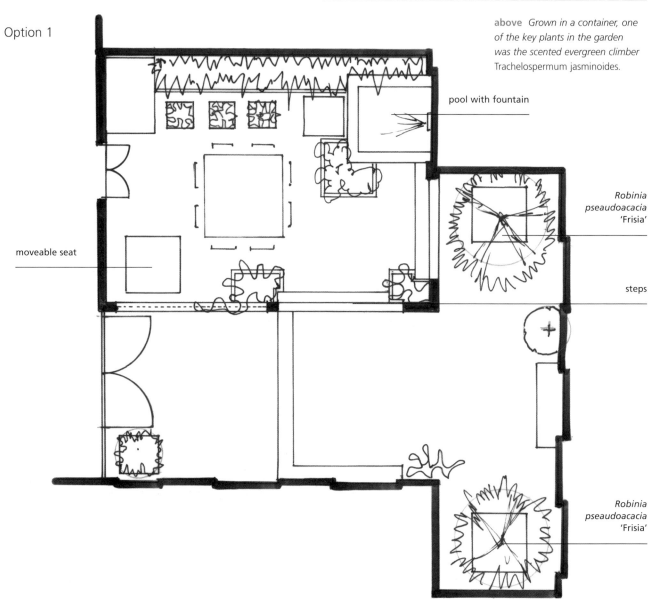

pool with fountain

Robinia pseaudoacacia 'Frisia'

steps

moveable seat

Robinia pseaudoacacia 'Frisia'

The design was for a garden attached to a French 17th-century townhouse with an extension which formed an "L" within the remaining walled enclosure. A 19th-century metal conservatory was being used as a studio, but the owners wanted it converted into a summer entertainment room that would be an extension of the garden. The scale of the conservatory in such a small space was out of proportion, but it did provide outside privacy for eating and entertaining during the long hot summers.

The French have a flair for the combination of very modern design with traditional elements and this was evident in the furnishings of the house. It was this mood that was to be recreated outside, although a certain amount of minor detail was left to the clients so they could express their own individuality.

Everything surrounding the garden focuses your attention upwards because it is surrounded by high buildings, so it was necessary that the design had a very simple but bold treatment. Both the conservatory and the courtyard were treated as rooms – so the result was a room within a room which was reflected in the design. A pool within a fountain provided a focus point and lowers the eye away from the surrounding buildings. A movable seat allowed the family to use the space to suit their individual needs.

The planting scheme was simple with all the plants being restricted to containers. These included *Robinia pseudoacacia* 'Frisia', *Trachelospermum jasminoides*, *Dryopteris filix-mas*, *Buxus sempervirens*, *Wisteria sinensis*, *Myrtus communis* subsp. *tarentina*, and *Sinarundinaria nitida*.

Option 2

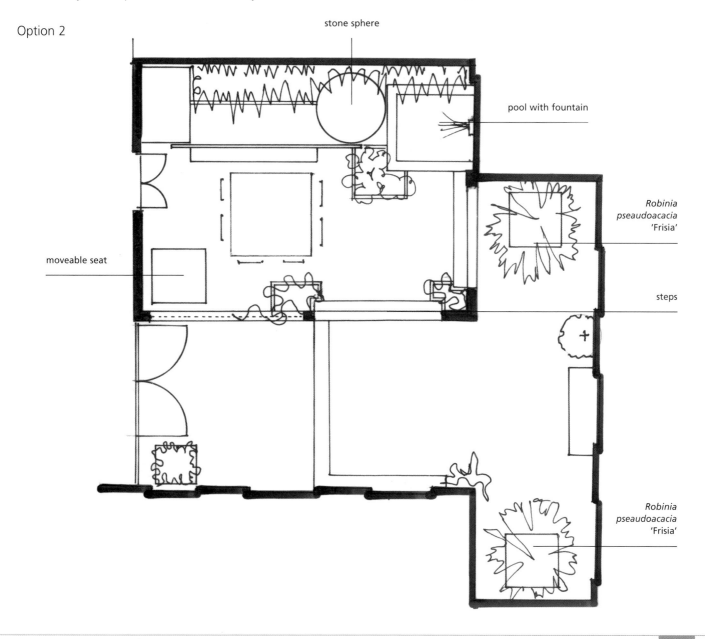

stone sphere

pool with fountain

Robinia pseaudoacacia 'Frisia'

moveable seat

steps

Robinia pseaudoacacia 'Frisia'

Garden Stage

Anthony Noel

dimensions: **5 x 12m (17 x 39ft)**
soil: **clay**
aspect: **southwest facing**
key features: **lawn/gravel square, stone walls**

The owner wanted to re-create an exterior stage or outside room using traditional materials in which to experiment. The garden was inspired by Hidcote, Sisssinghurst, and the cottage garden surrounding the farmhouse where he lived as a child. A dash of fantasy was inspired by Versailles, (large urns, elaborate topiary), and also his former career as an actor and set designer.

The old York stone path made a square around the lawn, or later, gravel square. The narrow passage near the house was paved horizontally to diminish any feeling of narrowness, using old bricks laid in an undulating fashion to suggest age. Around the edges, in fact everywhere in the garden, including pots, urns, and walls, stale milk and yogurt were applied to encourage moss and lichens.

Against the far wall was an old-fashioned honeysuckle, to the left of a disused gate (with a stone urn surrounded by hostas) was a rectangular raised bed, and, above it, a boxwood hedge. In the corner towered an urn planted with *Cordyline* 'Torbay Dazzler'. Separating the two beds was a boxwood totem pole and a tree paeony. Along the ground was a line of the silver Japanese painted fern. The long wall was planted with *Rosa* 'Madame Alfred Carrière' and decorated with terracotta masks. At the other, more sunny, end of the long wall was a Mediterranean silver and grey bed. Apart from permanent shrubs, climbers, topiary, bulbs, and herbaceous perennials, each year the garden would have four seasonal moods based on the bedding plants chosen.

raised bed

left *This small small garden is packed with predominantly white planting, and stylish features, including pots, urns, and topiary.*

right A view looking out of the house underlines the sense of the garden being an exterior stage or outdoor room.

wall fountain York stone path

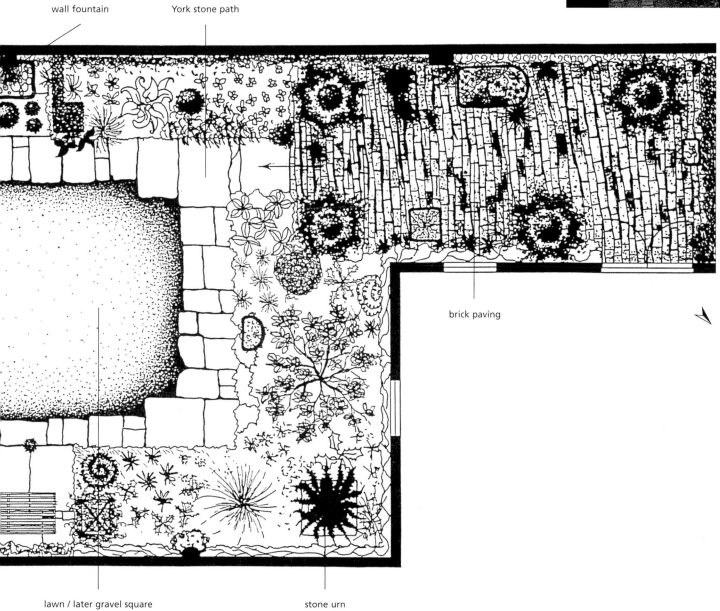

brick paving

lawn / later gravel square

stone urn

Sunken Garden

Balston & Co

dimensions: **38sq m (125sq ft)**
soil: **imported neutral topsoil**
aspect: **east facing**
key features: **semi-circular retaining wall, water fountain**

The owners wanted to create a small urban garden that was largely decorative but which had seating in the area that catches the sun in summer. Water could be included as well as stainless steel to form a sheet cascade. Privacy was an important issue but there was limited scope to increase it owing to planning and party wall requirements. The plan had to cater for the possibility of a future external staircase down from the floor above and a possible conservatory. The owners had limited gardening skills, but they wanted a scheme that created year-round interest. The available plot was in a tightly area enclosed by the surrounding properties and overlooked.

It was necessary to provide a strong low-level focus to bring the eye down, away from the surrounding buildings. A lower level of a semi-circular area of paving was formed with a plinth to display plants in containers. A semi-circular retaining wall with a fixed seat formed the transition between the two levels, the upper one providing a planting area. A central stainless steel fountain spanned the two levels, and trelliswork provided a support for climbers.

Shade and moisture-loving plants, many of them evergreen, provided year-round interest. Dogwood and maple trees provided the structural interest with low-growing herbaceous plants – ferns, hosta, and *Heuchera* – providing ground cover. Climbing roses, hydrangea, clematis, and ivy covered the trellis topped walls.

above *The elevation shows how different levels and dramatic planting can create interest in even the smallest of urban gardens.*

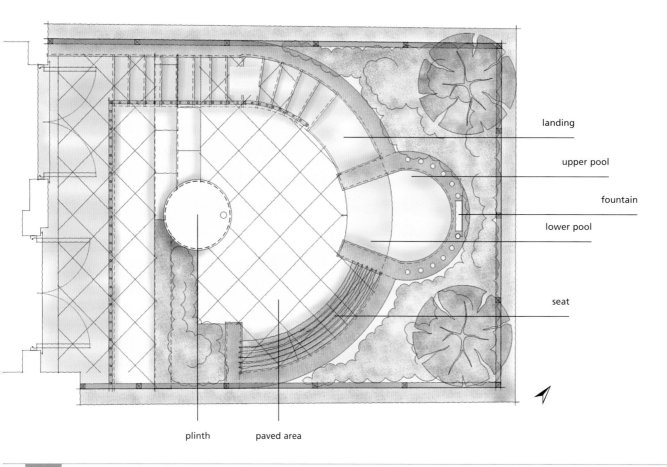

landing

upper pool

fountain

lower pool

seat

plinth   paved area

Bauhaus-Inspired Garden

Youn-sun Chun

dimensions: **6 x 6m (20 x 20ft)**
soil: **imported**
aspect: **shady**
key features: **suspended pergolas, low benches**

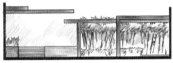

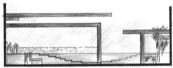

above *The elevations show how the blocks of black bamboo* (Phyllostachys nigra) *relate to the structural but unplanted pergola to provide vertical emphasis.*

The brief was to create a garden based on an existing design or art work. The pattern of the garden is based on a rug in the Bauhaus style. The patterns and colour regime are identifiable as an inspirational source. Because the garden is in a small restricted space, the design had to maintain a level of simplicity and use a restricted colour and planting palette.

The garden was paved on different levels with each surface or level paved in coloured concrete of a slightly different hue. Earth colours and terracotta shades were used to create a warm and comfortable atmosphere. Simple steel pergolas floated above the

garden at a higher level. These were to remain unplanted as architectural features giving scale and vertical emphasis. Low benches provided seating. Lighting under the benches and to the steps provided a hidden glow to restrict glare.

Planting was restricted to simple blocks of black bamboo (*Phyllostachys nigra*). These were planted for the black stems, and they linked to the pergolas overhead. In addition, the foliage moves and created sound with wind disturbance. The planting was evergreen and purposely understated. Lighting from the ground beneath created visual interest after dark.

Woodland Garden

Arabella Lennox-Boyd

dimensions: **20 x 7m (66 x 23ft)**
soil: **poor, slightly acid; improved with organic material**
aspect: **northeast facing**
key features: **meandering pathway**

The garden is long and narrow and is largely shaded by the neighbouring house and garden walls. A meandering brick pathway was created to provide a "journey" through a scented woodland-style garden, through a dividing *Taxus baccata* hedge, and on to a small brick edged lawn. The lawn at the far end of the garden was not overcast by the shadow of the buildings, and therefore was a great area for small children to play and sit in the sun. To the east of this cross-shaped lawn was a small, York stone terrace.

The woodland garden and the lawn garden were planted in two different styles as two different rooms. The woodland garden contained an existing *Magnolia grandiflora*, and was further planted with various small trees, each giving the garden some seasonal interest, privacy, and colour. The under storey and groundcover

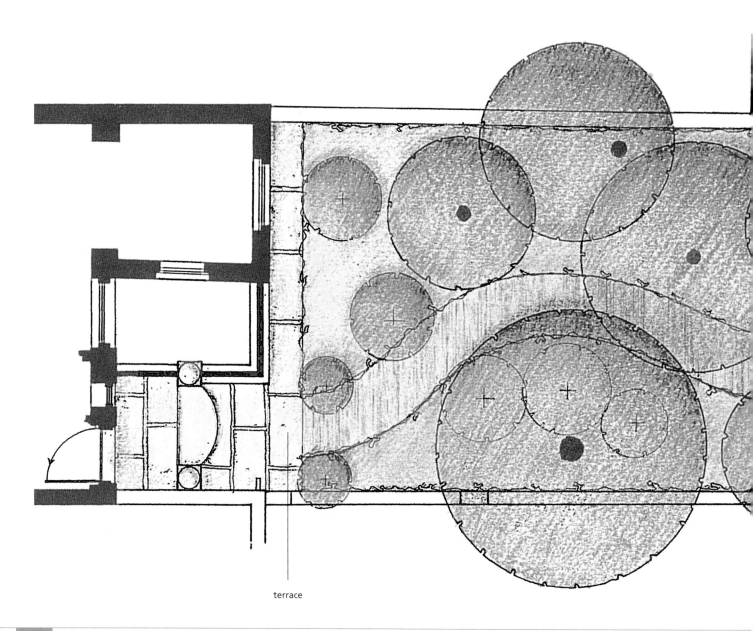

terrace

planting provided a profusion of colour and scent. Jasmine, *Philadelphus*, viburnum, honeysuckle, daphne, and *Hamamelis* supplied the scent, while camellia, hydrangea, spiraea, *Anemone*, hellebore, iris, hosta, wisteria, and clematis provided the colour. The combination of these plants within a structure of skimmias, euphorbias, elaeagnus, and a yew hedge gave a woodland feel.

The lawn area was planted with sun-loving plants. A profusion of roses gave colour and scent, along with ceanothus, rosemary, *Agapanthus*, bergenia, lavender, rock rose, clematis, and *Centranthus*. Some woodland planting was mixed into this area to provide a transition from one area to the other. The walls were furnished with climbers, and an abundance of spring and summer flowering bulbs increased the interest and magic in this small garden.

above *Among the small trees designed to give seasonal interest, privacy, and colour was a Japanese crab apple* (Malus floribunda).

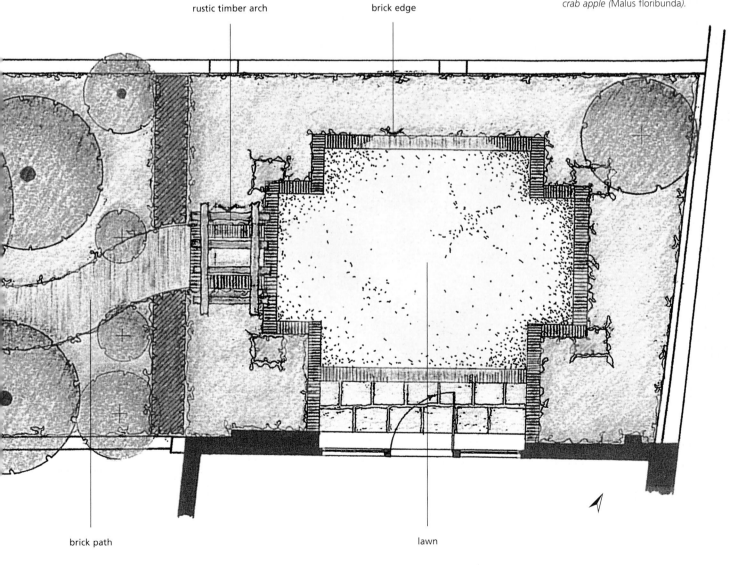

rustic timber arch   brick edge

brick path   lawn

Terrace House Garden

Catherine Heatherington Designs

dimensions: 13 x 5m (43 x 16ft)
soil: clay
aspect: north facing
key features: deck, paved area

The owners wanted a low-maintenance garden in a contemporary style suitable for children. They didn't want a lawn and preferred light colours and interesting textures in the planting, like those provided by grasses and bamboos. A view from the dining area was crucial – they wanted to feel as if the garden was part of the house. The house was overlooked, and while the neighbours on one side were to be screened, the other side was to be left open as the children talk with their neighbours over the fence.

A diagonal design was used to make the small area look bigger by bringing movement into the garden. The eye was taken around the space rather than going straight to the end of the garden. The steps were shallow and wide to make it easier for small children. The lines of brick through the paving echoed the lines of the deck board, and created a link between the two areas.

The shrubs and perennials planted included hebes, *Aucuba japonica* 'Crotonifolia', *Ceanothus* 'Italian Skies', *Euonymus fortunei* 'Emerald Gaiety', *Alchemilla mollis*, and *Milium effusum* 'Aureum'. Several plants were used for their architectural elements, such as *Calamagrostis* x *acutiflora* 'Overdam', bamboos, and *Fatsia japonica*.

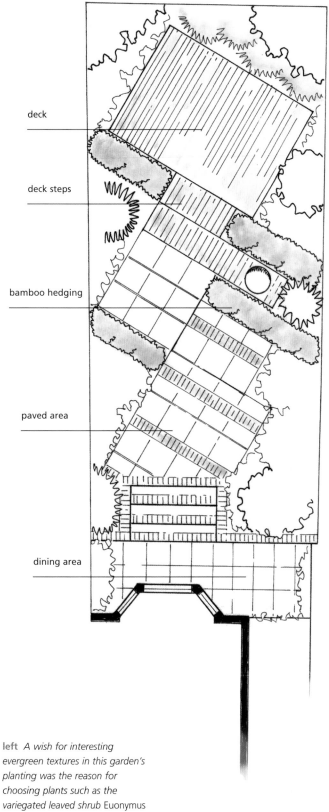

deck

deck steps

bamboo hedging

paved area

dining area

left *A wish for interesting evergreen textures in this garden's planting was the reason for choosing plants such as the variegated leaved shrub* Euonymus fortunei *'Emerald Gaiety'.*

A Garden of Circles

Lotti Kierkegaard – Elizabeth Banks Associates

dimensions: **7 x 5m (23 x 16ft)**
soil: **loam**
aspect: **south, southwest facing**
key features: **terrace, water feature**

right *Low maintenance planting in this garden included bamboos – here, the variegated dwarf species Pleioblastus variegatus.*

The plan for this garden was to create a visual focus at the end of the house, where floor-to-ceiling glass doors allowed views from the kitchen. The planting was to be low maintenance. The garden had several neighbours to screen, however the owner also wanted to allow sunlight in.

The very linear structure to the house interior and architecture was offset with a geometric circular pattern that encompassed both planting and seating, and cut through the square paving layout. The wooden bench was custom built to the specific radii and the terrace was paved in light coloured paving setts. A concrete water feature in the same light colour as the paving material mirrored both the colour and the circular pattern of the design. By letting the box hedge follow the radii of the circular patterns of the design, greenery and planting was placed close to the house for added visual interest. The level of the box hedge started low and gradually raised up, which introduced movement in the small garden.

The planting included box hedging, bamboos, an existing cherry tree, grasses, and herbaceous perennials, creating specific colours for each season – yellow in spring, blue and pink in summer, reds and oranges in autumn, and white in winter.

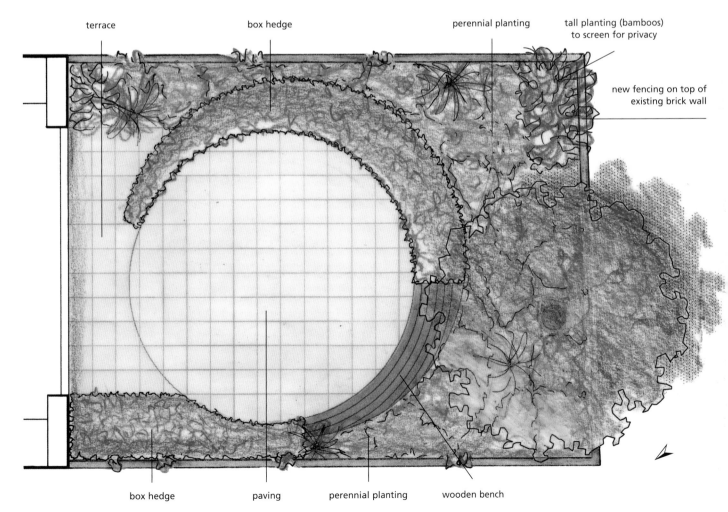

terrace box hedge perennial planting tall planting (bamboos) to screen for privacy

new fencing on top of existing brick wall

box hedge paving perennial planting wooden bench

"Sun Worshipers"

Clarke Associates

dimensions: 4.5 x 4.5m (15 x 15ft), 1.4 x 6m (5 x 20ft)
soil: slightly alkaline clay, loam
aspect: east facing, open to south and southwest, sheltered
key features: raised deck

right *The main area of planting included perennials such as ferns, euphorbias, and grasses – this is the clump-forming grass* Miscanthus sinensis *'Morning Light'.*

Option 1

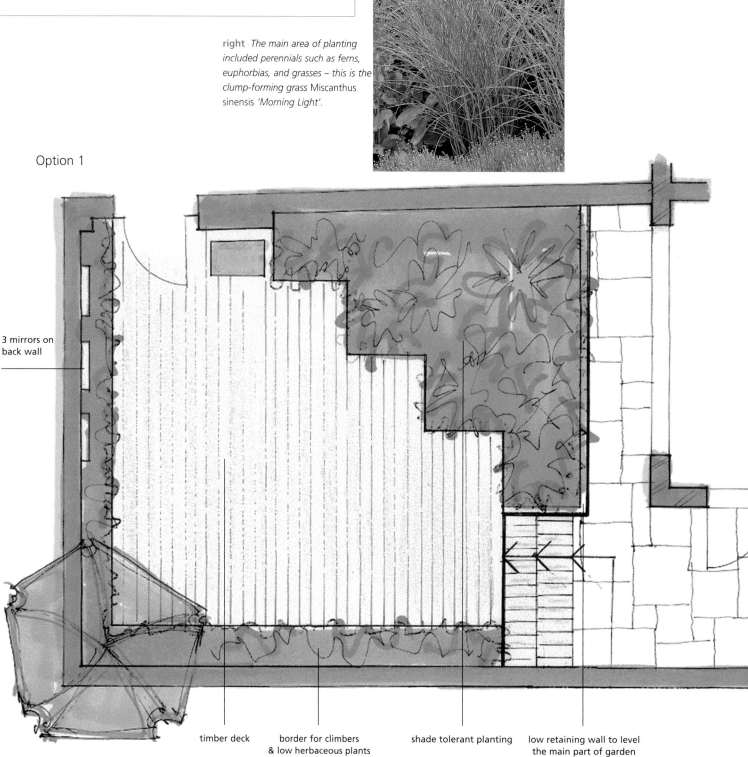

3 mirrors on back wall

timber deck

border for climbers & low herbaceous plants

shade tolerant planting

low retaining wall to level the main part of garden

The existing space was to be transformed into a glorious garden with lots of leafy green plants. There should be room to eat in the garden, it should be safe for babies to play in, and nothing should get in the way of sunbathing.

The focus of the garden was built around a timber deck – rather than the more traditional lawn – principally because it wouldn't suffer compaction and water-logging in wet weather or when garden furniture and bikes were dragged across it. The deck was lovely to walk on in bare feet, and it dried out and warmed up more quickly than grass. The deck created an upper level in the sunniest part of the garden and provided the maximum amount of sunbathing space. The windows overlooking the garden from inside were echoed by introducing three square mirrors along the back wall, creating virtual windows into the outside world but without compromising privacy. The paving chosen for the lower level was reclaimed flagstone in a traditional pattern but a more contemporary style would also have worked well. All garden and household storage was restricted to the utility area.

Planting on the sunny walls was restricted to evergreen climbers and a single layer of plants at low level which did not encroach too much on the deck. The main area of planting was fairly shade tolerant with ferns, grasses, euphorbias, and other perennials. A soft, warm colour on the walls completed the transformation, bringing sunshine into the garden even on grey rainy days.

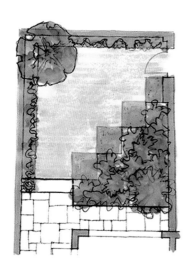

Option 2

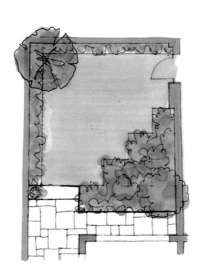

Option 3

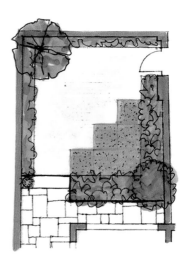

Option 4

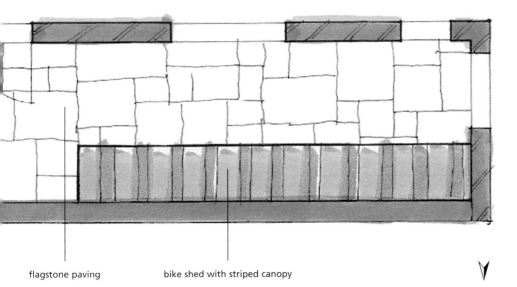

flagstone paving   bike shed with striped canopy

above The garden's designer worked on four alternatives ideas for the focal point of the garden. Option 1 was the preferred scheme – the plan for this option has been placed sideways on.

Four Formal Gardens

Simon Dorrell

dimensions: **9 x 9m (28 x 28ft) approx. each garden**

soil: **clay**

aspect: **south facing**

key features: **sunken gardens, pergolas**

A series of interconnected gardens were designed to reflect the extensive formal gardens in the historic setting of Hampton Court Palace in outer London. The four small gardens needed to provide shelter for tender plants and to provide intimate sitting areas.

The site of the small gardens lies on the perimeter of an area of lawn and specimen trees. There is a striking view of a substantial house, and the site is adjacent to an early Victorian yew hedge that separates it from the recently designed double herbaceous borders and the extensive, newly created, formal water gardens beyond.

Two pairs of sunken gardens were created, each linked by two "squares" covered with an oak pergola. The sunken gardens were

1st garden

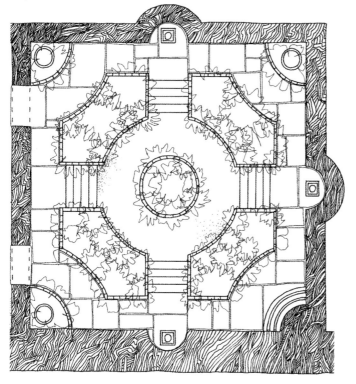

2nd garden

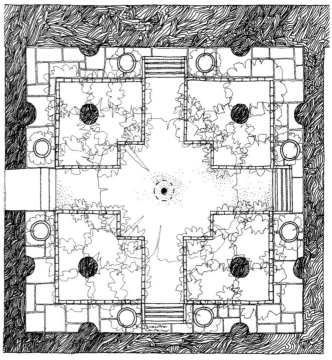

extensively paved in geometric patterns using stone, with areas within the paving left exposed for the planting. Brick retaining walls were topped with stone coping.

Oak benches were strategically placed to make the most of the views outside of the gardens. Terracotta pots provided focus points within the gardens in keeping with their formal style.

The exuberant planting within the formal yew hedged enclosures consisted of tender and half-hardy shrubs, perennials, and annuals selected for their smaller size, in keeping with the scale of the gardens.

right *The series of interconnected gardens were surrounded by formal yew hedging (*Taxus baccata), *to provide a dark contrasting backdrop.*

3rd garden

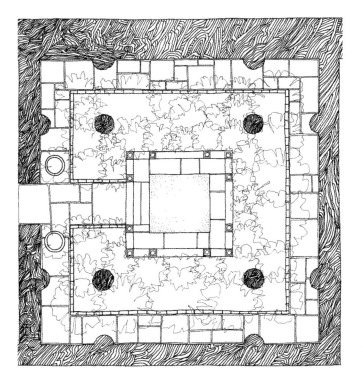

4th garden

Fibre Optic Garden

Sarah Eberle – Hillier Landscapes

dimensions: **main garden 10 x 10m (33 x 33ft)**
soil: **poor**
aspect: **north facing.**
key features: **decking, fibre optic lighting**

right *Timber decking provides a sophisticated but sharp contrast to the bold, textured planting in this garden.*

The owner of this garden wanted a contemporary interpretation that allowed the garden to become an extension of the conservatory so it could be used for entertaining and family meals. He has a love of technology and is interested in contemporary lighting and irrigation. He also requested a timber deck.

The original garden held no features in itself being introverted and enclosed by the garage and timber fencing. Some screening was required to improve privacy. There was also a drop in level between the rear of the house and level at the entrance to the garage to consider.

The garden is based on a small "amphitheatre" that provides seating opportunities as well as a sense of a "sunken garden". The main "use" area was away from the house to take advantage of available sun and light. The pergola formed a strong architectural feature that provided a sense of volume to the space. The scheme included a small water feature – a vertical polished steel cone which formed a curtain of water. This added to the rich textural emphasis.

The design used fibre optic lighting as an integral part of the construction. The fibre optic tubes were inset into step risers to the rendered retaining wall and into the uprights of the pergola and along each curved beam. The fibre optic tubes had the option of being clear or coloured and time controlled.

The planting was intended to be highly textural. A strong feature was the tree that pierced the lower deck which was underlit with paving lighters. Specimen plants were used to give an immediate effect and sense of scale. To the northern boundary the planting was designed to have a deterrent effect.

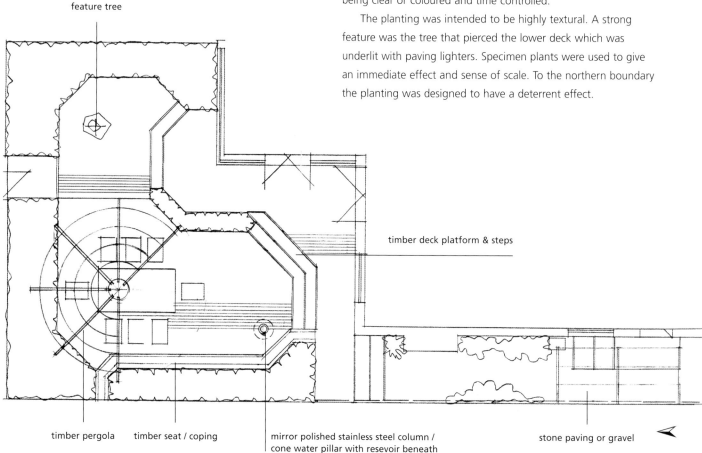

feature tree

timber deck platform & steps

timber pergola   timber seat / coping   mirror polished stainless steel column /
cone water pillar with resevoir beneath

stone paving or gravel

Divided Garden

Nigel Fuller

dimensions: 7 x 7m (23 x 23ft)
soil: neutral
aspect: northwest facing
key features: circular terrace, pool

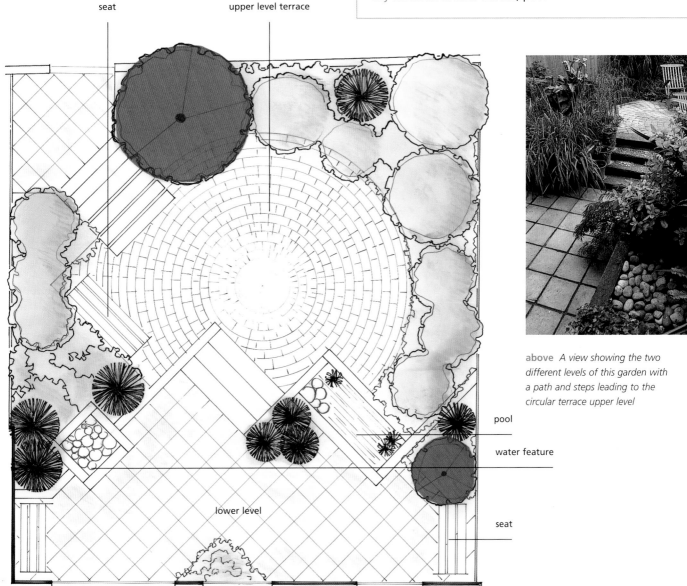

seat   upper level terrace

pool

water feature

seat

lower level

above *A view showing the two different levels of this garden with a path and steps leading to the circular terrace upper level*

A terrace was requested for entertaining and the owner wanted large architectural planting and a water feature. Curves were also part of his wish list. This was a new, previously undeveloped, site, and the builder had left it with only a steep path leading from the rear gate to the house; also, the owner required access from the house to the gate to be retained.

Working within the client's budget all the retaining walls were constructed from reclaimed timber. Leading from the house an area was paved using terracotta tiles. The garden was divided into two levels with steps at strategic locations to accomodate the slope between the house and the rear access. The upper level was transformed into a circular terrace of pavers. A pool was built to bring the sky into the shadiest part of the garden, and this water feature can be seen from the sitting room. The planting around the upper level was chosen for architectural features, and to provide year-round interest.

Multi-Level Garden

Sarah Layton – Allium Gardens Ltd

dimensions: **7.5 x 15m (25 x 49ft)**
soil: **heavy clay**
aspect: **east facing**
key features: **two-level deck**

Owned by a couple with three children under the age of five, the garden had not been used for more than four years because of an existing pond and the garden was too steep for children to tackle on their own or for an adult carrying a child. The family hoped to create a warm, interesting garden with child-friendly steps. They wanted a sitting area for eating, a visible play-space which was separate from the rest of the garden, a water feature for a calming atmosphere, and interesting, easily maintained planting.

The major feature in the garden was the two-level deck and step structure that gave access from the house. It created a spacious dining area that overlooks the garden and play area, as well as a mezzanine level that could be used as a dining space for the children. The gate at the top of the steps allowed the parents to close off the garden, and supervise the children from inside the house.

A bark floor play area was divided from the rest of the garden by low, brightly coloured trellis. As well as providing a soft landing, it was an ideal medium for the woodland plants that grew there and along the "woodland path" that ran to the centre of the garden. A small paved area was good for playing ball games, and a sunny bench, constructed of decking boards, allowed adult relaxation close to the simple urn fountain. This was a water feature that was safe for the children, and added the relaxing sound of running water to the garden. A mixture of evergreen and deciduous planting was used with strong architectural shapes chosen to give year-round interest.

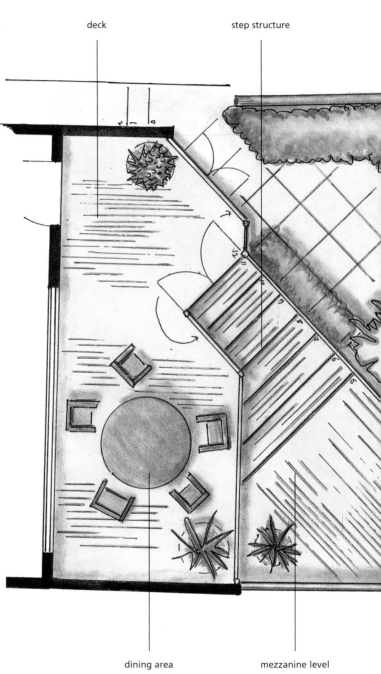

deck   step structure

dining area   mezzanine level

left A view of the small paved area of the garden, designed primarily for children's games. The planting has strong architectural forms.

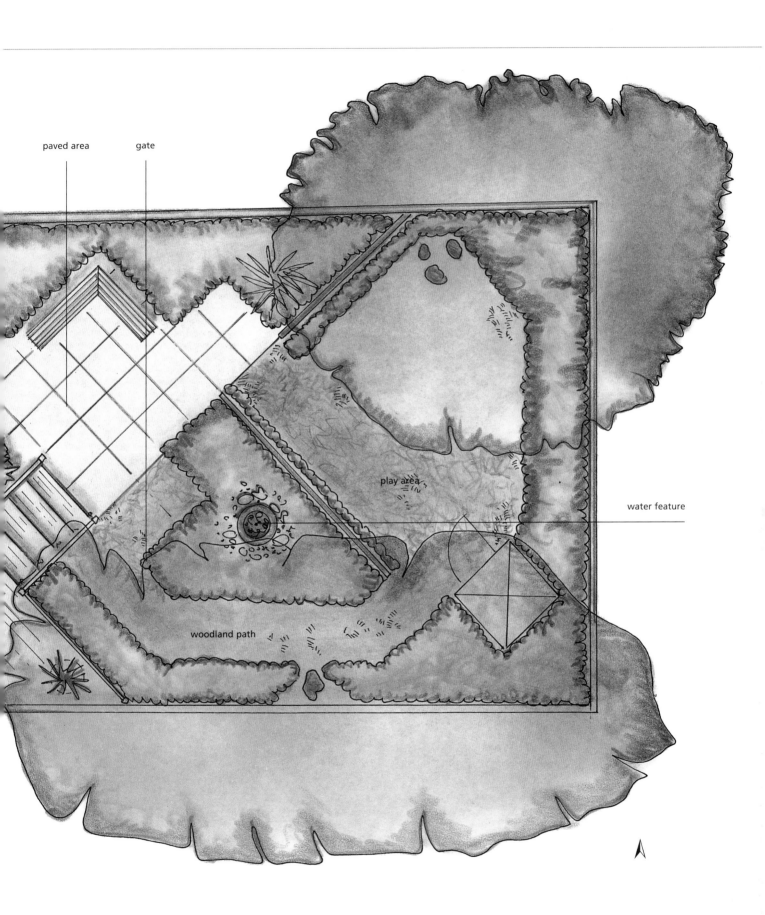

paved area

gate

water feature

play area

woodland path

Split-Level Garden with an Orchard

Christopher Maguire

dimensions: 250sq m (820sq ft) approx.
soil: alkaline, clay
aspect: northwest facing and southeast facing
key features: deck, ponds

above *This garden was designed on two levels: the lower has the ornamental pool, while the upper garden features a circular pond.*

The owner wanted an external space relating to their new dining room extension for sitting out and entertaining, and proposals for the area on the other side of the extension which, since the building work, no longer related to the house. The whole garden was on a hilly site that sloped in two directions away from the house; up on the north westside and down on the northeast. The area into which the new dining room opened was already enclosed by a low retaining wall rising up to the northwest.

The northwest aspect and the bulk of the single storey mono-pitch roof of the house on the south side meant that direct sun into the courtyard was limited. However, the enclosing retaining wall and the change in levels was a positive advantage to be exploited.

The northwest garden was designed on two levels. The lower area deck for sitting, directly accessed from the dining room, with a small ornamental pond and minimalist planting of bamboos and ferns, with a large rock and pebbles cutting into the deck. Wide steps led to the upper garden, where a circular pond discharges water via a narrow channel and chute into the lower pond. Mass planting of box (*Buxus*) provided a three-dimensional partial "enclosure" to the circular pond and the east side, and on the opposite side strips of paving were edged by the evergreen perennial *Pachysandra*.

The areas on the southeast side of the dining room was a transitional space where wide paving steps defined the diagonal access to an orchard, and a deck "bridge" led to the back of the dining room wing. The planting was principally ornamental shrubs with a lot of evergreen material to provide year-round interest.

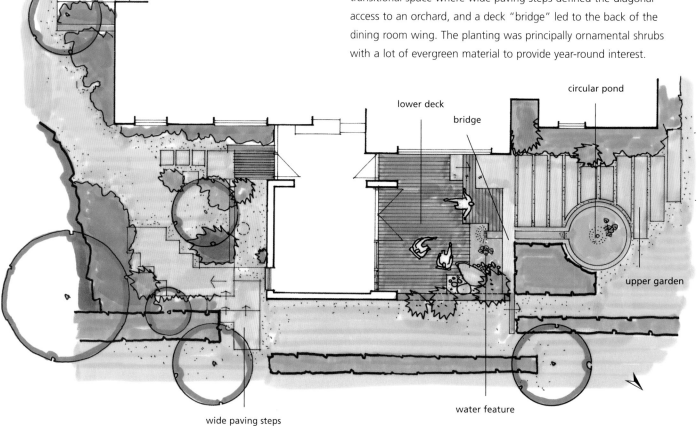

circular pond
lower deck
bridge
upper garden
water feature
wide paving steps

"Footfall"

Pickard Garden & Landscape Design

dimensions: **15 x 4m (49 x 13ft)**
soil: **sandy, loam, slightly acid**
aspect: **southwest facing**
key features: **unusual paving pattern**

left *This garden was designed primarily as a relaxing leisure space sandwiched between the building and a car park.*

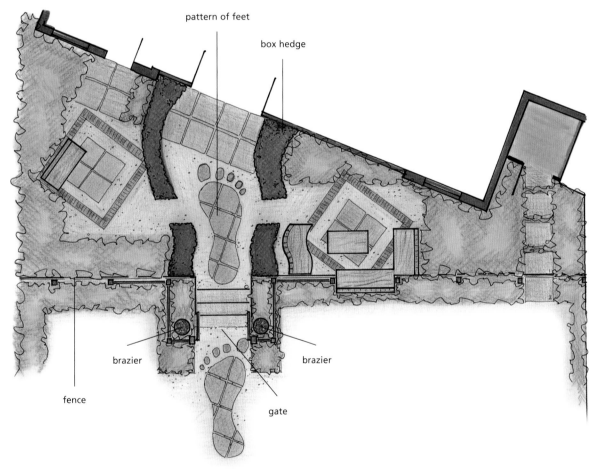

pattern of feet

box hedge

brazier

brazier

fence

gate

The clients, shoe designers, had a narrow and difficult space between the staff and customer car park and the entrance to their offices in which they wanted to create a contemporary (but not grimly modernist) garden. Visitors were often confused as to which of the two entrances to use and the garden was to guide them in the right direction. The clients also wanted a sitting area for their staff so they could take breaks or even work in the sunshine. They wished for a sense of fun to match their shoe designs.

The designers wanted to reduce the impact of the car park upon the sitting areas and offices. A solid division would have made the space feel small, dark and confined. Green oak, which is indigenous to this area, was used for a fence and gate that suggested division without being heavy and solid, and also for the benches and table supports in the seating areas. A pair of gas powered braziers stood on each side of the gate to light the car park and steps. A pattern of feet was laid into the walkway. The gate, braziers, and feet, combined with the sinuous low box hedge, left visitors in no doubt as to which entrance to use. The fence and tall ephemeral planting gave some separation, and a feeling of comfortable enclosure to those in the seating areas without stopping either the light or view.

left *The pool, constructed of reconstituted Portland stone, was surrounded by a curved hardwood wall.*

timber curved wall

camomile planted in between slate

concrete bench

den / studio

steps up to deck

hardwood deck

shallow pool

cherry tree

Almond Garden

Joe Swift & Sam Joyce – The Plant Room

dimensions: **6 x 4m (20 x 13ft)**
soil: **imported topsoil**
aspect: **southwest facing**
key features: **curved hardwood wall with integral seating**

The new house was bought with a standard garden design, but the owners wanted something a bit more adventurous. The brief was for a contemporary garden with a small pond, a summerhouse, an almond-shaped deck, and a selection of their favourite plants. The back of the house is largely glass, with a mezzanine level that overlooks the garden, so the garden also had to look just as interesting from above.

The features of the garden included a three-sided summerhouse, that fitted neatly into the corner and was constructed from marine plywood on two sides and toughened safety glass on the front. The roof was planted up with a *Sedum* mat. The seat, steps, and pool were constructed from a reconstituted Portland stone that was poured in situ. A filtration system was fitted to the pool to keep the water clear. A curved hardwood wall wrapped around one side of the garden, and integral seating followed the curve of the wall, which in turn became steps to the summerhouse and then the outer wall of the pool. To achieve the flowing lines of the bench and pool the large areas of concrete were poured on site. The shuttering needed to have several coats of paint to ensure the smoothest finish.

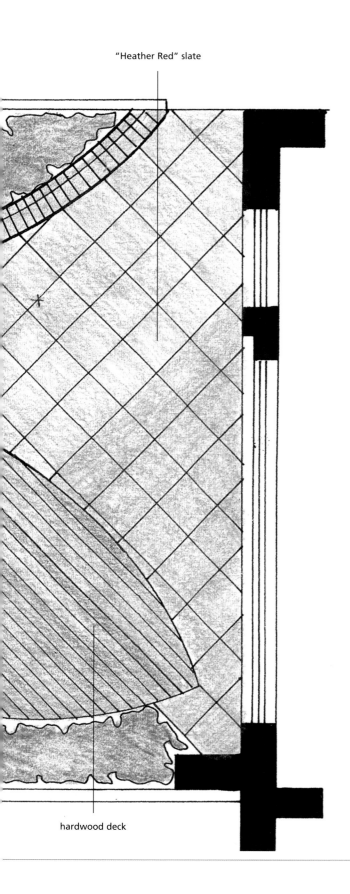

"Heather Red" slate

hardwood deck

above *A different view of this dynamic and lively space.*

Church Courtyard

Victor Shanley

dimensions: **3 x 5m (9 x 17ft) approx.**
soil: **sandy loam**
aspect: **mostly shaded**
key features: **water features, serpentine wall**

left *One of the key plants in this garden was the vigorous deciduous and brilliantly coloured azalea Rhododendron molle.*

The garden was to be used in part for extra mural teaching so it was felt that a serpentine wall would split the site and provide seclusion as a well as a dramatic feature. The wall was to be the site of three water features. Two of these were designed to fit into vertical slits, and the third was to be in the spirit of Paley Park in New York City.

A paved walkway was laid between the walls with waterfalls running down both internal faces. The curve of the wall took into account the position of the established evergreen holm oak (*Quercus ilex*). More planting was introduced such as *Rhododendron molle* subsp. *japonicum*, a honey locust tree (*Gleditsia triacanthos*), and *Pachysandra terminalis*; bamboos in square containers were placed along the walls. Some paving was laid out in a linear pattern to add an illusion of length and interest. Dogwoods were planted along the linear paving with groundcover of ivy. A further point of interest was six hardwood crosses with side plates of copper set in relief against the church wall and illuminated by low-voltage lighting from the rear. Several hardwood benches were supplied.

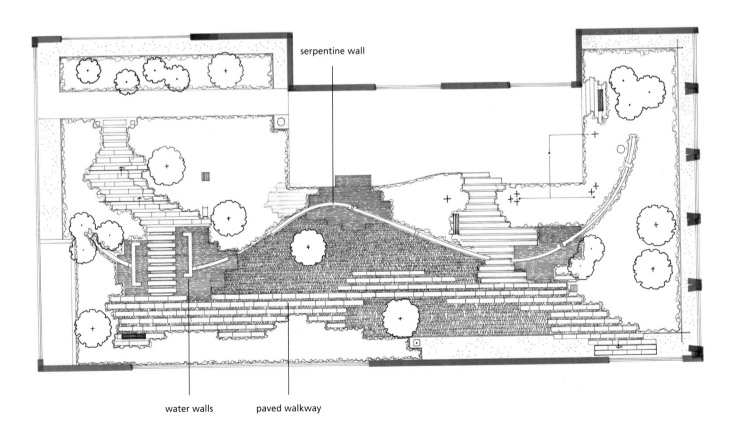

serpentine wall

water walls   paved walkway

A Taste of the Exotic

Natalya Scott

dimensions: **7 x 5m (23 x 16ft) plus side strip**
soil: **clay, enriched with manure**
aspect: **south facing**
key features: **decking, pergola, water feature**

The owner liked the established native plants in the garden which give the garden a country feel. She wanted a sheltered sunny seating area to use when taking a break from work and entertaining friends, and she wanted an existing brick patio in a bad state of repair replaced. Because the owner enjoys travelling it was decided to give the garden an exotic atmosphere. It was also necessary to provide a visual screen from a tower block.

Diagonal timber decking was laid from the dining room doors to a sun trap and seating area against the house wall. The diagonal pattern had the effect of visually widening the garden. The pergola was an integral part of the decking design and vertical stainless steel wires for climbing plants were suspended from the timbers. This provided shelter for the seating area and a visual screen to the tower block. An interesting vista from the dining-room glass doors was achieved by placing a sculpture at the end of the garden, with a pond and fountain behind it. Part of the pergola formed an arch which framed this view. The fountain provided the garden with movement, and the sound of trickling water was relaxing.

A line of olive trees screened the tower block and were a reminder of Mediterranean holidays. A potted banana plant shaded the seating area, and a line of palm trees emphasized the diagonal nature of the decking. A fig tree and zebra grass acted as a backdrop to the pond. Bamboo created a screen within the pergola structure.

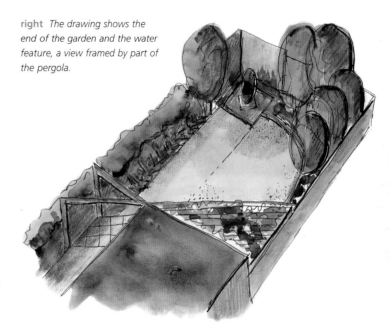

right *The drawing shows the end of the garden and the water feature, a view framed by part of the pergola.*

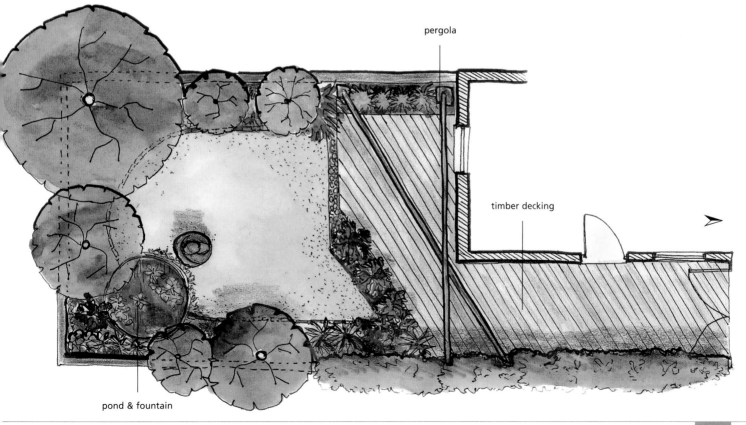

pergola

timber decking

pond & fountain

Roof Garden with Pergolas

Andrew Wenham

dimensions: **18 x 4m (59 x 13ft)**

soil: **soil-based container compost**

aspect: **east facing, windswept and exposed**

key features: **metal pergola, decking, water feature**

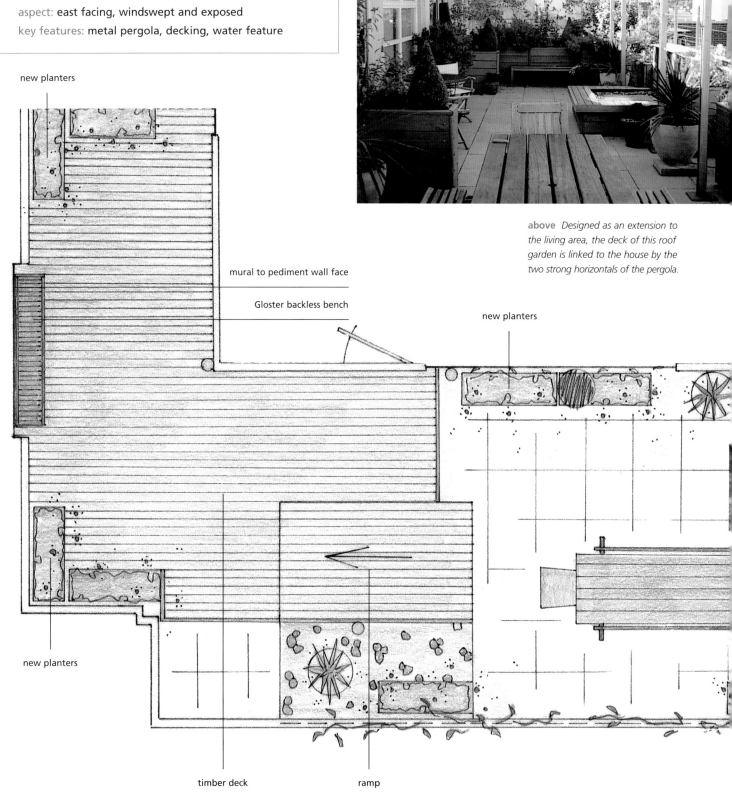

above *Designed as an extension to the living area, the deck of this roof garden is linked to the house by the two strong horizontals of the pergola.*

new planters

mural to pediment wall face

Gloster backless bench

new planters

new planters

timber deck

ramp

The owners wanted to break up the area of the roof garden and create interest without losing the sense of space, and they also wanted it screened from the views of neighbouring apartments. They preferred a contemporary design in keeping with the interior apartment and requested a water feature, plenty of planting space, seating areas and a dining table to seat eight, and lighting. They also wanted to make the planters and proposed decking accessible by wheelchair.

The garden was designed to be a living space/extension of the home, and it worked in that it "furnished" the space like a room. To provide an excellent contrast to the surrounding cityscape, strong horizontal lines were used in timber, cable, steel, and furniture. The deck was designed to wrap around the corner of the apartment and provided a ramp for possible wheelchair access. This also created a visual link to the main area. Two metal pergolas extended the contemporary feel of the apartment to the exterior. They created divisions and added depth to the space. A full-length mirror suggested a garden beyond where the pergolas met the building.

The water feature, combining other elements from the garden in a contemporary style, consisted of a vertical stainless steel sheet, and horizontal slate surface across which water runs. A western red cedar surrounded it.

Reclaimed timber planters were cut to the required height, stripped, and given a grey umber stain. The grey colour was an excellent foil to the plants. A silver metallic paint was used for the pergolas and screen. Again, this colour acted as a foil for the brighter colours of the plants, which were chosen primarily in shades of orange and purple. Among the plants chosen were azalea, bergenia, rock rose, cotoneaster, elaeagnus, escallonia, hebe, ivy, jasmine, juniper, lavender, honeysuckle, rosemary, skimmia, and wisteria.

Although there was a concern that the wisterias wouldn't do well in such an exposed situation, after being planted they flowered profusely, perhaps because the foliage was kept in check by the wind. It's always worthwhile experimenting with plants which don't naturally suit a particular aspect because every now and then they can surpise you and flourish.

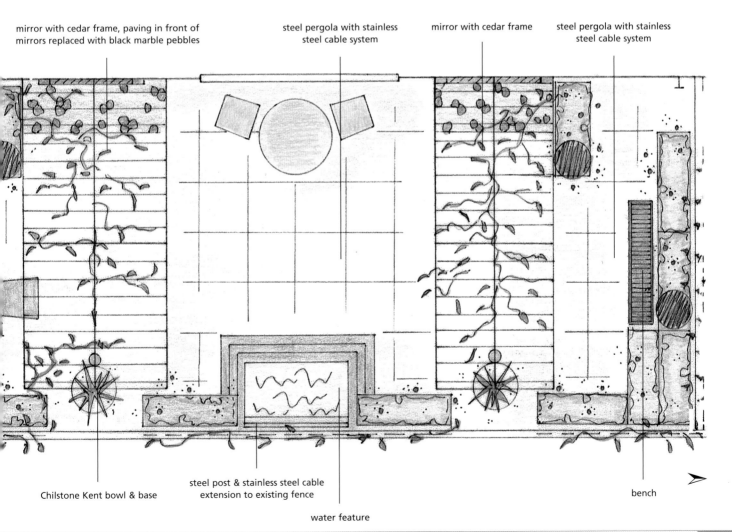

mirror with cedar frame, paving in front of mirrors replaced with black marble pebbles

steel pergola with stainless steel cable system

mirror with cedar frame

steel pergola with stainless steel cable system

Chilstone Kent bowl & base

steel post & stainless steel cable extension to existing fence

water feature

bench

Two Gardens

Keith Pullan

dimensions: **10 x 6m (33 x 20ft)**
soil: **well-drained, slightly silty loam, neutral**
aspect: **west facing, sheltered**
key features: **paved areas, trellis construction**

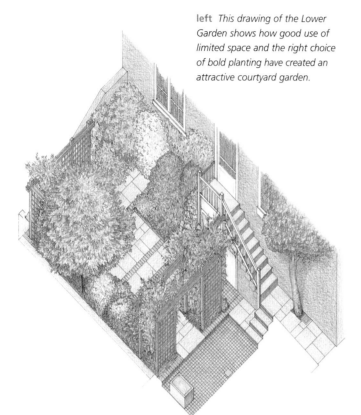

left *This drawing of the Lower Garden shows how good use of limited space and the right choice of bold planting have created an attractive courtyard garden.*

The garden is in two areas. In the Lower Garden the owner wished to make the most of the available space in the courtyard, and have an attractive, relaxing garden with areas for sitting and entertaining that included a water feature and an existing sculpture.

Trellis panels, posts, and overhead beams were used to increase the feeling of enclosure and privacy. They were also used to screen the potting shed and "utility" area and to form an archway into the main garden. Bamboos planted within these timber structures accentuated the sense of division. An existing stone trough was reused, along with a lion's head mask, to create a water feature positioned as a focal point on entry to the garden. The owner's sculpture, a carved wooden figure, was positioned as a second focal point to be seen across the garden from the archway entrance.

It was important to maximize all the space available by using climbers and tall vertical plants to disguise the boundaries. Climbers planted on walls and trellis included *Rosa* 'Veilchenblau' and *R.* 'Goldfinch', clematis, and a honeysuckle. The bamboos *Fargesia dracocephala* and *F. nitida* added vertical interest.

The Upper Garden is a small terraced area positioned away from the house at a higher level. It is used as a tiny "potager", divided into two levels. A row of dwarf fruit trees and a central path edged with alternate clipped balls of box (*Buxus*) and paving slabs provided structure on the lower level. Centrally placed steps led up to a paved seating area with salad crops and herbs to each side, and fruit trained against a high back wall. An informal mixture of additional shrubs, perennials, and grasses complete the planting.

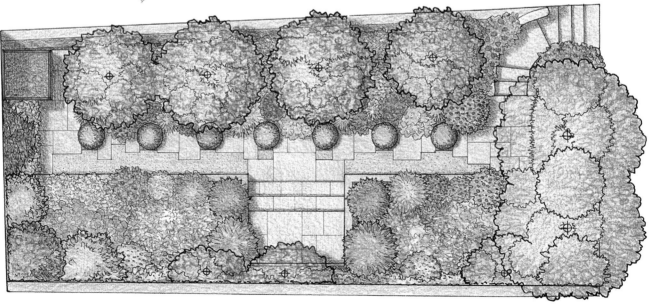

Upper Garden

Lower (house) Garden

Contemporary Formality

Cleve West

dimensions: **25 x 11m (82 x 36ft)**
soil: **sandy, loam, slightly acid**
aspect: **west facing**
key features: **deck, raised beds**

A formal garden was desired to complement the 16th-century house but the owners also wanted a contemporary twist. The roots of two existing sycamore trees had undermined a retaining wall. This needed rebuilding to a new specification to withstand the pressure from the root system and from the raised area beyond. The sloping path to the front door also had to be redesigned to include steps to provide a safer access. The owners wanted a deck by a

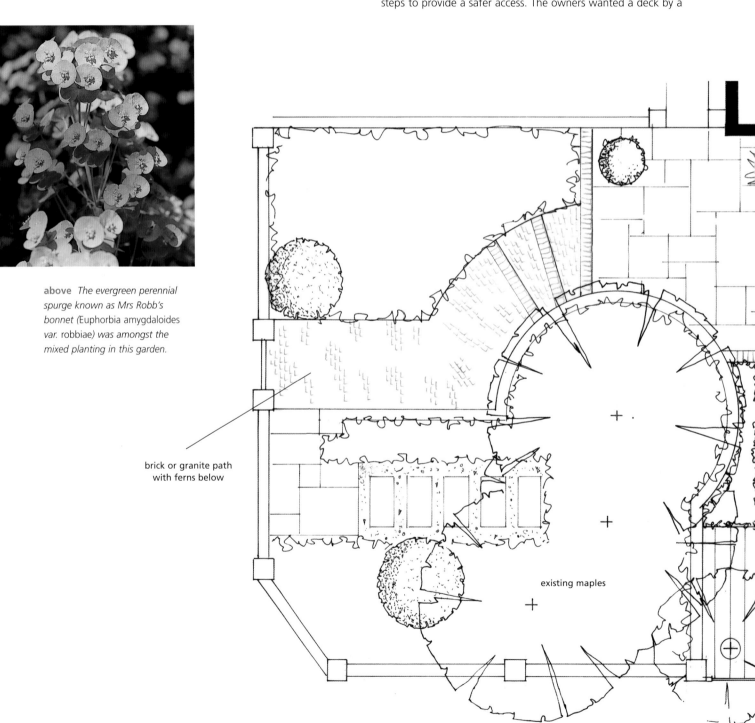

above *The evergreen perennial spurge known as Mrs Robb's bonnet (*Euphorbia amygdaloides var. robbiae*) was amongst the mixed planting in this garden.*

brick or granite path
with ferns below

existing maples

pool for sunbathing. All materials in the garden were to be reused where possible to minimize cost and to blend in with the house.

Along with the steps and deck, the design incorporated pleached trees, yew (*Taxus*) hedges, a timber raised bed planted with Irish yew (*Taxus baccata* 'Hibernica'), a raised planting of ferns, a brick or granite path with ferns below, seating, a deck over a pool, and a monolith feature. A general scheme of mixed planting was used in designated areas.

above *The part of the garden nearest the house, including the lawn, and the timber raised flower bed planted with Irish yew.*

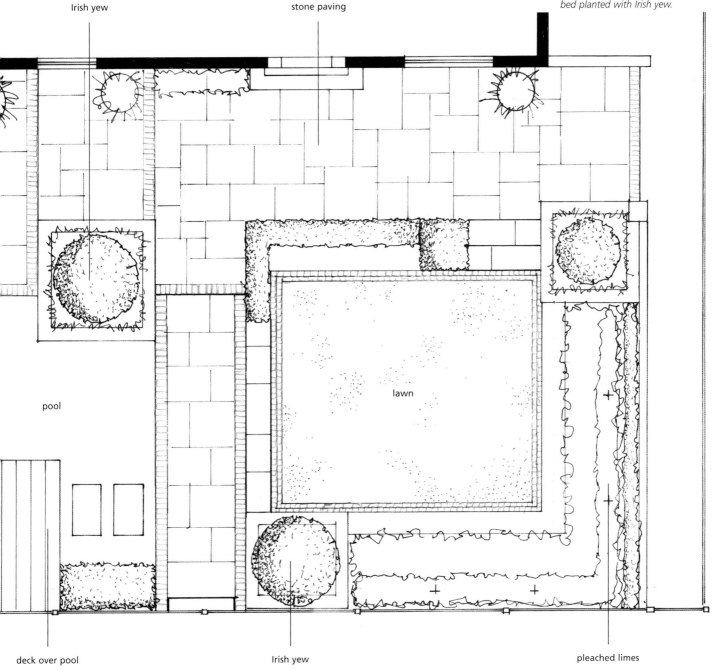

Irish yew   stone paving

pool

lawn

deck over pool   Irish yew   pleached limes

"Old Vicarage"

Michael Roberts Gardens & Landscape Designs

dimensions: **8 x 8m (26 x 26ft)**
soil: **imported neutral soil**
aspect: **south facing**
key features: **herb garden, water feature**

The owners required a dining and entertaining area with a small herb garden created from a section of tarmac covered parking area at the rear of the house. The overall design and hard landscaping had to meld with the weathered gritstone of the house.

The French windows did not have a threshold and the existing tarmac area was slightly dished to direct rainfall to a central drain, so the tarmac had to be removed to level the ground and add soil. However, the substrate under the tarmac consisted of solid rock and required three days of digging. Always expect the unexpected!

A small, water feature was placed in the corner of the garden to cover an old coal chute that had been covered with concrete. The 270-degree quadrant herb garden was edged with granite setts and was centred on a Renaissance sundial. The natural stone paving was randomly laid using three sizes. A matrix of silver granite setts was laid within this paving, and the perimeter along the remaining tarmac parking area was also laid with granite setts.

A low hedge of common box was planted along the perimeter to separate the garden from the parking area and as a protective barrier for children. Two large beds were planted with lavander. The shrub *Sarcococca confusa* and roses were planted against the west wall. The south-facing wall was planted with herbs, roses, and clematis.

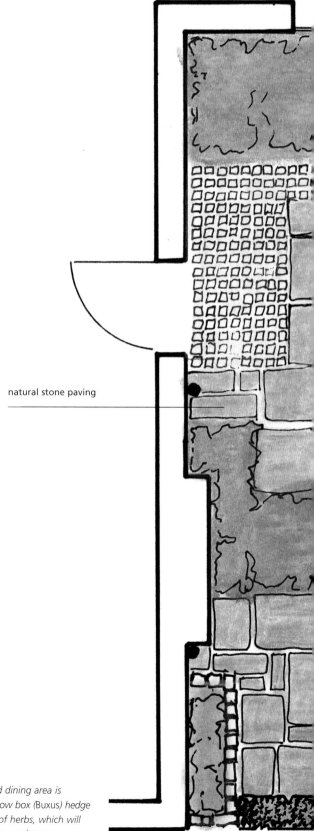

natural stone paving

left *The paved dining area is bordered by a low box (Buxus) hedge and a mixture of herbs, which will eventually create enclosure.*

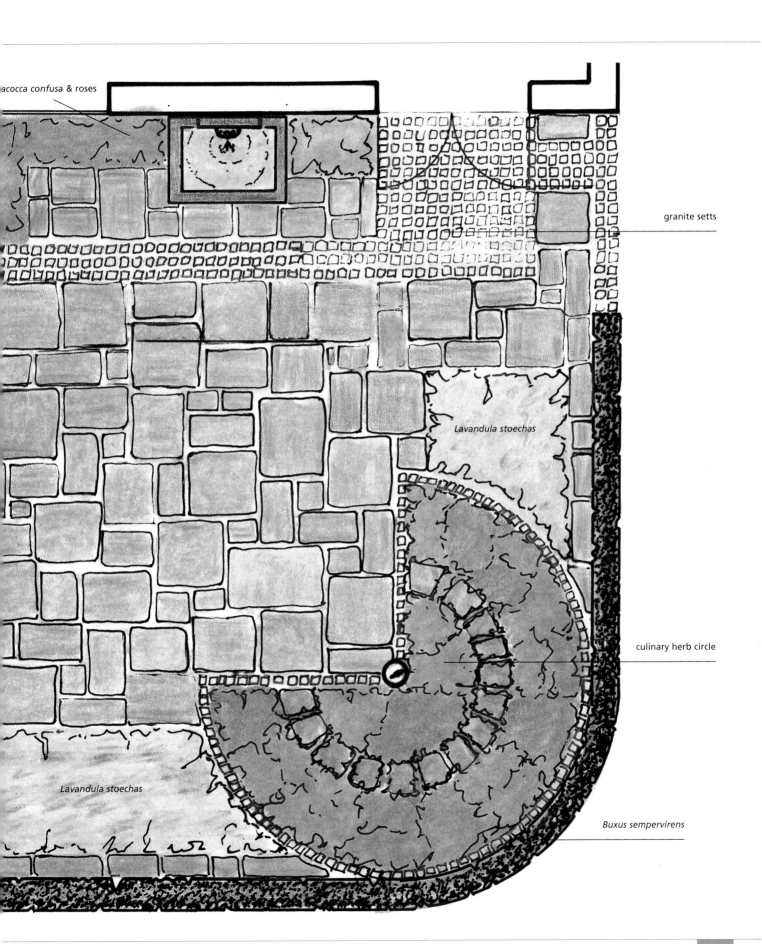

acocca confusa & roses

granite setts

Lavandula stoechas

culinary herb circle

Lavandula stoechas

Buxus sempervirens

Cobblestone Garden

Alison Dove

dimensions: **11 x 12m (36 x 39ft) plus strip**
soil: **n/a**
aspect: **southwest facing**
key features: **cobble paving, deck**

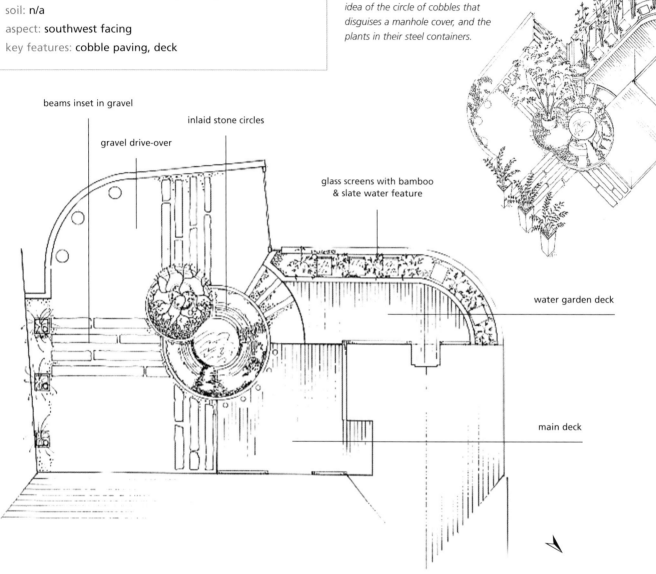

right *The drawing gives a clearer idea of the circle of cobbles that disguises a manhole cover, and the plants in their steel containers.*

beams inset in gravel

inlaid stone circles

gravel drive-over

glass screens with bamboo & slate water feature

water garden deck

main deck

A contemporary, low-maintenance garden was wanted to complement the modern interior of this rebuilt barn. It had to maximize the small amount of space, which included car access to the garage, and required an area for relaxed seating, a dining area, and moving water. A change of level was also desirable.

The small site was adjacent to springs, with a high water table, and enclosed by a high brick wall. Levels incorporated a curving slope to the integral garage and a steep drop to the back door. All this formed part of a larger conversion of a beautiful complex of farm buildings in a conservation area on the edge of countryside.

A sloping gravel driveway with inset beams carried the design to the boundary wall and echoed the beams in the house. Lights

inset in the gravel emphasized the curve of the driveway. A circle of cobbles housed a galvanized steel container in which a multi-stemmed birch grows. The container concealed a manhole cover. On a further circle of smaller cobbles stood a robust, round wooden table with curving benches. From the cobble circle a step rose to the deck which extended smoothly from dark interior floorboards.

All the planting was in containers, and tall square stainless steel planters with silver-stemmed brambles were set against barn weather-boarding. In front of the high brick wall, black bamboo (*Phyllostachys nigra*) stems rose between squares of smooth purple-black slate over which water flowed and disappeared. Behind these were panels of greenish sand-blasted glass, lit from below at night.

A Shared Garden

Barbara Hunt, Hunt Design

dimensions: **7.5 x 27m (25 x 88ft)**
soil: **chalk**
aspect: **northeast facing**
key features: **terraces, pergola**

Two neighbours wished to optimize their individual, very narrow, steeply sloping gardens by doing away with a defined boundary and sharing space. The scheme was to include a new garage for each property. One couple wanted a small lawn, the other liked the idea of a pool. Both wanted a larger, more comfortable place to sit.

The two properties form a corner portion of a terrace, and the gardens both slope steeply upwards from the houses towards a neighbouring road, with little level ground on which to sit. It was important that any scheme should be able to be divided with a boundary fence at some later date, should either neighbour move house. Although the neighbours obviously got on well, it was vital to provide some personal space immediately close to the house.

The properties were divided into zones, with zone 1 consisting of a sunken courtyard, a dark area that needed brightening. A nearby copper wall fountain provided sound, and planted trellis screens provided privacy. The trellis also contained a mirrored panel that bounced light back to the courtyard and reflected the falling water. The "mingling" area of zone 2 is used by both neighbours. Timber sleepers formed risers to the stepped terraces, and stepping stones crossed the terraces dressed with crushed gravel, through which plants could grow. Gravel paths on either side, separated by planting, formed Zone 3, which led to the garages. Zone 4 was a sunny sitting place from which to view the garden. Random York flags provided a terrace beneath a pergola, covered with fragrant climbers.

left *The planting scheme for this restricted space included scented climbers, such as honeysuckle (Lonicera periclymenum),* Trachelospermum jasminoides *(shown here), and Jasmine (Jasminum officinale), creating maximum impact in limited space.*

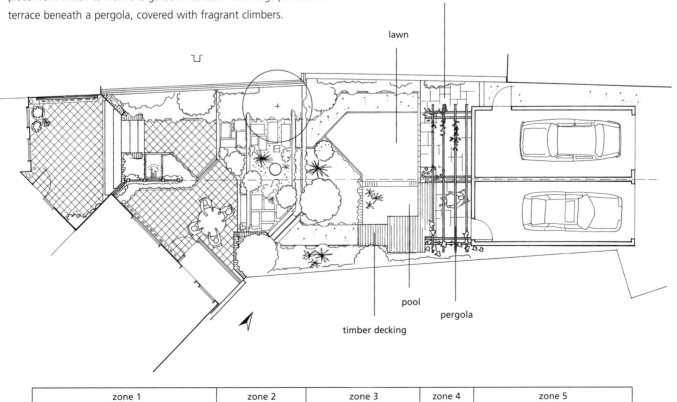

stone paving

lawn

pool

pergola

timber decking

| zone 1 | zone 2 | zone 3 | zone 4 | zone 5 |

Curving Pathway

David R. Sisley

dimensions: 8 x 10m (26 x 33ft)

soil: netural

aspect: north facing

key features: trelliswork, curved pathway

left *Evergreens – such as the shrub Azara serrata – dominate the planting scheme in this garden.*

The garden was adjacent to a converted coach house that had been divided into a number of small apartments. The owners required their own secluded garden space while maintaining views to the communal parkland beyond.

A curved pathway dominated the centre of the plot. Trelliswork was used to screen the garden without enclosing it excessively. The central trellis and its planting not only provided foreground interest with a mystery route to the water feature and seclusion for the sitting area, but it also incorporated surface water drainage from the large area of paving. There was an elevated floor level inside the property, and from here there was a view over the central trellis to the water feature and parkland beyond. Trelliswork rose to its highest point adjacent to the steps from the French doors, which provided a privacy screen between this garden and the neighbouring garden. Brickwork was not included on the west boundary beneath the trelliswork to ensure that maximum sunlight could filter into the garden.

Evergreens were the dominating feature of the planting scheme. These included *Azara serrata*, *Viburnum davidii*, *Fatsia japonica*, and *Osmanthus delavayi*. Trees included *Sorbus vilmorinii*, and the hop tree, *Ptelea trifoliata*, and among the climbers was the chocolate vine (*Akebia quinata*).

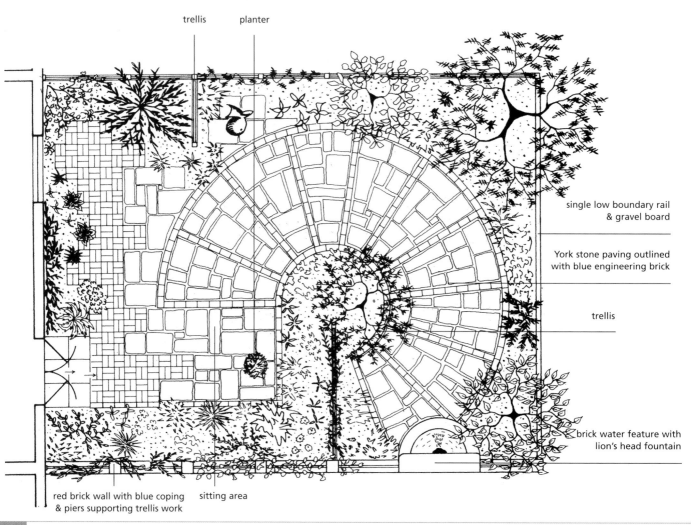

trellis   planter

single low boundary rail & gravel board

York stone paving outlined with blue engineering brick

trellis

brick water feature with lion's head fountain

red brick wall with blue coping & piers supporting trellis work   sitting area

Neon Roof Terrace

Woodhams Landscapes

dimensions: **5 x 8m (16 x 26ft)**
soil: n/a
aspect: **east facing**
key features: **neon water feature**

planting area   main terrace area

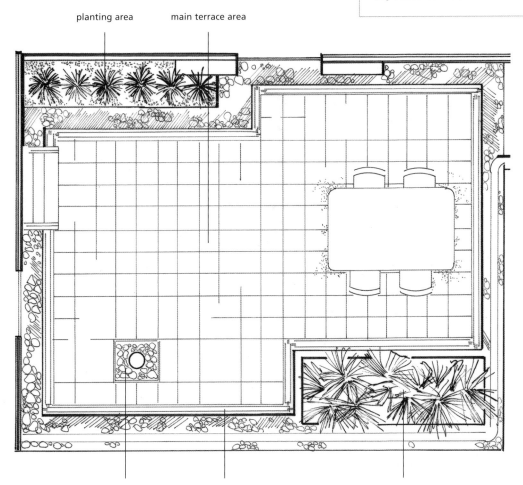

water feature   band of blue neon tube   planting area

above *Ambient blue lighting and a perspex column water feature set in white pebbles are two of the key features in this innovative contemporary roof terrace.*

The brief from the owner of this roof terrace was to create a visually exciting exterior room. He wanted it to have an electric feeling both at day and night. Because the terrace is on a roof the total weight of the materials was a main consideration. All the plants were in containers to help reduce the weight load.

Black slate paving created the main terrace area, which had to be set on a firm concrete base to make sure it was completely stable. The paving was surrounded by a band consisting of an electric blue neon tube that had been set within a metal channel and covered with a frosted glass. This feature delineated the shape of the paved "room" and provided the electric feeling requested

when lit up at night. Pale green glass mulch formed a final band around the terrace.

A column of perspex set in white pebbles formed a water feature, and it included ambient lighting to liven up an otherwise quiet corner of the terrace. To achieve the same velocity of the night-time neon light during daylight, the furniture was powder-coated in an electric blue colour.

To give definition to what would have otherwise been a plain rectangular shape, two areas of planting were created using powder-coated metal troughs, and planted with *Ophiopogon planiscarpus* and *Stipa gigantea*. A layer of the glass mulch ties them in with the paving.

"Garden of Walls"

Vladimir Sitta/Maren Parry

dimensions: **20 x17m (66 x 56ft) approx.**
soil: **sandy**
aspect: **sunny until early afternoon**
key features: **rock outcrops close to surface**

right *The designer has made a feature of the steeply graded rocky outcrop on which the garden stands.*

The garden is located on a steeply graded rocky outcrop in a Sydney suburb, and the owners wanted somewhere for the children to play. Extensions to the house required appropriation of the original garden space. The existing rocky outcrop has become the setting for the garden. The aesthetics counter the "traditional" suburban character of house, which offered a "heritage" face to the street.

The decoration and patterning have been left to the innate qualities and relationships of the materials used. The sandstone flagstones were covered by a filigree of lichens. The rocky outcrops oozed mossy water. The rendered walls had a flowery patina. White pebbles moved underfoot. Sheltering crevices nurtured unfurling ferns.

The walls grew fringes of succulents and grasses. A series of rising and overlapping walls created pockets of level ground, and semi-secret gardens were incrementally revealed as one walked through.

Tall foxtail grass planting concealed handrails and prevented dangerous play, while promoting intimate play spaces for the children of the family. As this plant reaches maturity, it could be fenced. Other plants included the gum *Eucalyptus haemastoma*, the fern *Doodia aspera*, *Agave attenuata*, *Liriope muscari*, the bower plant (*Pandorea jasminoides*), *Wisteria sinensis*, and species of cat's paw (*Anigozanthos*). There was also an existing Canary Island date palm (*Phoenix canariensis*).

left *Succulents and grasses grow out of the garden walls, while the rocks ooze mossy water. The effect of the planting is to soften what otherwise might be a harsh landscape garden.*

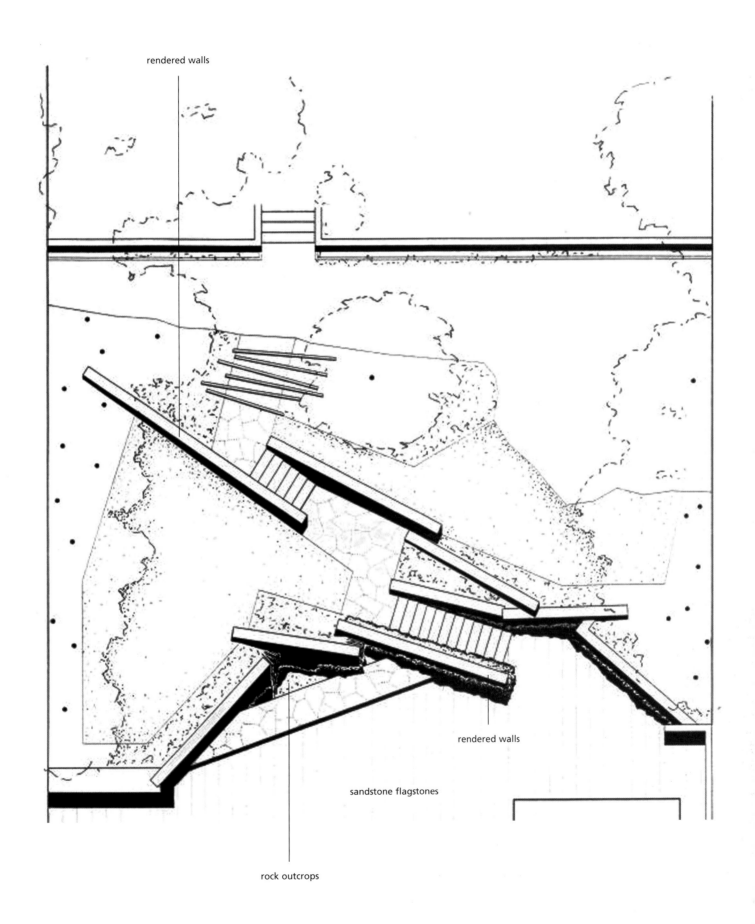

rendered walls

rendered walls

sandstone flagstones

rock outcrops

Minimalist Urban Garden

Helen Billetop Garden Design

dimensions: **5 x 6m (16 x 20ft)**
soil: **loam, neutral**
aspect: **northwest facing**
key features: **deck, natural slate bench**

right The simplicity of this garden's design is well illustrated by this view of the timber deck, designed for evening and weekend relaxation.

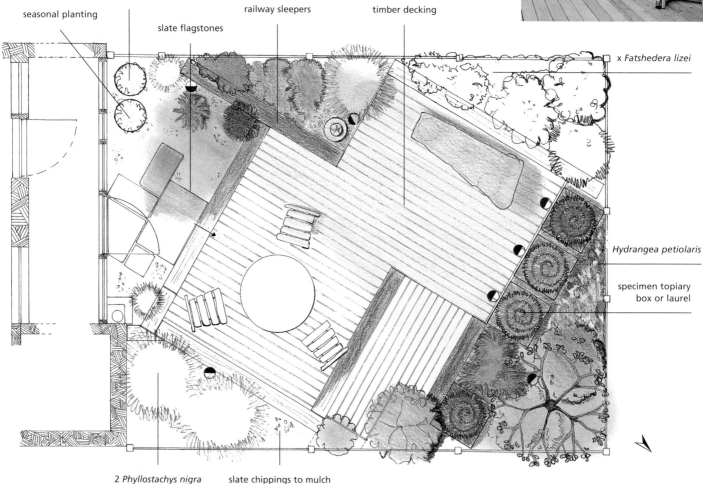

seasonal planting
galvanized steel planter
slate flagstones
railway sleepers
timber decking
x *Fatshedera lizei*
Hydrangea petiolaris
specimen topiary box or laurel
2 *Phyllostachys nigra*
slate chippings to mulch

The owners wanted a simple and modern garden to reflect the minimalist and stylish interior of a town house. A timber deck to echo the refurbished and stripped floorboards in the house was important to them, as was lighting because they often use the garden in the evenings. Low-maintenance planting was requested, especially architectural and evergreen plants for structure and texture throughout the year. The site at the back of the garden was being developed, so the inclusion of a new tree to give a vertical accent as well as offer some screening was agreed to in the brief.

The garden was level and laid to grass, and no features or plants were retained. Stepping up onto the deck, which occupied the centre of the garden, added a level, and vertical elements were introduced with the tree and the bamboo. A natural slate bench on solid hard wood cubes provided sculptural interest and a focal point from the house. Natural slate pavers were used in front of the conservatory and matching slate chippings were spread through the planting for easy maintenance. Stainless steel planters, with evergreen palms, *Chamaerops humilis*, and dwarf bamboo co-ordinated with the bistro-style furniture. The lights on the timber deck reflected off the steel planters by night.

The bamboo *Phyllostachys nigra*, added height, texture, and rustled in the breeze, as well as screening the corner of the fence and wall of the conservatory. *Hydrangea petiolaris*, x *Fatshedera lizei*, and ivies screened the fence. Among other plants are irises and hostas.

Spanish-Style Garden

The owner's brief was to create a garden with a Spanish flavour that would enhance the architecture of the house, located in California, thereby creating an authentic interior-exterior connection. Although the garden was on a small plot, there was a wide variety of micro-climates, with the most important aspect being the dry climate that is prominent in the region.

Because of the small size of the plot, the landscape was planned from the inside out to "expand" the interior views. Accentuating the architectural theme of the residence, the garden represented the quintessential Mediterranean landscape. Warm terracotta and buff colours were prominent in the paving materials, garden walls, and the large urns that flanked the long walk. Among the key features were an enclosed side garden with a water fountain, as well as a rear dining terrace. Elegant landscape lighting linked the interior and exterior spaces and illuminated the garden scene for after-hours use.

Bernard Trainor Design Associates

dimensions: **2286sq m (7500sq ft)**
soil: **clay**
aspect: **full sun to shade**
key features: **side garden with fountain, dining area**

Water is a key element in the Spanish garden and in this case the water feature was strategically placed outside the dining room to remind one of the importance of water in this climate.

Continuing with the Mediterranean theme, dry-climate plantings of lavender, thyme, and rosemary were nestled beneath edible fruit trees, such as figs, olives, and a pineapple guava. The architectural plantings, including cordyline, acanthus, olives, and phormiums, were at one with the landscape walls and structural elements in the garden.

urn   urn   water feature   enclosed side garden

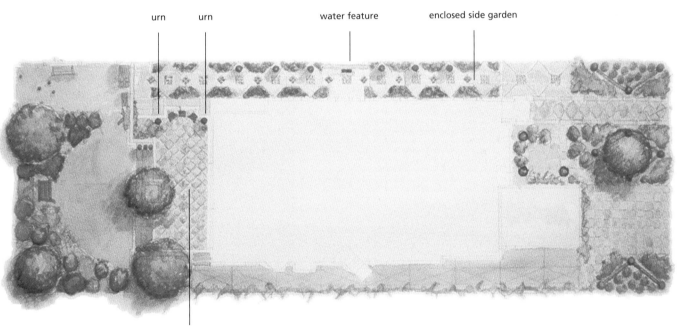

dining area

left *This view shows how well the Spanish-style house has been linked with the garden, especially through the use of Mediterranean, dry-climate planting.*

Child-Friendly Garden

Mark Lutyens

dimensions: **5 x 4m (16 x 13ft) approx.**
soil: **improved with compost**
aspect: **south facing**
key features: **children's play area**

The end of the garden had been a building site for a year or more, and to compensate for this the builder of the new adjoining house had offered to cover the blank end wall with a standard trellis. Instead, the owners wanted a design that would be more exciting and incorporate a children's play area.

There was an unusually large and sculptural *Pyracantha* growing at a higher level than the main garden which was to be kept. To take the weight off the roots of the plant, it was decided that the principal surface would be timber deck, not paving. Because the only access to the garden is through the house, the materials were also limited to what would fit through the passageway. The trellis panels were just slightly too large and had to be dismantled to get them into the garden.

The design was intended to suggest a small bothy at the end of the garden, half-hidden by vegetation. It included a lot of trellis, a false window, a small shed with a play platform on the roof, and a sand pit. At a higher level there were horizontal canes lashed to vertical steel cables.

Planting was not a key element of the scheme, but it needed to be robust enough to withstand children, obviously not be toxic or spikey, complement the rather good planting in the rest of the garden, and grow reasonably fast to cover the walls and trellis. A lot of vines and climbing roses were planted, along with softer aromatic evergreens such as lavender, rosemary, and, at the children's level, *Lotus* syn. *Dorycnium*.

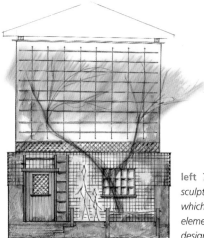

left *The wall trellising and sculptural firethorn (*Pyracantha*), which was one of the few existing elements retained in a garden designed as a children's play area.*

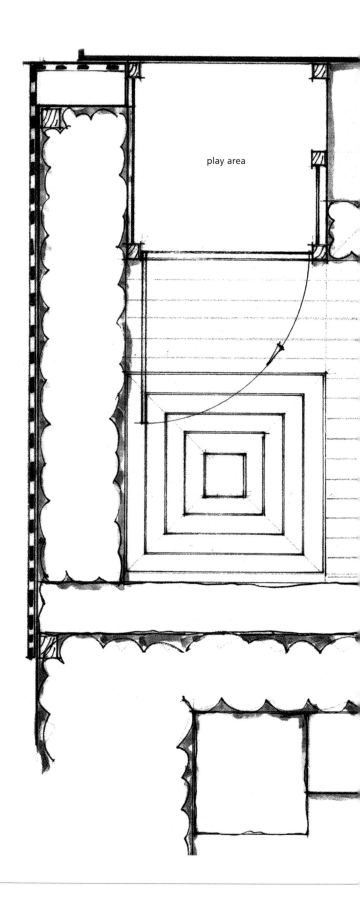

play area

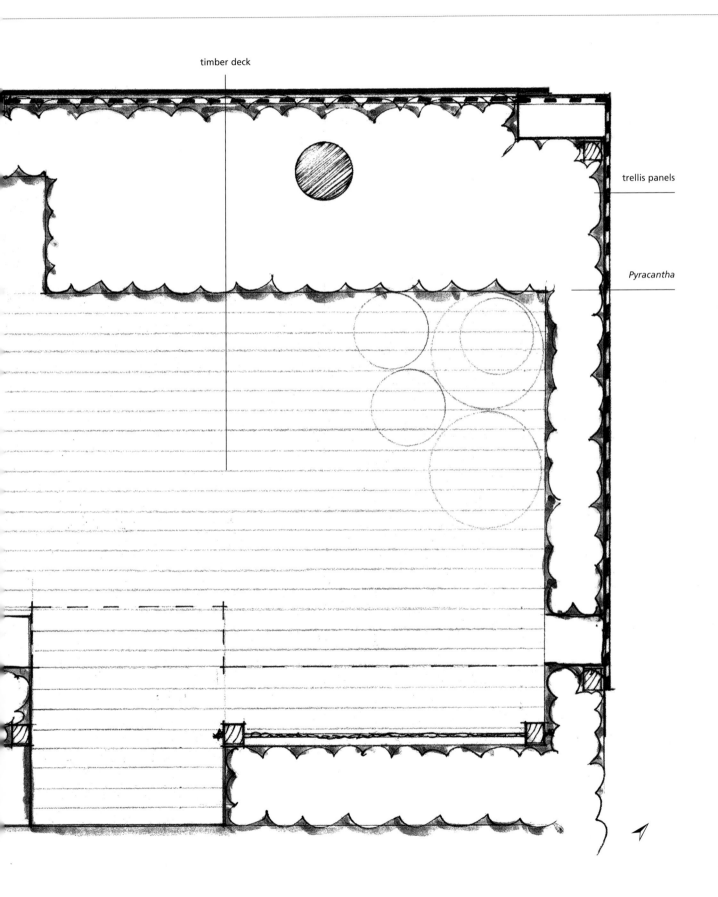

timber deck

trellis panels

Pyracantha

Seaside Garden

Douglas Coltart

dimensions: **225sq m (738sq ft)**
soil: **sandy loam, slightly acid, free draining**
aspect: **south facing at front of house, east facing at side**
key features: **circular patio, fire pit**

The owners of this seaside garden wanted a storage area for canoes and a canoe trailer, a hedge removed to open up sea views, a semi-private seating area, colour introduced through plants, and a water feature. They preferred natural materials such as stone and liked curves and flowing lines. They wanted a visual division from their neighbours, but not a physical one, because they mow their grass.

A storage area or structure large enough to house 12 canoes with a trailer would detract from the main part of the garden, therefore a new entrance was created so that they could be hidden behind the new gates. Putting the canoes "away" and bringing in a new entrance allowed the existing gate to be blocked off and the creation of a semi-private seating area. This was enhanced through the building of a wall which not only gave an air of permanence to the garden but increased the sense of privacy. The wall to the front of the garden was the main structure – it was built with concrete block and either faced in sandstone or given a "dry dash" finish. More than half the height of the wall was solid concrete inside (due to the pounding of waves during winter), with effective planters in the top section.

A circular patio was built of multi-coloured slate. This was edged with salt, as was the adjacent fire pit. There is a carved stone plaque on the wall set behind the area of herbaceous perennials, which would only be visible during the winter and spring. Two small reflecting ponds were created in the planted areas, and sculptural timber features divided this garden from their neighbours but still allowed access between. Metal edging was used to define beds and paths – this gave much better flowing curves than the traditional timber edging and pegs. It also provided a dark line (dark brown in colour) which accentuated the shapes of the garden.

The planting consists of a combination of seaside and salt-tolerant plants with herbaceous plants, which die back and are dormant during the winter periods when the winds are at their most salt laden. Perennials were selected for the front area to introduce swathes of colours. The planting within the wall were mainly alpines, which are more permanent in nature and soften the lines of the front wall. The planting to the side of the house was herbaceous again, in the form of grasses and ferns.

left *With stunning views of the sea available, it was understandable that the owners' brief for this garden included the removal of an existing hedge.*

timber gates

boulders

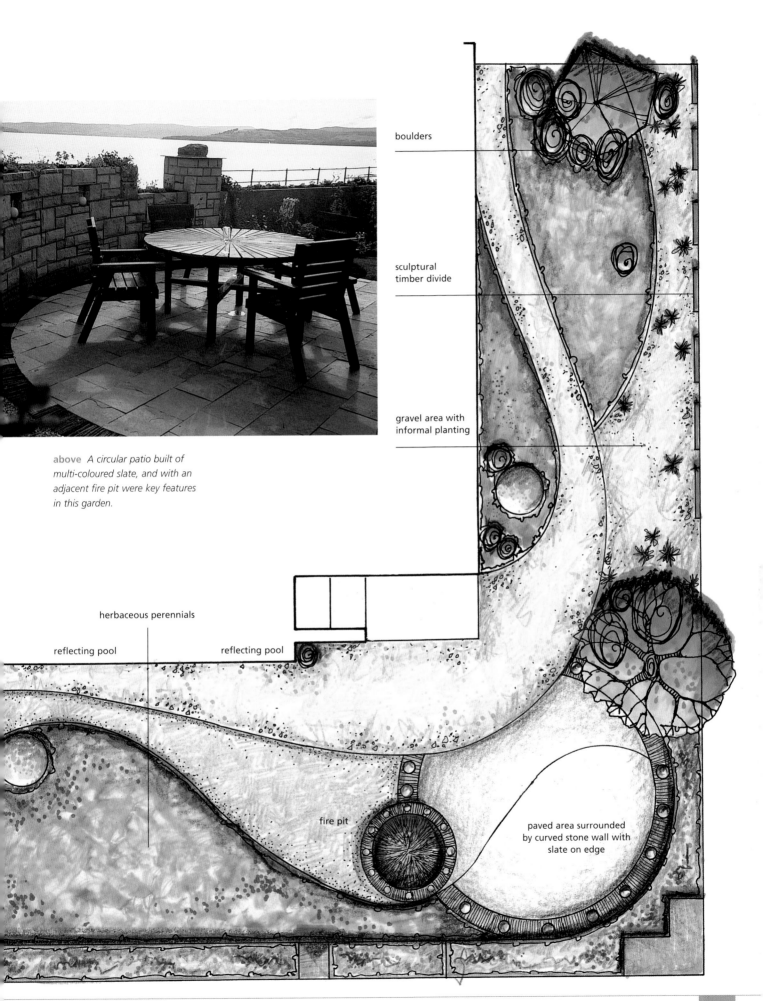

boulders

sculptural
timber divide

gravel area with
informal planting

above *A circular patio built of
multi-coloured slate, and with an
adjacent fire pit were key features
in this garden.*

herbaceous perennials

reflecting pool

reflecting pool

fire pit

paved area surrounded
by curved stone wall with
slate on edge

"Conversations"/Wildlife Garden

Paul Cooper

dimensions: **both gardens 8 x 16m (26 x 52ft)**
soil: **both gardens neutral**
aspect: **both gardens south facing**
key features: **wigwam-style figures/a large pool**

These are two different garden. The owners of "Conversations" requested a design for a garden that would amuse and entertain, as well as be an enjoyable garden for holding parties. An amusing atmosphere was achieved by creating wigwam-style figures, who appeared to be dancing and in conversation. The figure "frames" were clothed in planting of climbers, and were positioned on circular paving designed to create a spotlight effect. Trellis was used to define the spaces and to create areas concealed from view. Paving was also used to create an area for entertaining, and built-in seating provided areas for relaxation. A two-way pool was divided by a reverse topiary trellis screen – a figure is a cut-out of a trellis panel with planting defining the form. The planting included *Bergenia cordifolia*, which was chosen to represent faces of an

"Conversations"

right *The drawing shows the wigwam-style figures in deep "conversation" on circular paving, as if in a spotlight.*

audience, while yellow sedge was planted around the circular paving to highlight the spotlight.

In the second garden, the owner wanted a modern-looking wildlife garden in a surbuban setting. The garden was designed around the key feature of a large pool that was defined by a curved deck, a rocky bank, and a pergola walkway. At the far end the pool merged into a small meadow with woven wooden spheres, intended to represent seeds. In the centre of the pool three "Rock Props" stood like wading creatures, and acted as a water feature. Planting was a mix of evergreen shrubs and herbaceous, becoming less formal towards the rear of the garden. Marginal and aquatic plants featured. Paving provided a sitting area near to the house from which paths become gravel as they led to the more informal part of the garden.

right *Key planting for the wildlife garden included the clump-forming perennial Ligularia 'The Rocket', often used as a marginal plant.*

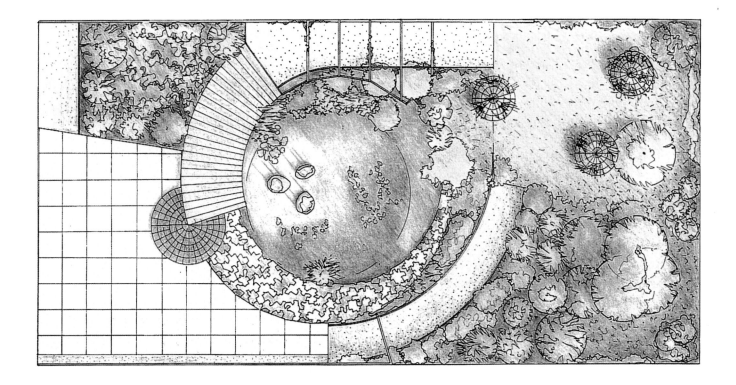

Wildlife garden

left *The far end of the wildlife garden showing the large pool with the three "Rock Props" standing like wading creatures at its centre.*

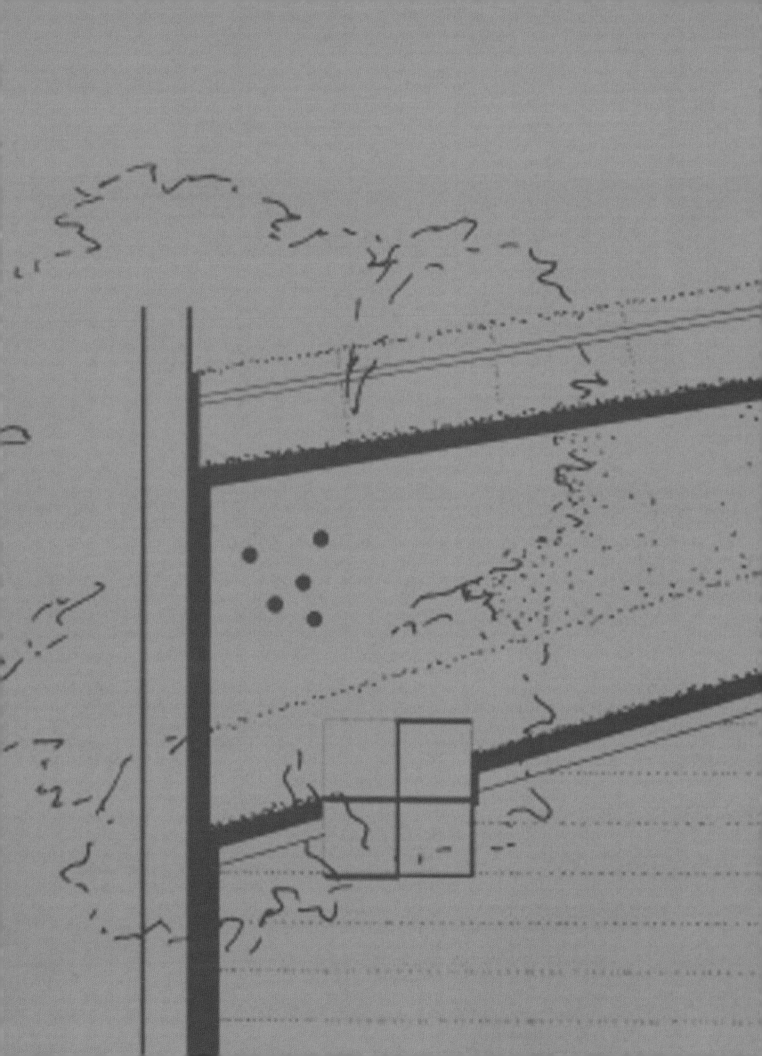

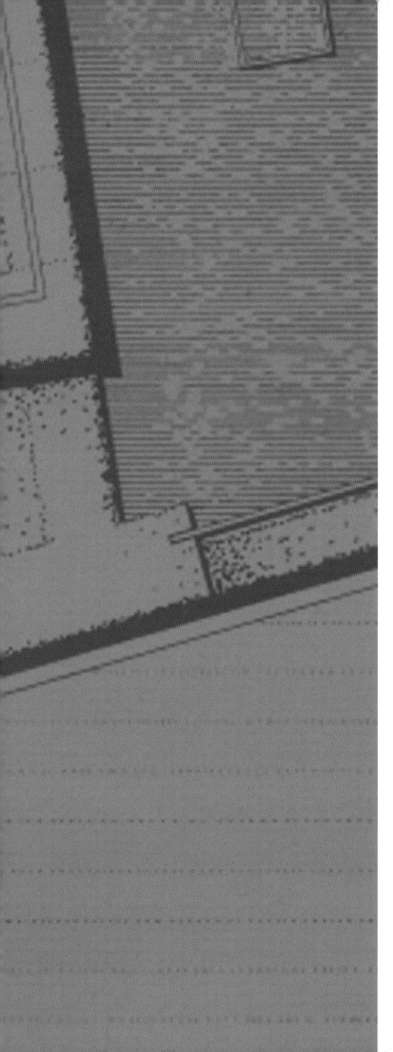

Water has been an important contributor to the success and charm of gardens throughout the ages, a valuable resource for life, and a glittering, tactile, mercurial element for designers to exploit and manipulate. It is a dynamic and formless material, shaped and channelled by containment or plumbing to create anything from still reflective pools to powerful jets, cascades, or streams.

With bubble jets or smaller scale wall spouts it is the noise that attracts. These features are ideal for restricted spaces or for gardens used by young children. For larger gardens, reflecting pools need to be substantial in order to make the most of surface patterns and light play. For planted pools water depth is an important consideration as different species require different depths.

Whatever the reason for using water, play up the scale as much as possible, consider the edge detailing of the water feature, as this is a key factor in defining design quality, and consider the location of water carefully as this can be a major undertaking in terms of time and cost.

The garden that opens this section, designed by del Buono and Gazerwitz, shows a substantial pool used as an integral part of the subtle and elegant design. The water is used as a complementary surface, exaggerating the length of the garden, and providing an opportunity to grow selected specimen water plants.

Water Gardens

Limestone Garden

del Buono-Gazerwitz Landscape Architecture

dimensions: **12 x 7.5m (39 x 25ft)**
soil: **clay**
aspect: **west facing, open**
key features: **long, still pool**

A new garden was created to work in conjunction with the extensive refurbishment planned for the house, working in tandem with the building and the architecture of its new extensions. The new garden was conceived as an extension of the architecture of the house to the outdoors. Thus the limestone paving was extended seamlessly outside, while a new double-height extension to the building entirely constructed in glass was reflected in a long still pool spanning almost the entire length of the garden. A small section of the proposed new paving was cantilevered over the pool. By laying it lower than the surrounding paving, it read as a small, solid jetty suspended over the water.

To maximize privacy, a wall-mounted steel wire structure was designed to support climbers and create a sense of enclosure. The garden also has no direct link to the communal gardens beyond so a retractable, steel staircase was designed to fit onto the face of the rear perimeter wall, creating a link to the woodland beyond.

All planting was set in large rectangular blocks carved out of the proposed limestone paving. Sculptural, multi-stemmed *Amelanchier lamarckii* specimens added height, colour, and flowers at different times of year. A range of large leaved shrubs and perennials were selected to maximize the contrast between the garden's geometry and the softness of the planting. Japanese iris (*Iris ensata*), planted within a linear container set inside the long pool, broke the surface and added colour and greenery to the water.

left *In order to add colour to the scheme, the Japanese iris (*Iris ensata*) was planted in a linear container inside the long pool.*

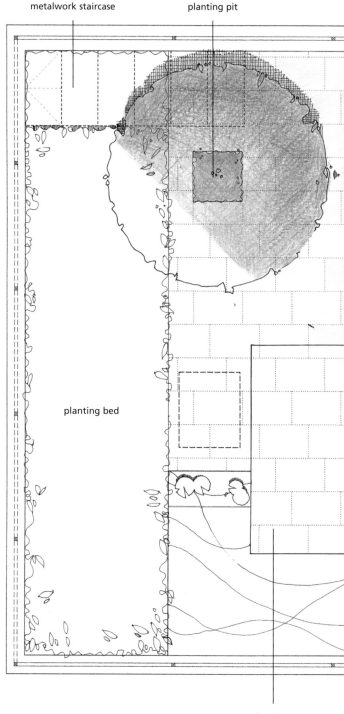

metalwork staircase   planting pit

planting bed

sunken terrace
coursed limestone paving

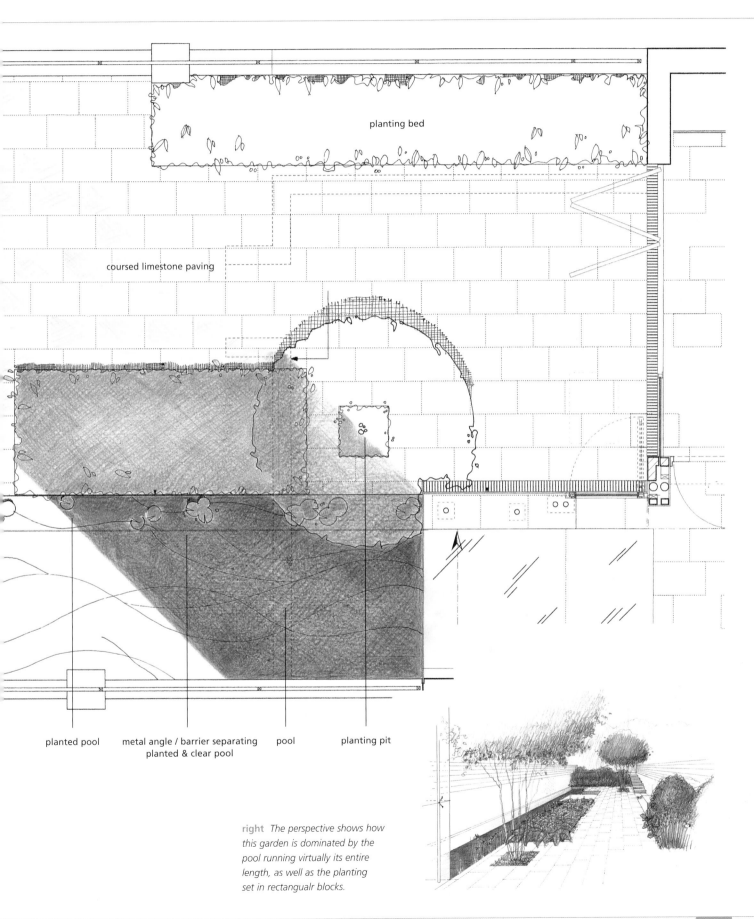

planting bed

coursed limestone paving

planted pool   metal angle / barrier separating   pool   planting pit
                      planted & clear pool

right *The perspective shows how this garden is dominated by the pool running virtually its entire length, as well as the planting set in rectangualr blocks.*

Electric-Blue Courtyard

Paul Dracott Garden Designs

dimensions: **10 x 8m (33 x 26ft)**
soil: **sandy loam**
aspect: **east facing**
key features: **steel walkway and pergola, water feature**

The request for this garden was to create a space suitable for entertaining clients, reflecting the modern image of the company, within a family garden. The new layout was to divide the lawned garden and utility area and enclose a courtyard that could reflect contemporary interior decor. Modern materials, vibrant colours, and a child-safe moving water element were all to be included.

The new design aimed to create an extension to the office with a strong focal point to lead visitors out into the courtyard. This was achieved by mounting a stainless steel water shoot in a rendered wall, and framing the resulting water sheet with a *Trachycarpus* and *Miscanthus*. The water sheet then fell through galvanized grid into a shallow rill and flowed towards the house beneath a steel walkway. The rill was sandwiched between hardwood decks and the entire courtyard was enclosed with rendered wall painted lilac. This separated the courtyard from the small lawned garden with access out of the courtyard via a bespoke gate of galvanized grid.

A pergola of stainless steel poles and cables above one deck eased the transition from office to courtyard and created a sense of security. The courtyard was then given another dimension by the use of blue strip lights beneath the rill grid, blue uplights to the pergola, and white lighting within the planting.

Planting was simple and architectural, with emphasis on foliage, form, and texture with a subtle purple tinge. All planting areas were mulched with plum slate to associate and link the planting with coloured vertical elements in the garden. The shrubs planted are *Chamaerops humilis*, *Fargesia murielae*, *Yucca filamentosa*, and *Phormium tenax* 'Sundowner'. The perennials include *Epimedium* x *versicolor* and *Calamagrostis brachytricha*.

above *The garden is seen at its most dramatic at night when the key feature of blue strip lighting comes into its own.*

right *Seemingly a different garden in daylight; this view of the stainless steel pergola marks the transition from the office to the courtyard.*

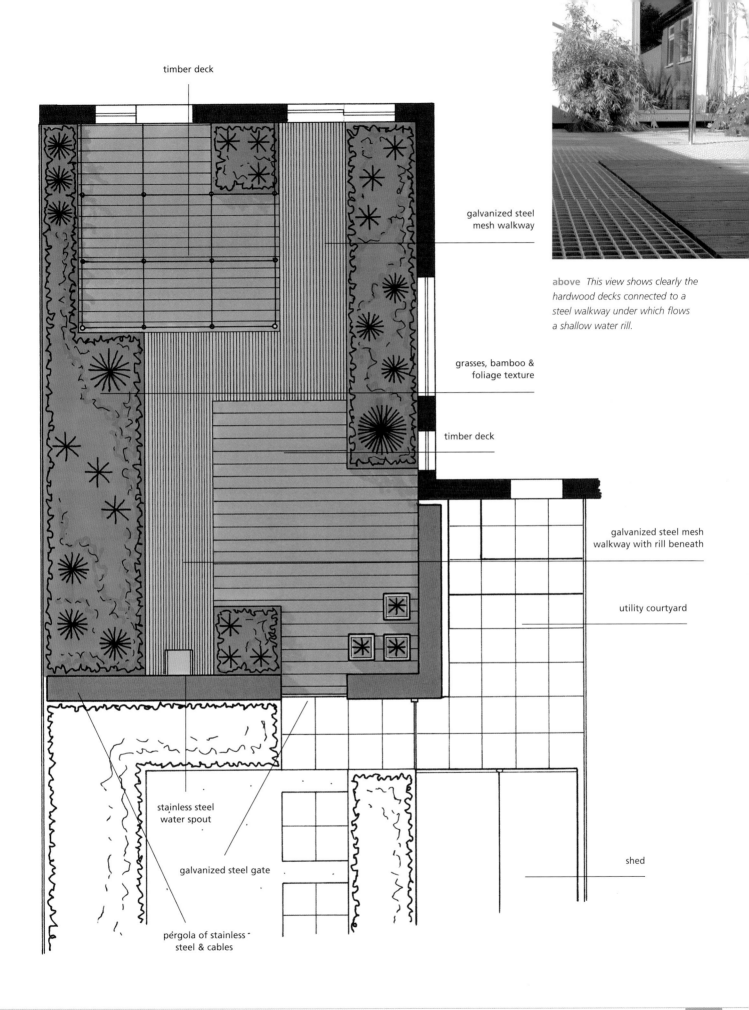

timber deck

galvanized steel
mesh walkway

above *This view shows clearly the hardwood decks connected to a steel walkway under which flows a shallow water rill.*

grasses, bamboo &
foliage texture

timber deck

galvanized steel mesh
walkway with rill beneath

utility courtyard

stainless steel
water spout

galvanized steel gate

shed

pérgola of stainless
steel & cables

Barn Courtyard

Alison Dove

dimensions: **9.5 x 8.5m (31 x 28ft)**
soil: **alkaline clay, replaced with (alkaline) topsoil**
aspect: **southwest facing**
key features: **pool, stone bridge, terrace**

The owners requested a modern, low-maintenance garden for the family to enjoy during breaks from working in Holland, which would largely coincide with school holidays. The garden is the small courtyard of a barn conversion, surrounded by buildings on all four sides. These vary between the traditional dark, pitch-painted weather-boarding of the main two-storey house, the mellow old brick of an adjacent low barn, and the more modern red brick of the parents' house. There are no views, and the garden can get extremely hot in mid-summer. However, overhead structures or trees were not wanted by the client as large windows overlook the garden from the modern, minimalist sitting room. There were also several manhole covers to hide.

Paths were made of smooth Cotswold gravel edged with pale Indian sandstone. Water flowed from a carved stone bowl into a narrow, deep rill, beneath a pale Indian stone bridge and into a long, narrow reflecting pool in front of the large house window. Leaving the pool the water flowed into the shadiest corner, where it disappeared into a recessed bowl. In this shady corner a small seating area could be reached from the office door.

Lavender and *Convolvulus cneorum* spilt from a narrow bed beside the rill. Beyond this a generously proportioned pale stone terrace was fringed by four tall curled obelisks, each containing a climber, the glossy *Trachelospermum jasminoides*, visually linking the lower brick wall with the dark weather-board above. Between these was a simple but elegant iron bench.

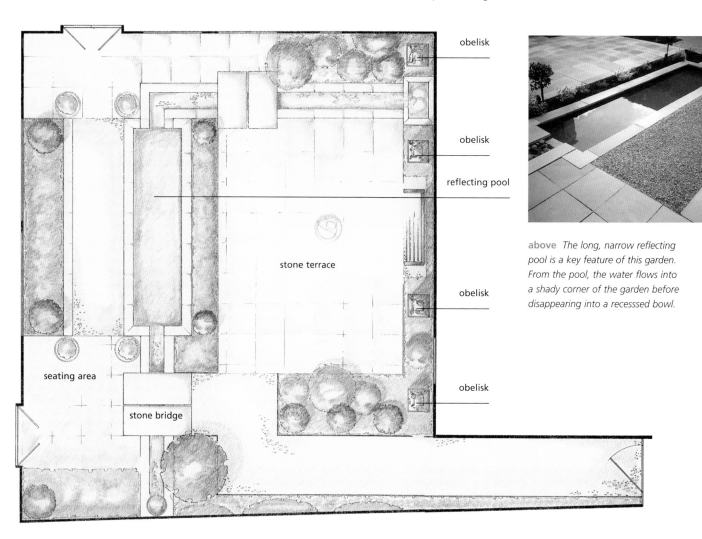

obelisk

obelisk

reflecting pool

stone terrace

obelisk

seating area

obelisk

stone bridge

above *The long, narrow reflecting pool is a key feature of this garden. From the pool, the water flows into a shady corner of the garden before disappearing into a recesssed bowl.*

Teahouse Garden

Christopher Maguire

dimensions: **900sq m (2953sq ft) approx.**
soil: **alkaline (chalk subsoil)**
aspect: **south to west facing**
key features: **Japanese-style teahouse**

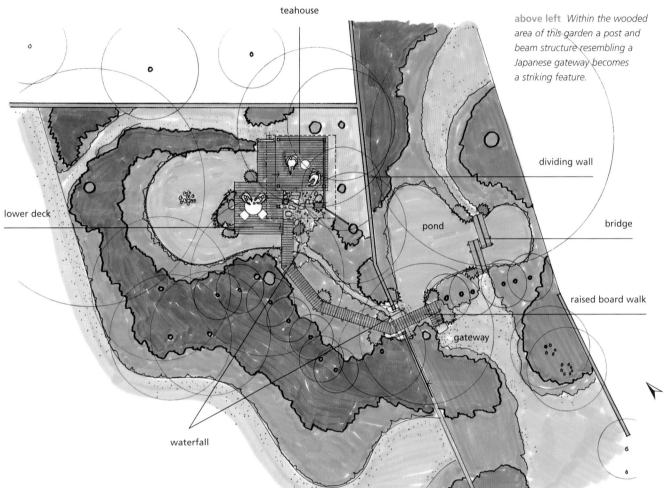

teahouse

above left Within the wooded area of this garden a post and beam structure resembling a Japanese gateway becomes a striking feature.

dividing wall

lower deck

pond

bridge

raised board walk

gateway

waterfall

The owner of the garden wanted a Japanese "teahouse" structure within a wooded area, which is only a small part of a large garden. It is bounded by a lawn and existing borders to the south, a boundary wall to the northeast, and a dividing wall between an upper and a lower wooded area within the owners property.

There were a number of large box trees, a mature *Robinia pseudoacacia*, a large Scot's pine (*Pinus sylvestris*), sycamore, laurels, and an ancient yew. The space is divided in two by a north-south wall, and there is a large drop in level from west to east. The walls, mature trees, and the two wooded areas at different levels provided restraints, but they also provided a strong structure to which the design could relate.

An interpretation of the forms of a teahouse was created with a post and beam structure in Douglas fir and cedar shingles roof, which has a deck floor and enclosing rendered walls on two sides. The other sides opened to a lower deck and a pond. This fed a stream flowing to a waterfall into a lower lake, crossed at its narrowest point by a board bridge. From there a bark path led to a point where there were long views out of the site. A Japanese-style gateway marked the transition between the two levels and was linked to the teahouse by a raised board walk.

A mixture of trees, shrubs, perennials, grasses, ferns, climbers, groundcover plants, and water/marginal plants were chosen which are suitable for a woodland setting.

A Calming Garden

Nigel L. Philips Landscape & Garden Design

dimensions: 23 x 28m (75 x 92ft)
soil: sandy loam. slightly acid
aspect: northeast facing, open
key features: grotto, waterfalls, summerhouse

The owner of the garden required an area for a summerhouse and a separate garden for relaxation and enjoyment by an elderly group of up to 10 people. Some of the group would be in wheelchairs. A fall in the ground level had to be considered in the plan.

Two brick and stone terraces defined areas for entertaining, with one of them being accessible by wheelchairs. Stone steps were used between the two levels. A grotto, waterfalls, and pond created an attractive, calming feature. Along with the summerhouse, a pergola arch was used in the design.

Besides the existing magnolia and juniper, a pear (*Pyrus salicifolia* 'Pendula') was planted. Shrubs in the planting scheme included rosemary, rock rose, lavender, potentilla, and ceanothus. A variety of perennials were chosen, and bog planting was used near the pond.

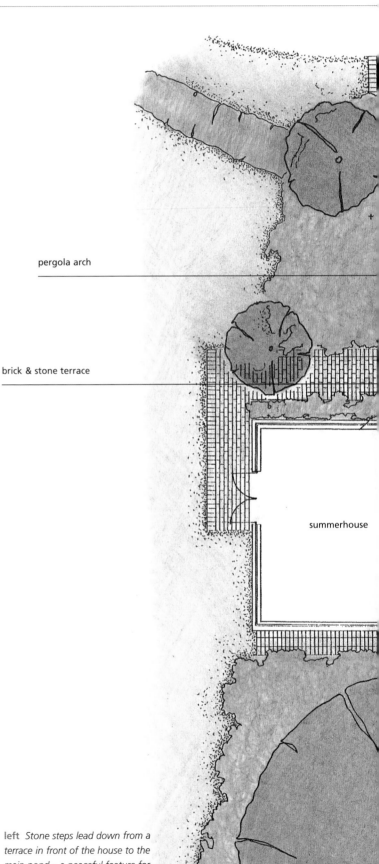

pergola arch

brick & stone terrace

summerhouse

left *Stone steps lead down from a terrace in front of the house to the main pond – a peaceful feature for people to relax by.*

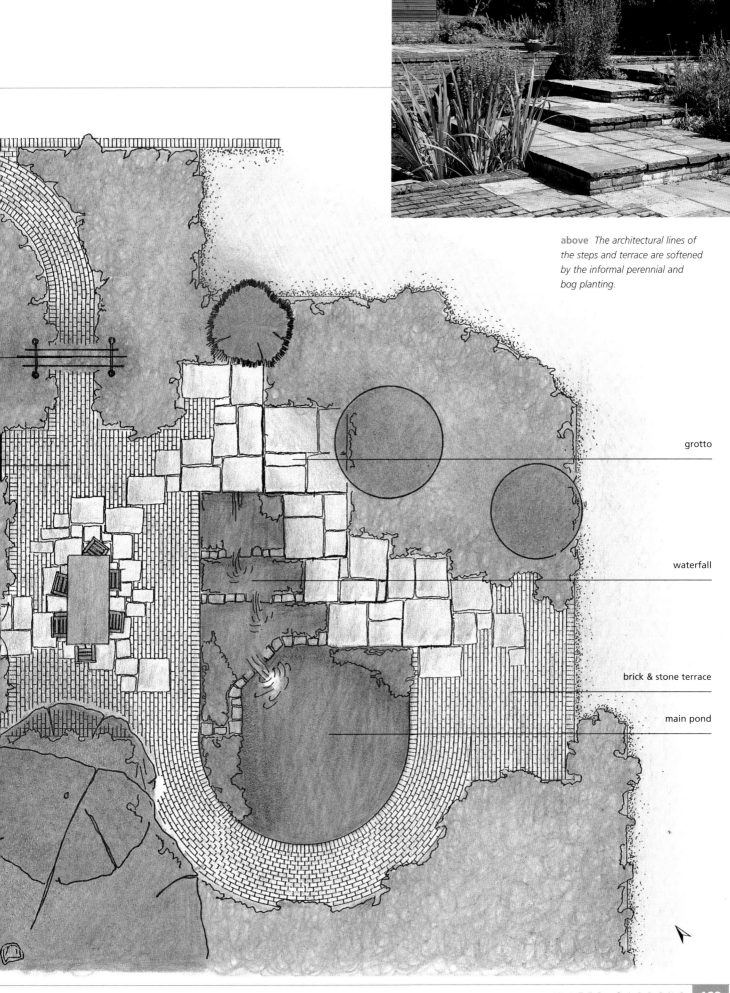

above *The architectural lines of the steps and terrace are softened by the informal perennial and bog planting.*

grotto

waterfall

brick & stone terrace

main pond

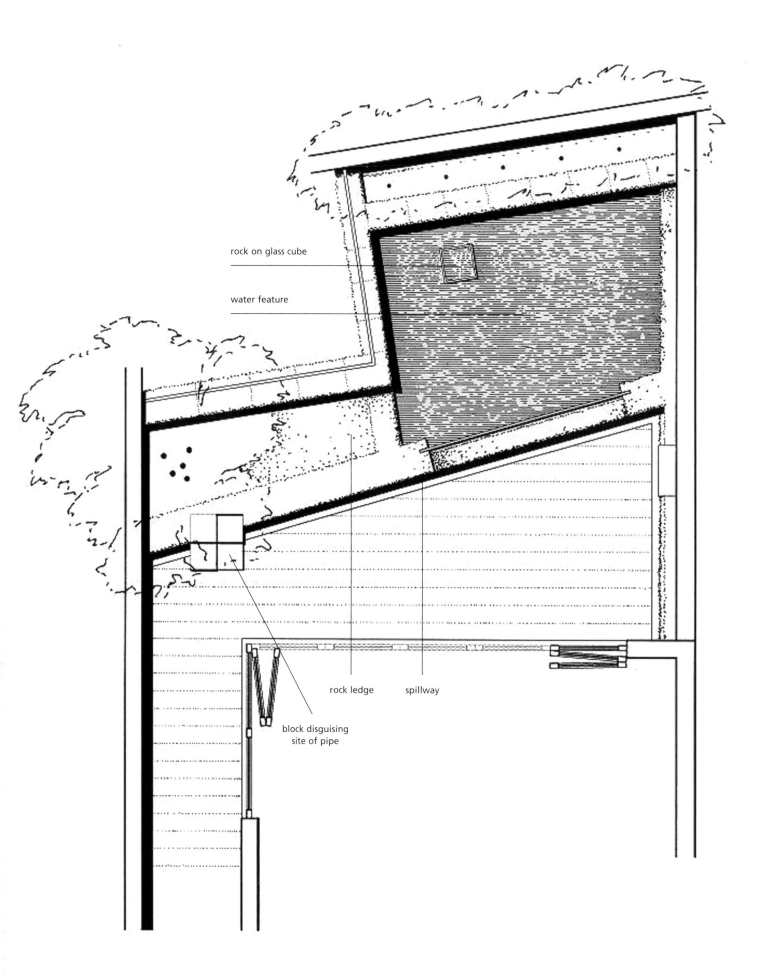

rock on glass cube

water feature

rock ledge   spillway

block disguising
site of pipe

Out of Rock

Vladimir Sitta/Maren Perry

dimensions: **6 x 4m (20 x 13ft) approx.**
soil: **imported**
aspect: **mostly sheltered**
key features: **rock ledge, water feature**

left *The "Blue Rock" nesting on a glass cube was added to the garden in order to enhance its restrained colour palette.*

The owners of this Australian garden wanted to reduce the feeling of claustrophobia. The garden has an awkward shape and consisted of only rock – no soil – and ugly brick walls. What makes this garden very site specific is the existence of the sheer rock.

The rock was been used as the base for a pool and retaining walls. A rock ledge originally finishing near the kitchen was pushed back at an angle and excavated to allow for a body of water to cover virtually the entire area. The flow of water over the spillway filled the space and the kitchen with a pleasant sound – much treasured in a dense urban environment with ambient noise generated by vehicles and air conditioning. The water was set at the eye level of the sitting person, and to enhance its effect the spillway was made of glass. This transparency compensates for a spatially constrained backyard. At night the spillway and the source were lit. The "Blue Rock" nesting on the glass cube of the source was a late addition to enhance the restrained colour palette of the garden.

The excavation exposed an unused pipe that runs across the garden. The removal of the pipe left an unsightly scar, which was filled with a large rectangular block, not disguising, but rather mysteriously covering a "secret" passage. Black pebbles and black granite tiles extended from the kitchen.

The planting was chosen for very modest spatial demands, while attaining the desirable height. It included black bamboo (*Phyllostachys nigra*), Moso bamboo (*P. edulis*), and baby's tears (*Soleirolia soleirolii*).

right *The water feature, created out of the garden's sheer rock, is complemented by a key plants, including the bamboos* Phyllostachys nigra *and* P. edulis.

Garden of Continuity

Arabella Lennox-Boyd

dimensions: **13 x 10m (43 x 33ft)**
soil: **average**
aspect: **west facing**
key features: **water canal, stepping stones**

The design for the garden was to be in the modern idiom and should convey a sense of peace and continuity. A design was inspired by the year of the millenium. A central feature based on water was chosen for its timeless, tranquil quality. In contrast, included in the design are ancient olive trees, which have thrived on the arid shores of the Mediterranean since before the start of the modern calendar. These elements, subtly alluding to the millenium, were inspirations for the garden.

The main feature was a water canal which surrounded an inner grass space, with both edges of the canal having been trimmed with cut slate. Six gnarled olive trees in stainless steel containers were spaced equally within the canal in such a way that they appear to float on the water's surface. Slate stepping stones at each end made bridges to the island lawn.

Another feature was the imposing rectangular structure which drew the eye towards the back of the garden. Here, a sculpture by William Pye, "The Vortex of Water", rested on the top of a turf mound surrounded by borders of the giant feather grass (*Stipa gigantea*) and tawny herbaceous perennials.

At the front of the garden, towering pillars of Italian cypresses (*Cupressus sempervirens*), festooned with climbing roses, punctuated boldly planted beds, including *Iris* 'Indian Chief', the alkanet *Anchusa azurea* 'Loddon Royalist', and the oriental poppy *Papaver orientale* 'Orangeade Maison', flanked a small lawn. A carefully clipped bay hedge on the north boundary provided a dark contrast to the silver olives, water, and vibrant planting.

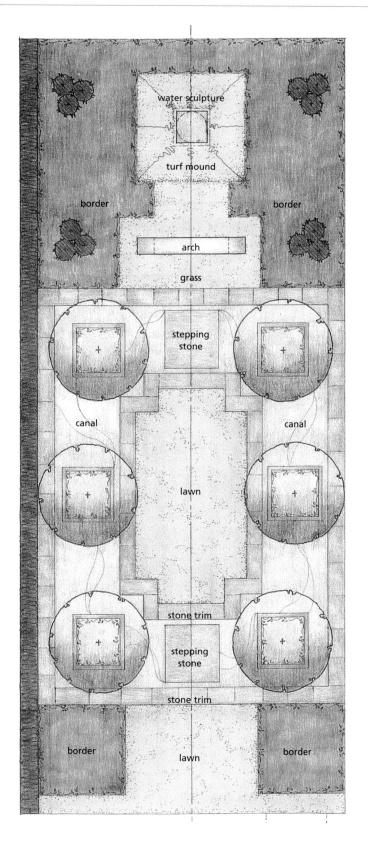

Water Meadow Garden

Mark Anthony Walker Associates

dimensions: **12 x 14m (39 x 46ft)**
soil: **slightly acid**
aspect: **open, exposed**
key features: **timber decking, ceramic poles**

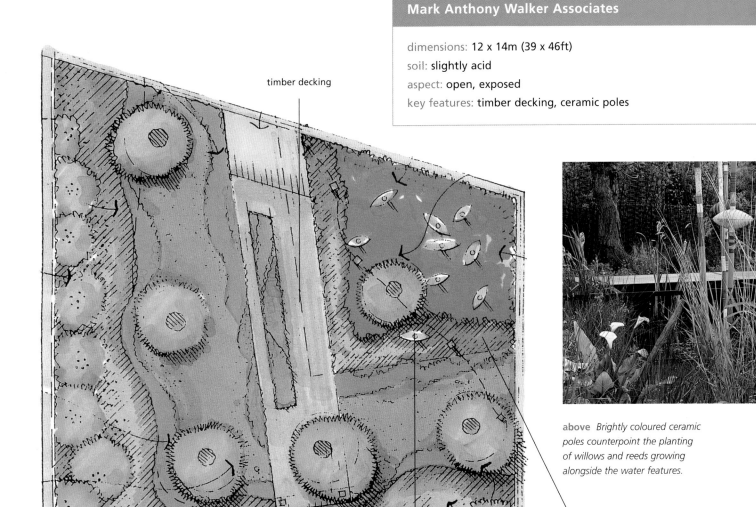

timber decking

water feature

ceramic poles

above *Brightly coloured ceramic poles counterpoint the planting of willows and reeds growing alongside the water features.*

A garden with a water meadow theme was conceived as part of a larger surrounding landscape, and it was inspired by the aesthetic and sculptural qualities characteristic of a wetland landscape. A marginal garden between the large garden and the landscape was created that seamlessly blended into the surrounding countryside.

The viewer's eye was drawn to the centre of the garden by a timber deck, and the garden was designed to be viewed from all positions along the two open boundaries. The design of the timber deck was restrained, functional, and modernist in style to contrast with the gnarled trunks of the pollarded willows. The deck visually "floated" over the meadow planting beneath, and was designed to be non-interventionist, with trees and reeds growing through slots

and portals. Sculpture was included in the garden. The brightly coloured ceramic poles (by sculptor Jonathan Keep) echoed the upright character of the pollarded willows, and added scale and texture to the scheme.

A restrained planting palette and mass planting of single species created an expansive and natural effect. Some trees either planted or existing acted as "living sculpture". Sculptural and mature pollarded willows implied the corner of a larger field, forming the framework of the space. Much of the planting was characteristic of a wetland landscape. The russet browns and greens of the reeds and willows contrasted with flowering indigenous species such as sweet flag, kingcups, ragged robin, and water avens.

Double-Pond Garden

Keith Pullan

dimensions: **7.5 x 6m (25 x 20ft)**
soil: loamy clay, acid
aspect: **east facing, sheltered**
key features: **ponds connected by a waterfall, decking**

The small part of the garden next to the house consists of a paved terrace and lawn area which required no redesigning. However, the owner wanted an existing pond replaced and extended to an additional pond at a higher level behind the garage, with a bridge across the ponds to provide access into the garden from a gate at the rear. An informal design was requested, with a natural appearance to the ponds, including a cobble and pebble beach and boulders. Planting should again be informal and varied, and use should be made of existing plants where appropriate.

The ponds, with their waterfall connection, formed the dominant feature of the garden. A timber deck and bridge, with overhead timber beams, gave a more structured character to the upper pond, while boulders and a cobble beach added informality to the lower section. There was a gravel area at the far side of the pond providing space for a small bench seat. A gravel path led to the rear gate exit which was concealed by a trellis panel.

The existing mature conifer *Chamaecyparis lawsoniana* was a dominant, structural feature. Other existing conifers and shrubs provided an evergreen background to the garden. A Japanese maple (*Acer palmatum* 'Atropurpureum'), *Hydrangea macrophylla*, and a variety of perennials provided additional colour and interest. Climbers were provided on the overhead beams, including wisteria and an evergreen clematis. Pond plants were selected for contrast in foliage as well as flower.

left *The plants bordering the lower of the two ponds included a Rodgersia pinnata 'Superba' – shown here – and Iris sibirica; both in character with their position.*

boulder edge to pond

lower pond

border of mixed planting

gravel onto pebble & cobble beach

stone-sett edging

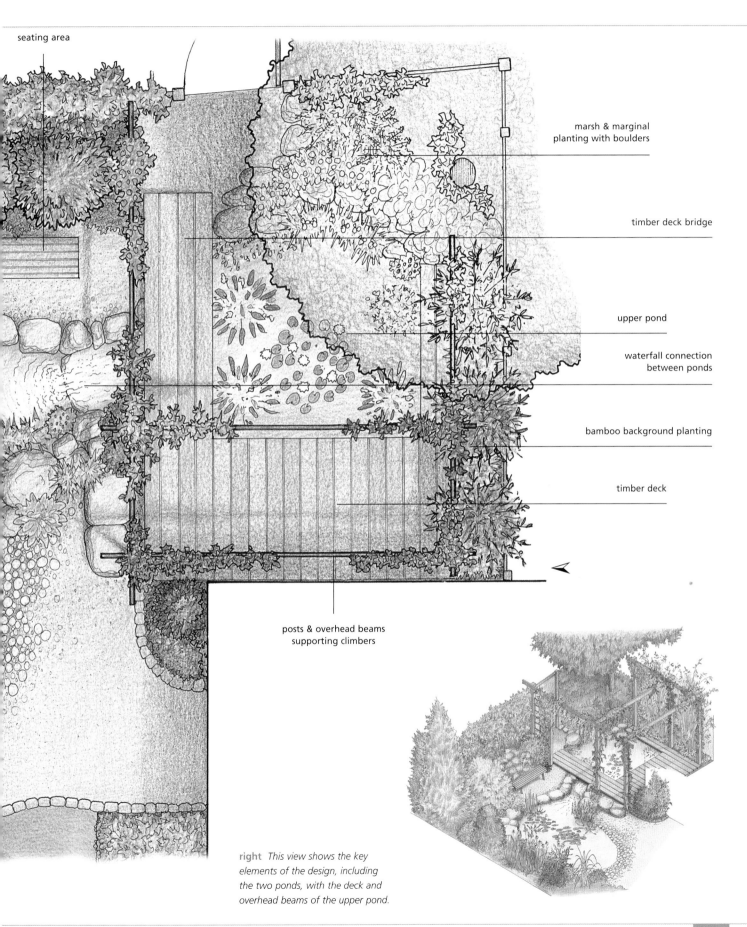

seating area

marsh & marginal
planting with boulders

timber deck bridge

upper pond

waterfall connection
between ponds

bamboo background planting

timber deck

posts & overhead beams
supporting climbers

right *This view shows the key
elements of the design, including
the two ponds, with the deck and
overhead beams of the upper pond.*

1960s-style Garden

dimensions: **22 x 5m (72 x 16ft)**
soil: **acid side of neutral**
aspect: **north facing**
key features: **fish pond**

The owners of a 1960s-style house wanted a garden that was different and that would also complement the house. They did not want grass, but requested water for fish, and they asked that the design include paving slabs of various sizes that the owner had acquired over the years.

The garden already had a narrow, flat, open terrace, and retaining walls of York stone had already been built. A water maze was designed within these constraints, constructed from butyl liner, and using the existing paving slabs.

The planting required a lot of colour with a Mediterranean or exotic feel, but all the plants had to be hardy and not take up too much room in a narrow area. Evergreens for structure included *Fatsia japonica*, *Viburnum davidii*, and *Choisya ternata*. Hibiscus and fuchsias were among the deciduous shrubs. Plants with big leaves that look good next to water were planted such as *Hosta sieboldiana*, *Acanthus mollis*, *Crocosima* 'Lucifer', *Melianthus major*, *Hemerocallis*, and *Eremurus robustus*. In summer pots of variegated agaves and colourful annuals would be placed at strategic points along the terrace.

left *The fish pond surrounded by bold architectual planting and, in the summer months, pots of colourful agaves and annuals.*

Option 1: wildlife garden (preferred)

Option 2: formal circular garden

Option 3: labyrinth or maze circular garden

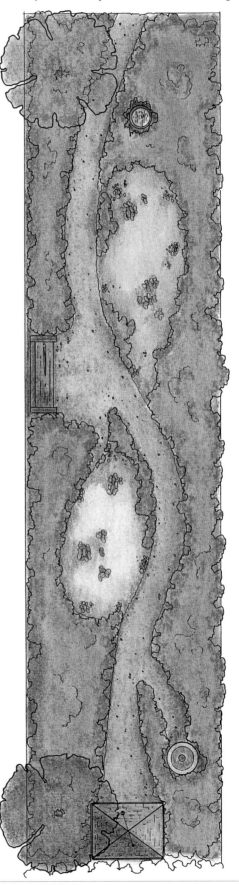

The thread of formal or axial design runs through garden history from the gardens of Islam, through the classical grandeur of Italy and France, and into the Beaux Arts symmetry prevalent in the early twentieth century.

Although Modernism introduced an asymmetrical alternative to the Western scene, symmetry has never died out, and has produced dramatic and powerful modern gardens. Scale and proportion are key factors in successful formal layouts, with axes and vistas relative to the views from the house often defining major routes in the garden. Sculpture and ornament are often used to punctuate important intersections, or, as focal points, to terminate routes and views.

In some gardens formal and informal elements can be combined to good effect, with asymmetrical geometry defined by formally clipped hedges, sharp edges to paving, and long rills or canals of water. This can increase the drama of a design through heightened contrast, which is in fact one of the key characteristics of the English garden. Beneath the weight of extravagant and romantic planting in the herbaceous or mixed border often lies a sharply formal or highly organized garden layout.

Michael Balston opens this section of the book with a garden that incorporates axial and symmetrically designed spaces within a wider context.

Formal Gardens

Gardens Within a Garden

Balston & Co

dimensions: **23,070sq m (6 acres)**
soil: **loam, with some acid areas; boggy close to the river**
aspect: **mostly south facing**
key features: **oval lawn, rose garden, kitchen garden**

right *Leading down from the terrace, the oval lawn was surrounded by Mediterranean plants and aromatic herbs.*

The existing garden originally formed part of a larger garden, but it was still substantial and contains some good trees, including cedar, walnut, oak and birch, as well as shrubs. The owner required a new layout to take advantage of the best of the remaining planting, but also to exploit the site better, opening up views to the river, creating a better relationship with the architecture of the 18th-century house, and incorporating a rose garden, kitchen garden, and mixed border. An existing swimming pool was to be incorporated, as well as a pool room.

The design included a box parterre, a terrace out of the conservatory, an elliptical lawn, changes in level, and metal arches to define the kitchen garden, rose garden, thyme lawn, orchard, swimming pool garden, and herbaceous border.

An important reception area required year-round planting interest and a number of evergreeens. Mainly shrubs with light flowers were used to show up against yew. The rose garden was planted with pinks to purples. The peak season was extended by choosing roses that bear hips and including late-flowering perennials for good autumn colour and bulbs for spring. The thyme garden is closely linked to the rose garden and is in co-ordinating colours.

The orchard had a wilder feel, created by longer grass with mown path, spring and autumn bulbs, and roses trained into trees. A simple planting scheme was used for the borders, with large blocks of individual varieties. For the oval lawn terrace area, aromatic Mediterranean plants were selected. Herbaceous plants and shrubs were planted around the swimming pool.

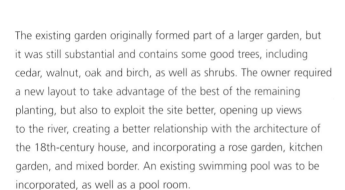

left *Although the peak season for the rose garden is high summer, planting interest was extended by including late flowering perennials, such as penstomen, hollyhocks, and phlox, and bulbs in spring.*

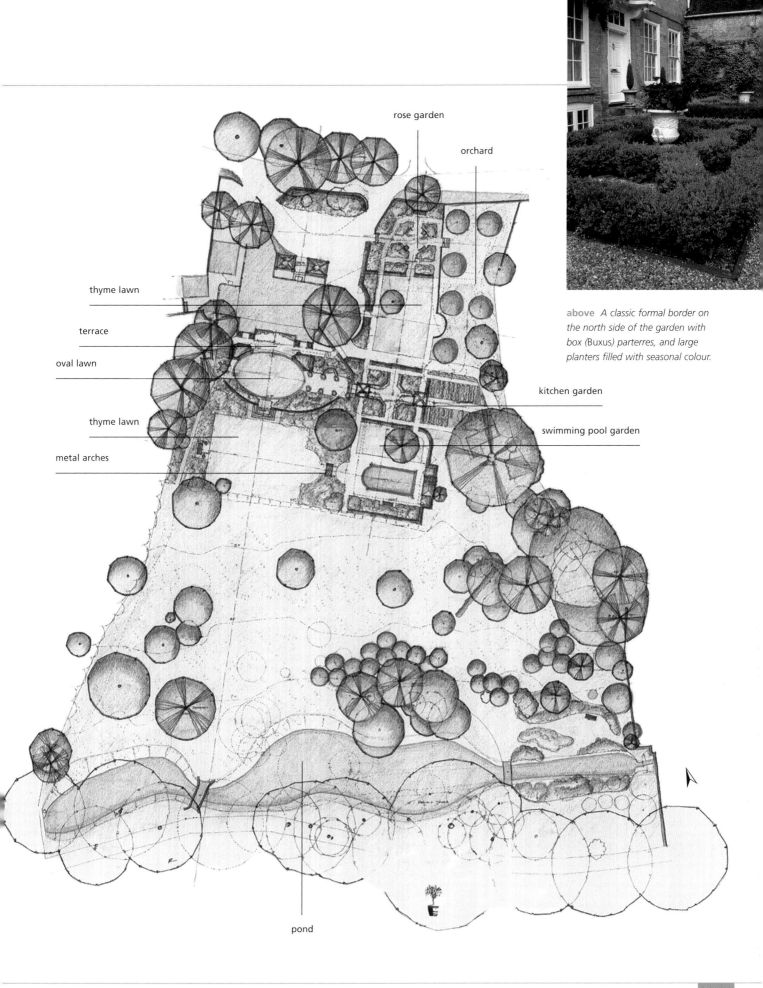

rose garden

orchard

thyme lawn

terrace

oval lawn

thyme lawn

metal arches

above *A classic formal border on the north side of the garden with box (Buxus) parterres, and large planters filled with seasonal colour.*

kitchen garden

swimming pool garden

pond

thyme

stainless steel arch
(with espalier tree)

box balls

"Lutyens" style bench

herbaceous perennials

carved stone balls

box

chequerboard planting & paving

buff river slabs for paving area

Espalier Garden

Douglas Coltart

dimensions: **5 x 5m (16 x 16ft)**
soil: **free draining, neutral**
aspect: **south facing**
key features: **stainless steel espalier**

left Slabs formed a paved area in this garden with gaps left for evergreen planting; the slabs were also used for raised beds around the perimeter of the garden.

The owners wanted a garden designed with a restricted budget, so the design had to be for a garden that could be built in two days by four people. The garden itself was small, but the owners wanted a structural framework that included some type of seating element, and a structure that would allow a plant trained as an espalier. The garden was within a terrace of other gardens and was backed by a hedge, and the owners requested a design that would provide a view from the house that would be distinct from the others. Because the garden was only accessible from the front, the components had to be of a size that would fit through the corridors in the house.

The structure for the espalier was created from a curved section of stainless steel tube, which had holes drilled along either side at regular intervals. Stainless steel wire was threaded through these holes and tightened to provide the horizontal wires for the espalier to be trained along. Slabs were used to form a paved area with gaps left for planting. The slabs were also used on edge to form raised beds. The paving included a seating area in front of the espalier, which framed a bench.

The planting was selected to provide an evergreen framework and act as a foil for herbaceous perennials. The small garden was bounded by a low yew hedge within which are standard holly bushes, with their balls above the hedging. The boundary was complemented by balls of box (*Buxus*). Plants include *Taxus baccata*, *Ilex* x *meserveae* Blue Prince, *Buxus sempervirens*, *Thymus vulgaris*, *Liatris spicata* 'Floristan Violet', and *Hosta* 'Sum and Substance'.

right An important feature of this garden was the espalier of curved stainless steel tubing; it framed the seating area and, in due course, would have a plant, such as a fruit tree or bush, trained along it.

Colonial Garden

Arabella Lennox-Boyd

dimensions: **12,140sq m (3 acres)**
soil: **sand mixed with loam, acid**
aspect: **sheltered**
key features: **long, sloping site**

The design for this coastal garden in Southampton, New York, was inspired by the beauty and climate of Long Island, with its colonial classicism, and by the needs of a young family. The garden was divided into a series of sheltered spaces, protected by hedges of *Ligustrum ovalifolium* and *Taxus x media* 'Hicksii', that separated play areas from lawns and guest spaces from the main house.

The approach to the house was important and called for a formal sense of arrival. A broad gravel drive was designed between existing pudding-shaped topiaries leading to a new, west-facing gravel courtyard with topiary of box (*Buxus sempervirens*) at its centre. Lines of summer flowering *Lagerstroemia* 'Natchez' framed the house, and leant a sense of symmetry to the asymmetrical architecture. The courtyard structure was reinforced by a cut stone trim, and a series of box cubes along a border in front of the house.

An axis across the courtyard led to a swimming pool for the house to the north and, to the south, guest-house gardens and swimming pools. An oval lawn to the west of the north pool was reached through twin borders surrounding a small square lawn for barbeques. The oval lawn was an all-purpose space, which allowed for summer parties and games of football.

To the north of the guesthouse was an intimate garden with concentric squares of cut stone trim, set in a fine lawn surrounded by borders of grasses and roses which alluded to the surrounding maritime flora. Trees in the garden provided a vertical element and flower from spring through summer, when fruit and colourful autumn leaves come to the fore. The guesthouse lawn, surrounded by grasses and perennials, afforded stunning views to the sea.

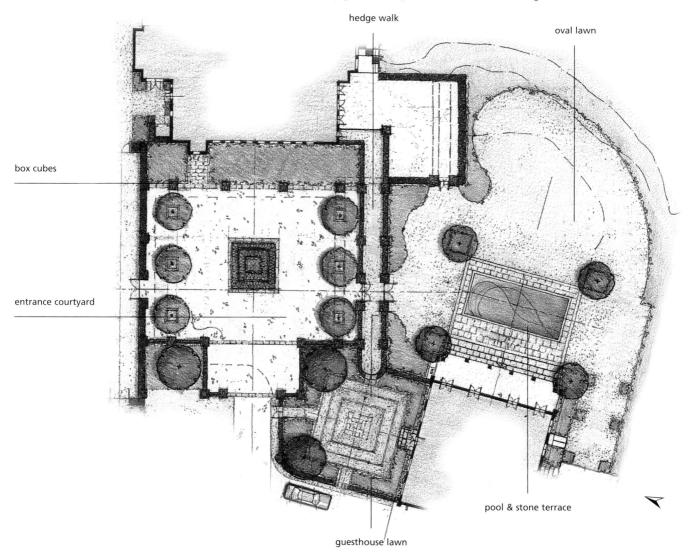

hedge walk

oval lawn

box cubes

entrance courtyard

pool & stone terrace

guesthouse lawn

Farmhouse Garden

Roderick Griffin

dimensions: **35 x 15m (115 x 49ft)**
soil: **chalk, imported topsoil**
aspect: **northwest facing, exposed**
key features: **circular terrace, formal pond**

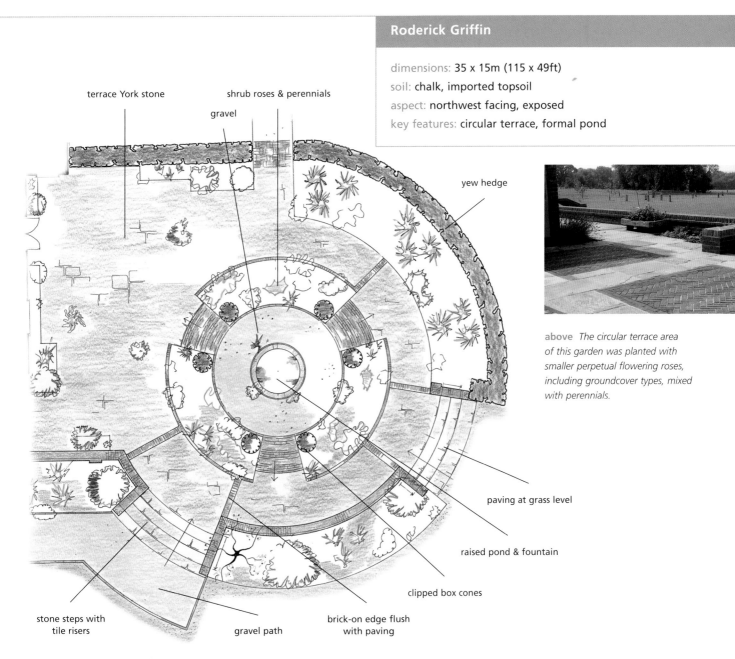

terrace York stone

shrub roses & perennials

gravel

yew hedge

paving at grass level

raised pond & fountain

clipped box cones

stone steps with
tile risers

gravel path

brick-on edge flush
with paving

above *The circular terrace area of this garden was planted with smaller perpetual flowering roses, including groundcover types, mixed with perennials.*

The house was created from a few remnants of farm buildings. No garden existed, only concrete-based cattle buildings and farmland. The owner requested a traditional garden to make the best use of the location, and he wanted it to include terraces, a formal garden, a large vegetable garden, and a rose garden. It should also accommodate various troughs, sundials, and pots from a former house, and have a formal garden pond.

In line with the traditional feel required, random rectangular York stone paving was used with dark red and orange multi-stock bricks, in keeping with the farmhouse walls. The retaining walls were of substantial construction in view of the "made up" nature of the ground. Coping details were chosen to reflect a detail used on the retained sections of the former barn buildings. Steps were formed using tile risers. Thin strips of roofing tile cut widthways were used without mortar as paving. It was decided that the formal pond would go within a walled garden area to the southwest of the house. The step and the tile plinth was designed to fill the void and accommodate the owner's sundial.

The circular terrace area was created to fulfil the request for a rose garden. This design introduced the owner to some smaller perpetual flowering roses, including groundcover types, mixed with perennials. In the planting area immediately in front of a yew hedge, the owner's favourite hybrid tea roses were interspersed with yuccas and edged with perennials. The yew hedge was planted to enclose and separate the front garden and driveway. It also created a good backdrop to the planting and provided shelter.

A Village Garden

Simon Dorell

dimensions: **105 x 90m (344 x 295ft)**
soil: **clay**
aspect: **north facing, open**
key features: **apple orchard, reflecting pool, Tudor parterre**

left Among the evergreen and deciduous trees planted in this garden were cherry trees – this variety is Prunus x subhirtella 'Autumnalis'.

The brief was to design a low-maintenance public open space for village residents and visitors. The area, formerly a pasture paddock, was bounded by village gardens, a patch of woodland, and farmland, with far-reaching views north. It was to include allotments, paths with all weather surfaces for the use of cyclists and pedestrians, and space for the possible later erection of a public meeting place.

A central "green" had a double avenue of holly topiary and elm, with regularly deployed "earthworks". There was a formal apple orchard and four grids of fastigiate trees, along with a reflecting pool and Tudor parterre. The allotments were of an elipitical shape.

The planting consisted of deciduous and evergreen trees and hedges, including elm, apple, pear, birch, cherry, poplar, willow, holly, box, yew, Irish yew, hornbeam, and false cypress. Deciduous and evergreen shrubs, predominantly viburnums and hydrangeas, were also planted, along with hardy perennials.

Tudor parterre   pool

earthwork   New Moon pool

Updated Garden

del Buono-Gazerwitz Landscape Architecture

dimensions: **300sq m (984sq ft)**
soil: **clay**
aspect: **sheltered**
key features: **sunken terrace, pool with stepping stones**

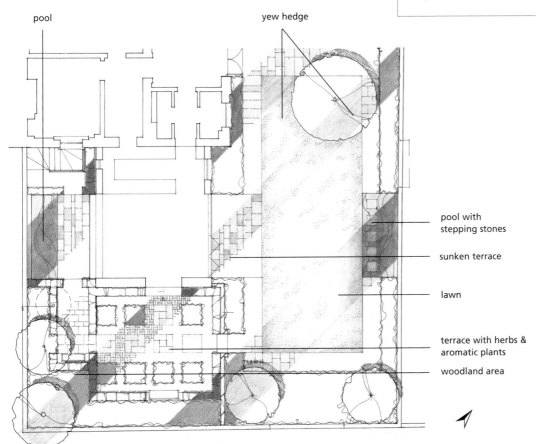

pool

yew hedge

pool with stepping stones

sunken terrace

lawn

terrace with herbs & aromatic plants

woodland area

above *The terrace, paved in York stone and brick, is used for dining. The planting includes culinary herbs and aromatic plants.*

This well-established garden was to be updated to reflect the refurbishment of the property carried out by its new owners. Previously owned by a keen gardener, the site contained many good, mature specimen shrubs and climbers as well as a few trees. The old brick walls surrounding it added enclosure as well as the character and atmosphere of a country garden. The design was to simplify the layout of the established garden, but retain several outstanding specimens.

Slick "Acero" stone continued out from the interior to form a new, sunken terrace overlooking the main lawn. A pool and fountain abutted the lawn, and was bisected by a row of stepping stones designed to appear to float on the water's surface. York stone and brick were used to form all pathways and steps.

"Rooms" within the garden each had a different feel. In the shade of an old pear tree the planting was limited to ferns and baby's breath (*Soleirolia soleirollii*) set against the backdrop of an evergreen climber trained on the brick walls. Another shady area under a birch was planted as a small woodland garden. A small terrace paved in York stone and brick and used for outdoor dining was planted with culinary herbs and aromatic plants. The borders surrounding the main lawn contained old-fashioned roses, potentillas, and tree paeonies. A mature yew hedge screened a service area and shed.

Cottage and Vegetable Gardens

Ryl Nowell

dimensions: **736sq m (2415sq ft) approx.**

soil: **sandy loam**

aspect: **south facing**

key features: **terrace, vegetable garden**

above *The area just outside the house shows the stone terrace with the garages in the background.*

The owner wanted a garden design that would reflect the design of the extension to the modern house to provide a private space with cottage planting. He also wanted to create a garden to link with the modern pavilion that includes a large entertaining space adjacent to the pavilion. There was to be a link between these two areas, along with access to the garage. A large vegetable garden and greenhouse were also requested. The garden was near the sea and on a slope, which had to be considered in the plan, along with the existing trees and established boundary planting.

A series of circles were used to establish the defined areas, incorporating a stone terrace and vegetable garden. Steps provided an easier transition between levels, thereby eliminating the slope of the garden.

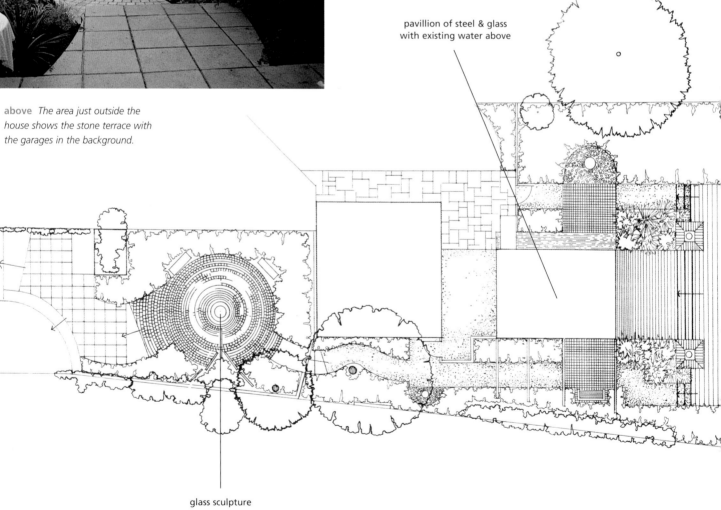

pavillion of steel & glass
with existing water above

glass sculpture

right *A pathway links the modern glass extension to the house with the garden.*

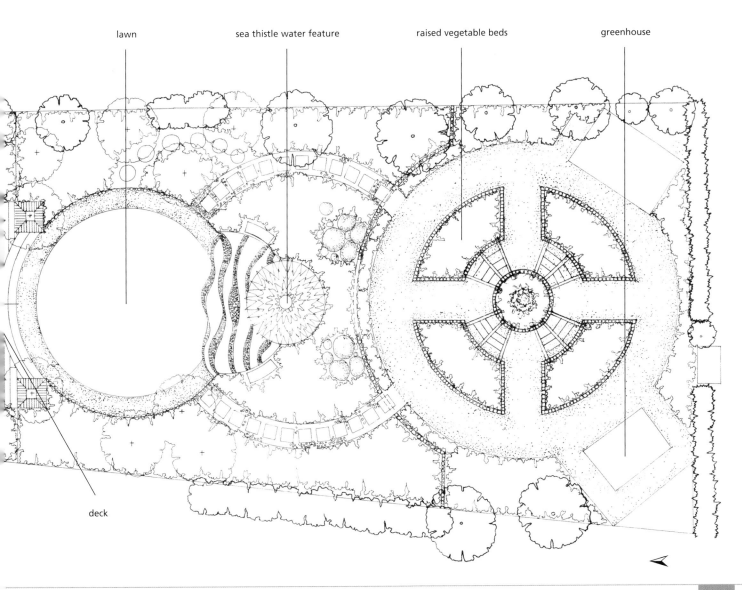

lawn

sea thistle water feature

raised vegetable beds

greenhouse

deck

A Sense of Arrival

Nigel L. Philips Landscape & Garden Design

dimensions: **15 x 17m (49 x 56ft)**
soil: **sandy clay loam**
aspect: **north facing**
key features: **paving, topairy**

The owners of this triangular-shaped front garden wanted a design that made sure that vistors were led directly to the front door of the impressive house. The garden needed to create an interesting and dramatic sense of arrival. They also wanted the planting to be pale colours ranging through white to cream to pale yellow with glossy evergreens. Existing light levels in the garden were low, and this issue was to be addressed in the plan.

A combination of brick paving and sandstone paving was laid with the contrasting colours of the materials clearly delineating a pathway to the front door. Brick edging was used to provide sharp lines around topiaried box spheres, which were planted in a grid throughout the garden. To provide visual interest and offset the symmetrical nature of the architecture, the pathway had rectangular sections extending out to one side, giving the illusion that some of the box spheres projected into the pathway – however, there was ample room in the pathway for visitors to come and go.

The planting scheme included an existing box (*Buxus sempervirens*) specimens, which was pruned into a topiary shape. Among the shrubs planted were *Buxus sempervirens*, *Prunus laurocerasus* 'Otto Luyken', *Sarcococca humilis*, *Viburnum davidii*, *Hydrangea arborescens* 'Annabelle', *Potentilla fruticosa* 'Vilminoriana', *Philadelphus* 'Beauclerk', and *Achillea* 'Moonshine'. Perennials included *Geranium renardii*, *Iris* 'White City', *Polygonatum* x *hybridum*, and *Sisyrinchium striatum* 'Aunt May'.

above and below right *A simple but striking design for a front garden. To provide visual interest and break the neat formality, rectangular sections create the illusion that the box (*Buxus*) spheres project into the pathway to the house.*

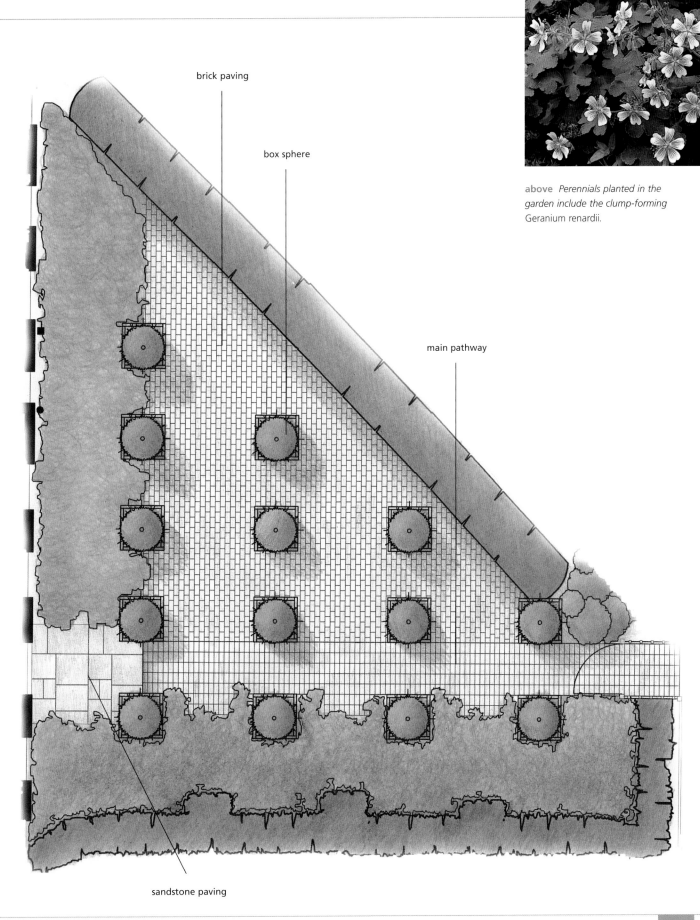

brick paving

box sphere

main pathway

above *Perennials planted in the garden include the clump-forming Geranium renardii.*

sandstone paving

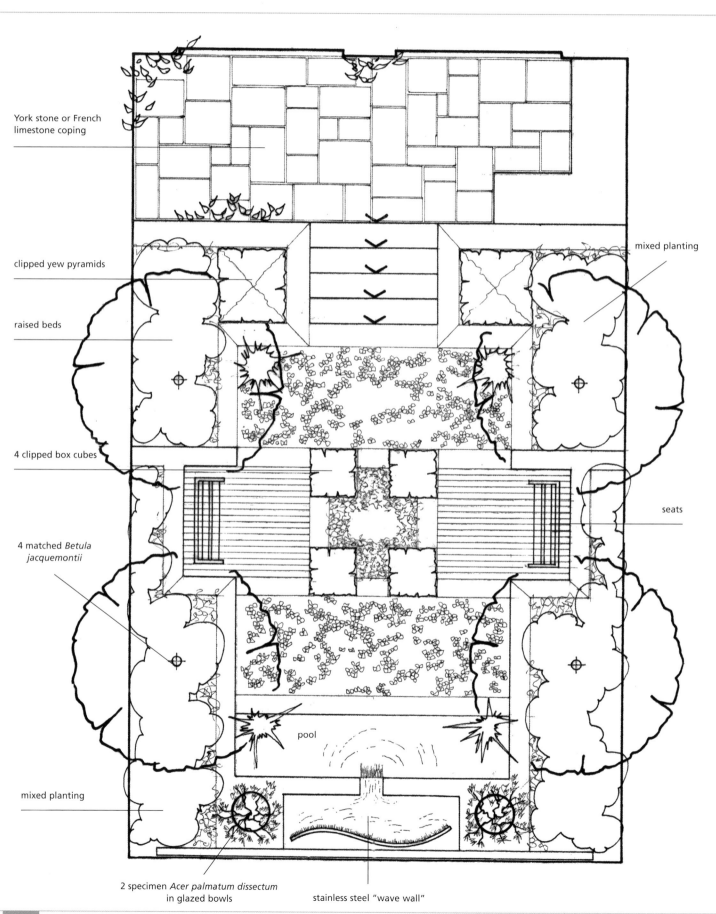

York stone or French
limestone coping

mixed planting

clipped yew pyramids

raised beds

4 clipped box cubes

seats

4 matched *Betula
jacquemontii*

pool

mixed planting

2 specimen *Acer palmatum dissectum*
in glazed bowls

stainless steel "wave wall"

Wave Wall Garden

David Stevens

dimensions: **9.5 x 15m (31 x 49ft)**
soil: **clay**
aspect: **south facing**
key features: **water feature, cubes of box**

The brief was for an equally contemporary garden but in a formal style that would compliment the regular façade of the building. Low maintenance was a consideration, a water feature of some kind was essential, and the prime function of the space was to be relaxation and entertainment. The garden is surrounded by brick walls, and the access is from the basement level which had been converted into a contemporary dining and living area.

Paved in random rectangular York stone to match the floor in the living area, a terrace of ample size was provided near the house, and from here broad steps, flanked by pyramidal yews, led up to the main garden level. To soften the overall hard landscape framework the flooring changed to buff coloured stone chippings, leading the eye across to the central feature of clipped box cubes surrounding a bed of thyme. Matching seats faced one another across the garden, fitting into the recesses within the raised beds.

The main focus of the garden, at the far end, was the stainless steel "wave wall". This was highly polished, with water welling up through the structure and rippling down the face into the raised pool below, which spilt into the lower pool set just below the main garden level. The whole feature was set against a concrete block wall, rendered and washed in a terracotta colour. Japanese maples were set to either side, planted in blue glazed bowls which stood out in sharp relief, looking as good in winter as they would in summer.

Four birch trees provided vertical emphasis, and also helped to break the views of surrounding properties. Fragrant climbers clothed the walls, while there was a proportional mix of shrubs and hardy perennials that provided colour and interest throughout the year with the emphasis on architectural form and foliage.

right *The key features of this garden, including the stainless steel "wave wall" at the far end, and the clipped box (Buxus) cubes surrounding a bed of thyme.*

Waterfront Garden

Acres Wild

dimensions: **50 x 85m (164 x 279ft)**
soil: **sand and gravel**
aspect: **south facing, exposed**
key features: **meandering hedge, gravel maze**

The design was to create a single, integrated garden from two existing gardens while retaining the possibility of converting it back to two at a later date. The owners wanted it to incorporate proposed building works (boathouse/garage and guesthouse), to remove all car parking to the west side of the site, to direct guests to the front door, and to provide shelter and enclosure for a wide variety of seating and dining areas. Views across the harbour had to be retained, and the garden was to create a foreground to the view. The sea breeze and tidal flow were main considerations.

Inspired by wind and wave patterns, a meandering "S"-shaped evergreen hedge integrated the two garden areas, providing partial enclosure. The hedge was broken in places to frame views of the estuary. A contrasting softer, grassy planting in front created an abstract of distant view in the foreground. Belts of salt and wind-tolerant plants reinforced the design and provide shelter from winds.

Timber revetments and a low earth berm on the waterfront protected the garden from high tides. In front the parking was kept to the west garden with an arrival garden on the east side. A directional gravel path led to the front door via a central gravel maze feature with a compass detail.

Warm orange sandstone paving with soft orange brick trims, walls, and step risers were chosen to match the house, along with sandstone setts and shingle for paths and the drive. Cedar decking was used in the pool garden. A nautical atmosphere was provided by sailcloth parasols and steamer loungers, ornaments, and sculpture, including an armillary sphere, made from stainless steel and polished wood.

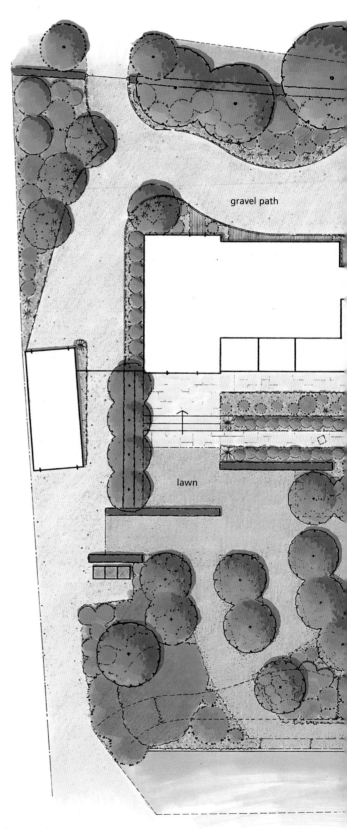

gravel path

lawn

left *A drawing of the view from the house across the lawn to the harbour beyond.*

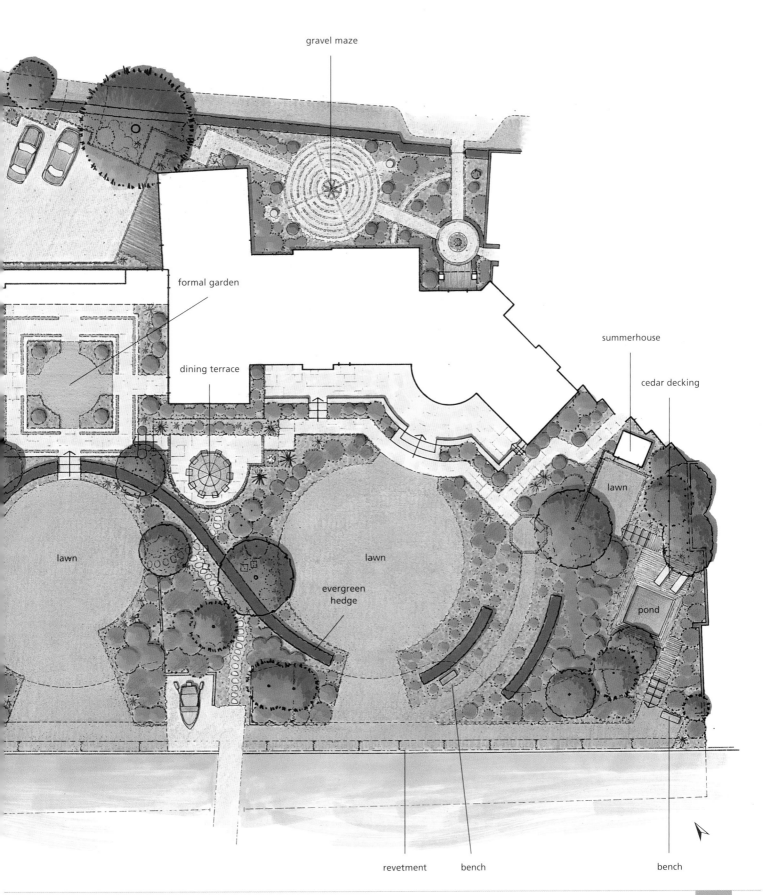

gravel maze

formal garden

summerhouse

cedar decking

dining terrace

lawn

lawn

lawn

evergreen
hedge

pond

revetment

bench

bench

Tree-Lined Garden

del Buono-Gazerwitz Landscape Architecture

dimensions: **23 x 48m (75 x 157ft) approx.**
soil: **clay**
aspect: **sunny and open**
key features: **terrace, lines of pleached lime trees**

The owners wanted to adapt the existing garden, which includes pleached lime trees, large London plane trees, and several flowering trees, so that it matches the new architecture of the house which has been extensively refurbished and expanded. A strong sense of enclosure arises from the large trees and brick walls and buildings. The garden also includes mature yew hedges and many more good specimen plants that the owners wanted to retain in the new garden.

Changing an established mature garden and adapting it to the needs and requirements of its new owners without losing its atmosphere or damaging the existing vegetation will create constraints on any design. The landscaping and choice of materials has to be carefully planned and carried out to avoid damaging the root systems of the established trees.

York stone was used to create the new terrace at the rear of the house, as well as for a second, sunny, new terrace situated at the front of the existing yew hedge at the other side of the main lawn. Hoggin with a York stone trim was used on all the paths, and to form a surface for a new play area for children at the rear of the site.

An additional line of pleached lime trees was added to one side of the garden. Holm oak (*Quercus ilex*), hollies, and the shrub *Pittosporum tenuifolium* were also added at the rear of the garden to enhance the sense of enclosure and privacy.

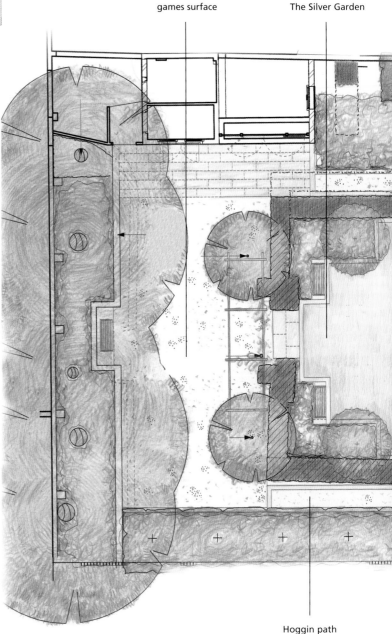

games surface   The Silver Garden

Hoggin path

left *This formal avenue of pleached lime trees complements the modern architecture of the house.*

right *The pleached limes enclose the garden space but also soften the impact of the high boundary walls. In this photo of pleached limes, clipped circles of box (Buxus) mark the transition between trunks and paving.*

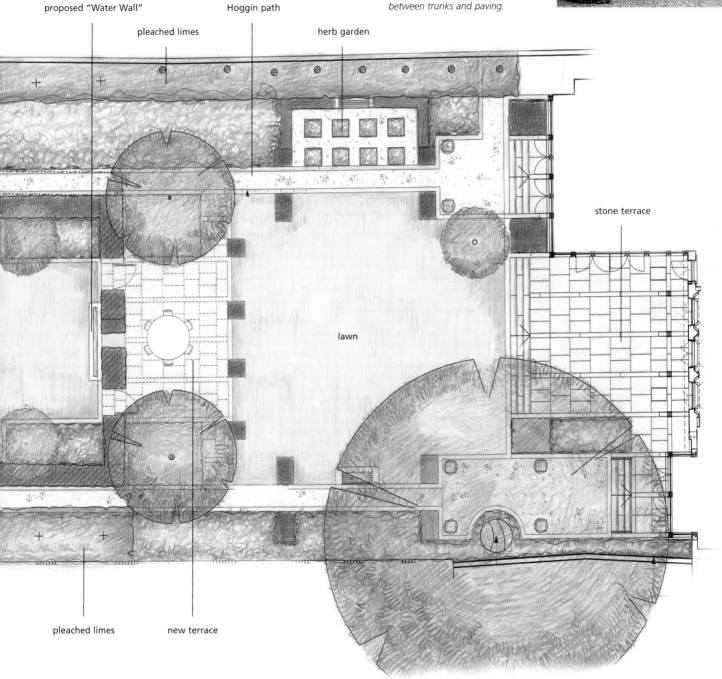

proposed "Water Wall"

pleached limes

Hoggin path

herb garden

stone terrace

lawn

pleached limes

new terrace

Town Garden with Rills

George Carter Garden Design

dimensions: 3.8 x 3.3m and 2.5 x 5.2m (12 x 11ft and 8 x 18ft)
soil: imported
aspect: mostly sheltered, midday summer sun
key features: rills of water

The owner required a light, green space with a colour scheme and style that offered a simple re-interpretation of formal early 18th-century garden design, echoing the classicism of the exteriors and interiors of the house.

The garden was accessible from the first floor reception rooms, and a balcony and staircase in iron had to be incorporated into the design. Any large plants had to be craned in over the mews walls to the rear of the site.

The existing high party walls were painted in an estate cream colour in keeping with the style of the house. Areas of paving were created, using cut Portland stone. Rills of water were used to reflect the sky into the space, helping to bring light into an otherwise dark garden. Seats made of grey-stained oak provided resting areas in the garden. The planting scheme was punctuated by including plants in lead containers. Cast-stone urns and obelisks added a sense of formality.

To add green to the perimeters of the garden, tall stilt hornbeam were used to provide a background to the garden. Below, the planting scheme incorporated shrubs and perennials in grey-green colours.

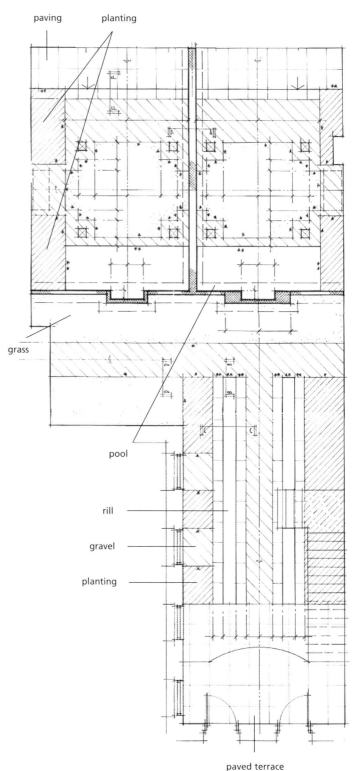

left *This town garden reflects the Palladian architecture of the house. The feaures include canals, an obelisk, pleached hornbeams (Carpinus betulus) and a standard cypress (Cupressus arizonica).*

"The Golden Jubilee Garden"

Barbara Hunt, Hunt Design

dimensions: **60 x 35m (197 x 115ft)**
soil: **sandy**
aspect: **open, sunny**
key features: **water feature, yew hedges**

right *The plants retained from the original garden included a mature tulip tree (Liriodendron tulipera); the flowers – shown here – are borne in midsummer.*

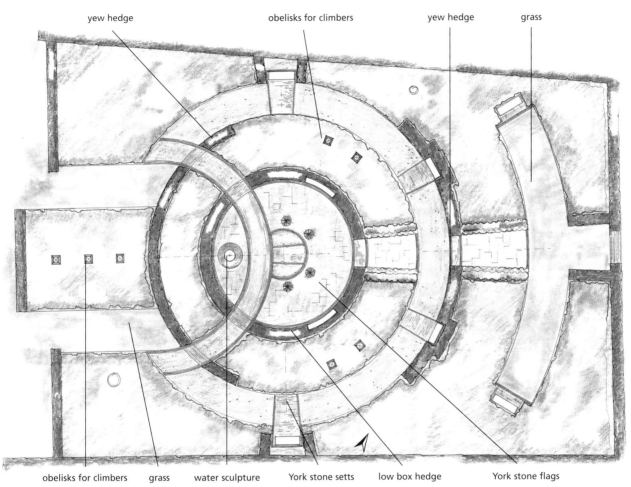

yew hedge obelisks for climbers yew hedge grass

obelisks for climbers grass water sculpture York stone setts low box hedge York stone flags

The development site is part of a larger public garden. The brief was to provide an area for herbaceous planting with high summer interest. The colour scheme for planting was to be in the pastel range – pinks, mauves, whites, silver – and a mature tulip tree was to be retained. The new garden was to include high-quality paved areas, ample seating, and water in some form, but not a pool. The design was to be fairly formal – a cruciform layout was suggested. Access had to be suitable for the disabled.

Buff sandstone flags and setts were used for the main paving, with edge details picked out in grey sandstone setts. The perimeter paths were laid in resin-bound gravel, providing easy access for the disabled. "Thales", a water sculpture by Barry Mason FRBS, was in mirror polished stainless steel.

The garden could be approached in two directions. From the main entrance off the long borders, the visitor was presented with a long vista terminating at the water sculpture. The false perspective of the narrowing path, cutting through a high yew hedge and edged with borders of lavender, added length and drama to the view.

The second approach was from the woodland garden. The views into the garden included green-grass paths and yew hedges. The visitor discovered the flowery, formal central space with its water sculpture by rounding the high yew hedges.

This peaceful central space was encircled by a low box hedge, into which were set simple stainless steel and teak benches. Other seats, sheltered by yew hedging were arranged around the perimeter walk that encircled the central area.

Garden of Ornamental Pears

Andrew Fisher Tomlin

dimensions: **9 x 29m (30 x 95ft)**
soil: **clay, poor loamy soil, improved with manure**
aspect: **east facing**
key features: **paving, avenue of trees**

The owners wanted to create a classic English garden with formal hedging to work with the simplicity and formality of the house and end mews house, which also belongs to the owner. The complexity of the new house design meant that a new paved area was required below ground level, and the design of this had to create light and also bring plants into the space.

New York stone and reclaimed London stock bricks were used to create different areas of paving, which allowed for flexible entertaining. The substantial, below ground-level area had access into the new basement family room and kitchen.

Regular planting of ornamental pear trees created an avenue edging of the garden. Box (*Buxus*) and other plants were planted to screen the rear house and add privacy to the area.

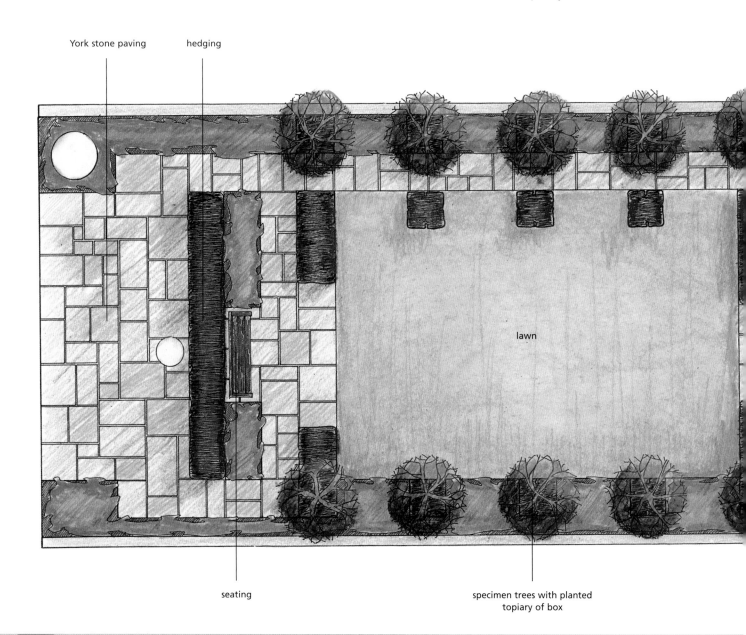

York stone paving   hedging

lawn

seating

specimen trees with planted
topiary of box

right *Along with clematis, hydrangea, and jasmine, climbers in this garden included* Rosa banksiae *var.* banksiae lutea.

far right *A key feature of this garden was the avenue of ornamental pears – the variety shown here is* Pyrus calleryana 'Chanticleer'.

climbers   tumbling plants

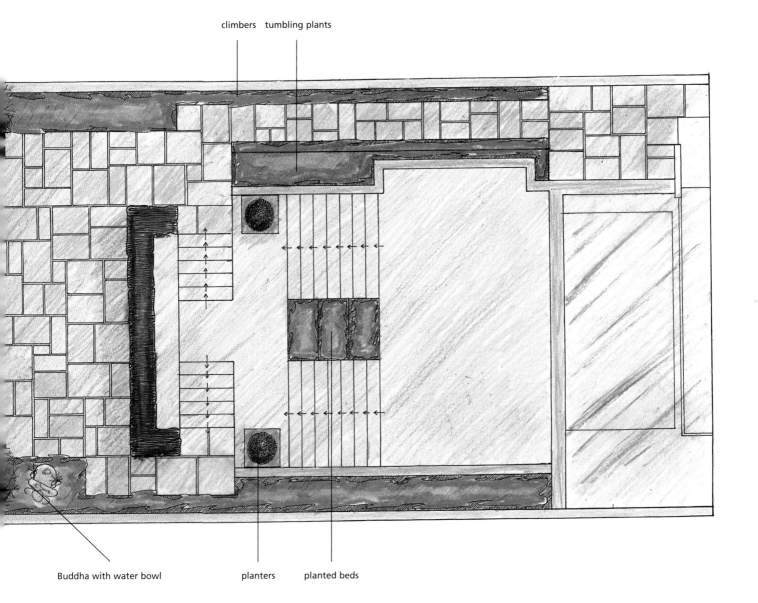

Buddha with water bowl   planters   planted beds

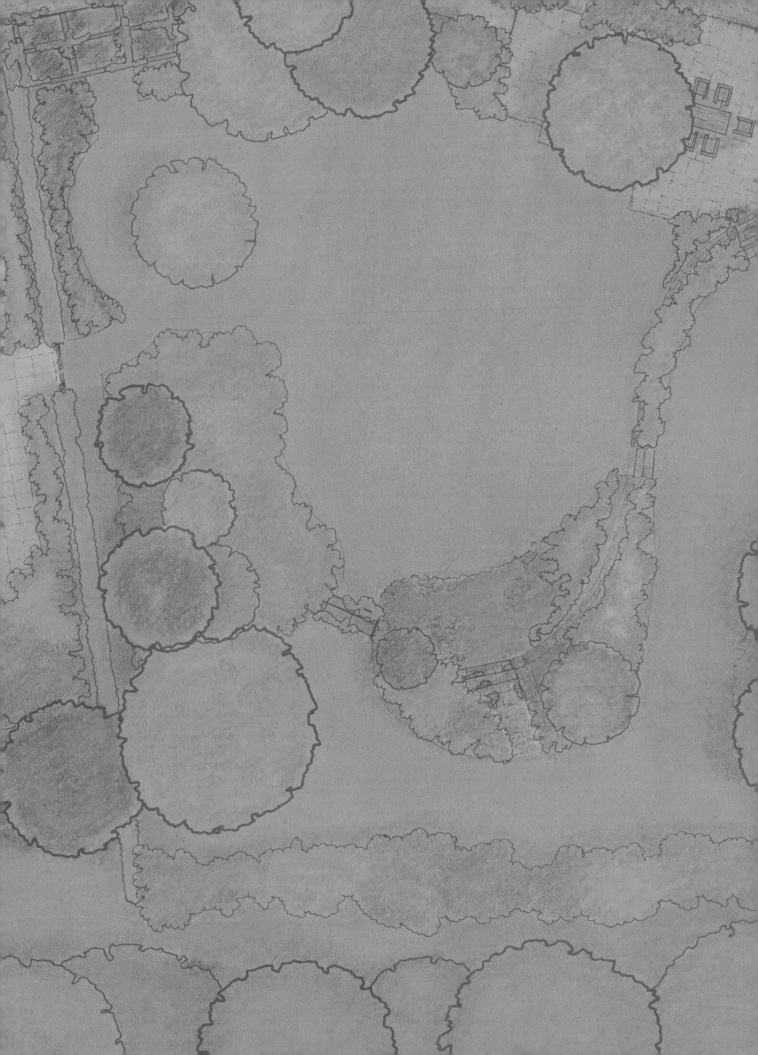

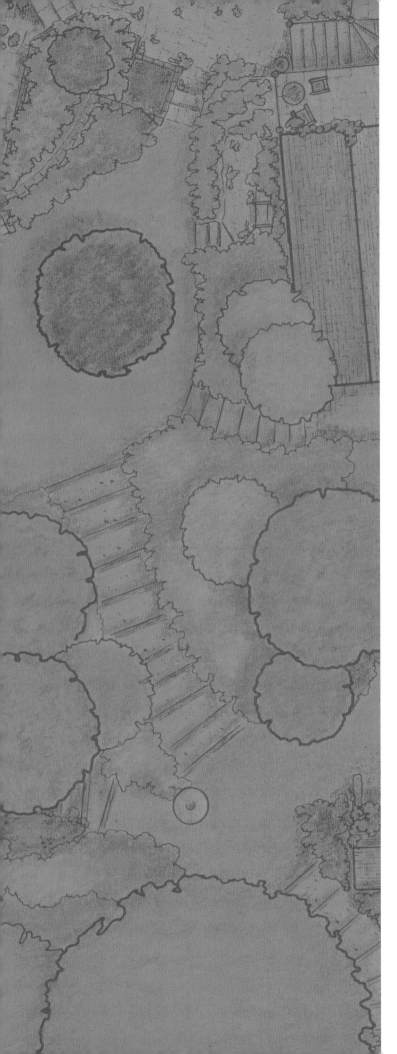

Not all country gardens are large, as many examples in this section will demonstrate. What makes these gardens of particular interest is the way in which they interact with the surrounding landscape. This relationship is a fundamental consideration in developing design solutions without the garden appearing alien and artificial.

It is useful to take the time to explore the surrounding countryside before developing a design, gaining a sense of what plants and materials are appropriate, the pattern of land form, which views are to be exploited, and which hidden or disguised. The orientation of the site and its prevailing winds are also important factors to be considered, as open views can also allow winds to damage the garden and its planting.

The majority of successful country gardens use more formal or controlled designs closer to the house with the garden becoming looser and wilder towards the boundaries. In effect, the garden becomes a transition between the "natural" and the man made.

Arabella Lennox-Boyd deals successfully with many of these issues in the garden that opens this section. Formal elements and spaces relate to the house or to key locations within the garden. Topography has been changed and softened in some areas to make the garden more usable, while areas of meadow and wilder planting relate the design to its wider location.

Country Gardens

Unified Gardens

Arabella Lennox-Boyd

dimensions: **5 hectares (12 acres)**
soil: **well draining**
aspect: **open, sunny**
key features: **terrace, yew hedges, pavilion, orchard**

A series of neighbouring properties near a lake were to be unified and developed into a garden, exploiting the views and creating space. The once separate buildings and parcels of land had been set at different levels to each other, creating a challenge for the design.

A large, imposing bank at the rear of the main house was moved back and sculpted into a series of large grass steps with banks to allow for better views from the house, giving a feeling of space, and improve the light. At the foot of the bank, beyond the lawn, a south-facing paved terrace was created, with pebble trims and details, to relate to the main house. Large planting beds around this terrace turned this space into the main garden area, used on a regular basis throughout the year. A small pavilion south of the terrace provided a covered place to sit near the house.

Large herbaceous borders surrounding a lawn led to a hedged vegetable garden beside an orchard. Retaining walls were needed to retain the soil where the old bank had been. Yew hedges were planted against the walls to soften the appearance of this area. In front of these hedges were large planting beds. Another south-facing garden, with an octagonal lawn, pleached trees, and deep planting bed, linked the other guest houses. Yew hedges screened the garages and retaining walls, and gave this space an intimate feel.

The circulation around the site was improved by extending the drive and removing various access points to the once separated properties. A parking and arrival courtyard was created, and the addition of the parkland trees and improved perimeter planting afforded the property more privacy and framed views of the lake.

right *Clipped evergreen yew (Taxus) hedges, similar to that shown here, were planted against rubble-filled walls to soften the appearance of this area.*

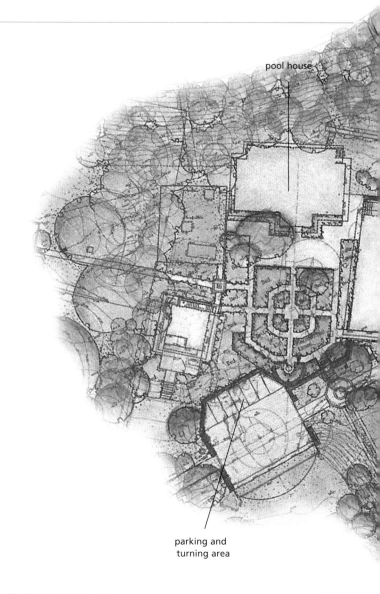

pool house

parking and
turning area

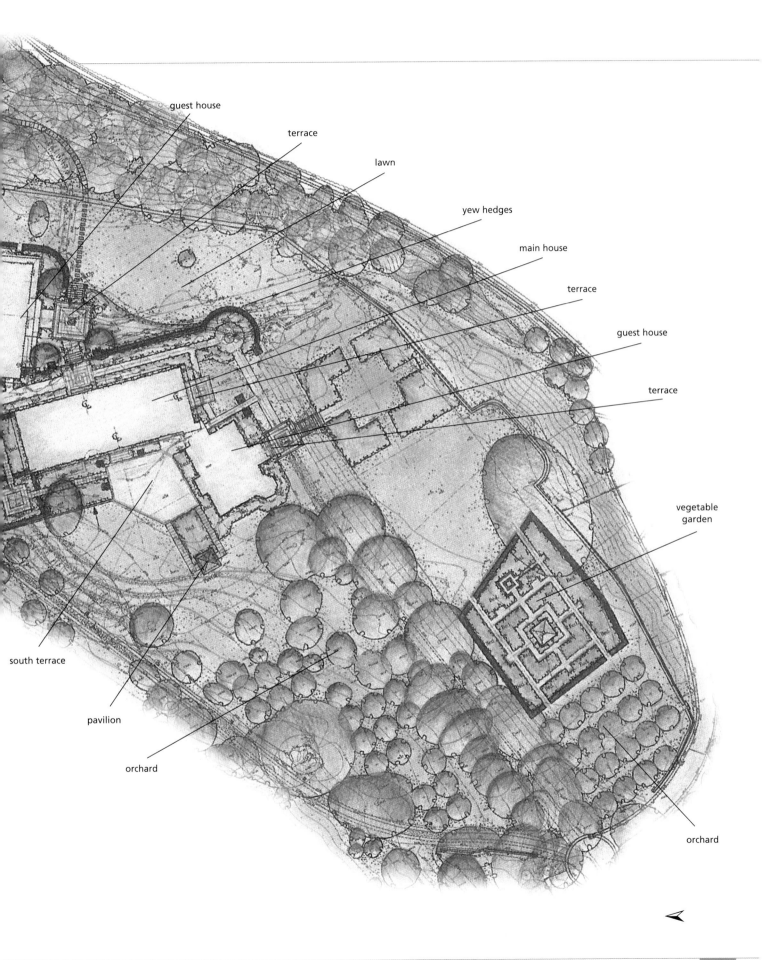

guest house

terrace

lawn

yew hedges

main house

terrace

guest house

terrace

vegetable
garden

south terrace

pavilion

orchard

orchard

"The Cresent"

James Aldridge

dimensions: **121sq m (30 acres)**
soil: **sandy to clay loam**
aspect: **southeast facing**
key features: **meadow, swimming pool, terrace**

The house has dramatic views of the South Downs and the Sussex Weald, and the garden includes several changes of levels, with the highest part of the site having 360-degree views. The owners wanted a garden that would make the most of these views.

A circular lawn with crescent-shaped steps leading to it was planned at a lower level of the plot. To one side of this lawn was a circular side terrace incorporating a William Pye water feature as a focus point. Spiralling sculpture walls led through woodland.

A semi-circular swimming pool and crescent pool house could be found beyond the woodland. From here extended a huge prairie planted with meadow flowers. The upper meadow was given further interest with mounds shaped like whale backs shoaling through the upper wild flowers like the backs of whales at sea. A spiral sculpture of stainless steel poles led to the high point with the 360-degree views.

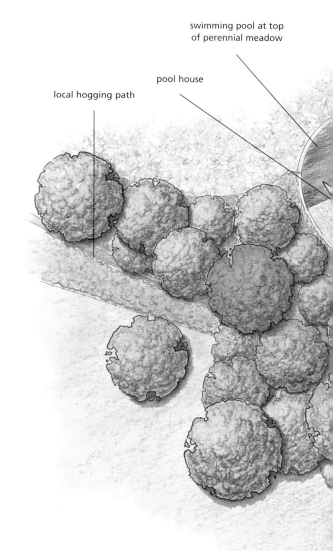

swimming pool at top of perennial meadow

pool house

local hogging path

left *Besides the meadow flowers in the prairie, it was envisaged that the planting would include a number of trees, includer alders (Alnus), beech (Fagus), and, shown here, common oak (Quercus robur).*

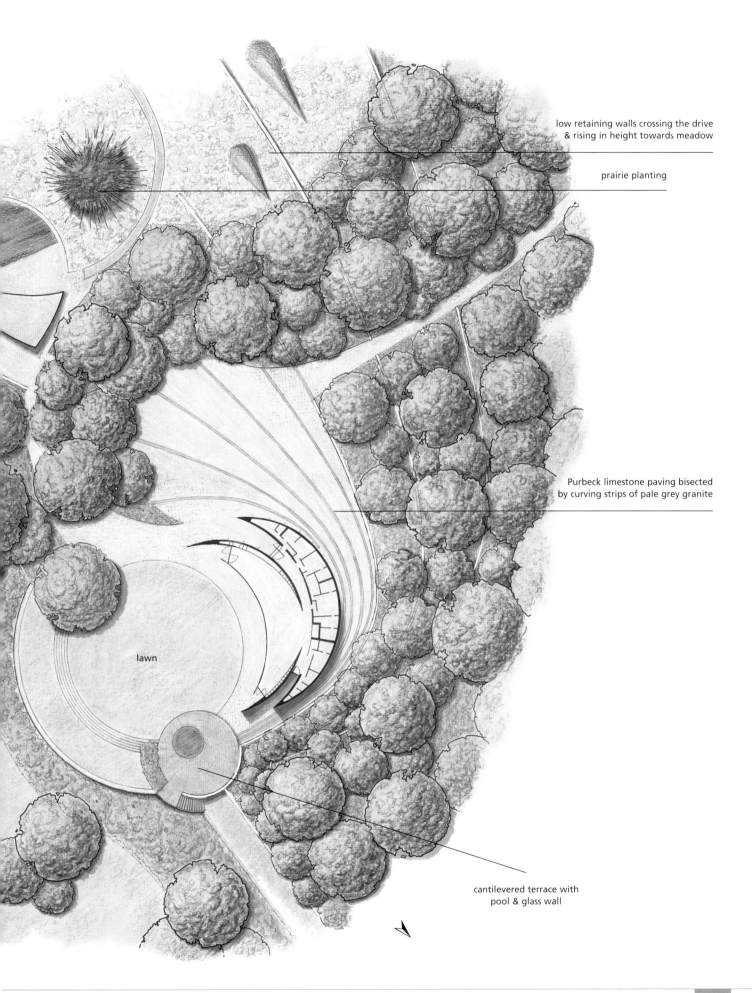

low retaining walls crossing the drive
& rising in height towards meadow

prairie planting

Purbeck limestone paving bisected
by curving strips of pale grey granite

lawn

cantilevered terrace with
pool & glass wall

"Wild Garden"

Acres Wild

dimensions: **60 x 40m (197 x 131ft)**
soil: **topsoil over solid chalk**
aspect: **east facing, open**
key features: **gazebo, deck**

above *The gravel path winds up to "the lookout" through expansive drifts of perennial planting, backed by a taller more permanent shrub structure.*

The brief was to create a "wild" garden of informal walks, focal points, and sheltered places to sit that would be easy to care for. The owners also wanted an exciting destination at the end of the garden to entice the clients up onto a windy hillside throughout the year. A steep slope, solid chalk, exposure to salt winds, and being in a very commanding position – where all can be seen but also all can see – had to be considered in the design.

The design created places of refuge to enjoy various views of the garden and surrounding landscape. The soft, flowing design was inspired by the rolling downland and coastal landscape context, with meandering paths and belts of shimmering grasses, and wind- and chalk-tolerant plantings enclosing a variety of seating areas as destinations and viewpoints. Movement throughout was characterized by a sense of closing in and then opening out. An oak-framed gazebo ("the lookout") provided the focal point of the design. Its clay-tiled pyramid-shaped roof reflected those of the house and Norman church in the village below.

Hard landscape was kept to a minimum and was primarily used for paths and seating areas to enhance the elemental character of site. Planed oak was designated for "the lookout", a deck, sturdy benches, retaining elements, and posts bound with hemp rope. Sleepers and Cotswold chippings were reserved for paths and steps, and Sussex brick pavers and random Purbeck paving were used for level surfaces.

The planting theme included plants that were shimmering, sheltering, sea-washed, and windswept in sea greens, bright greens and blues, whites, silvers, purples, yellows, and buff colours.

right *Timber and rope were used to link to the location. Here, planting encroaches on these features, and softens the geometric forms and lines.*

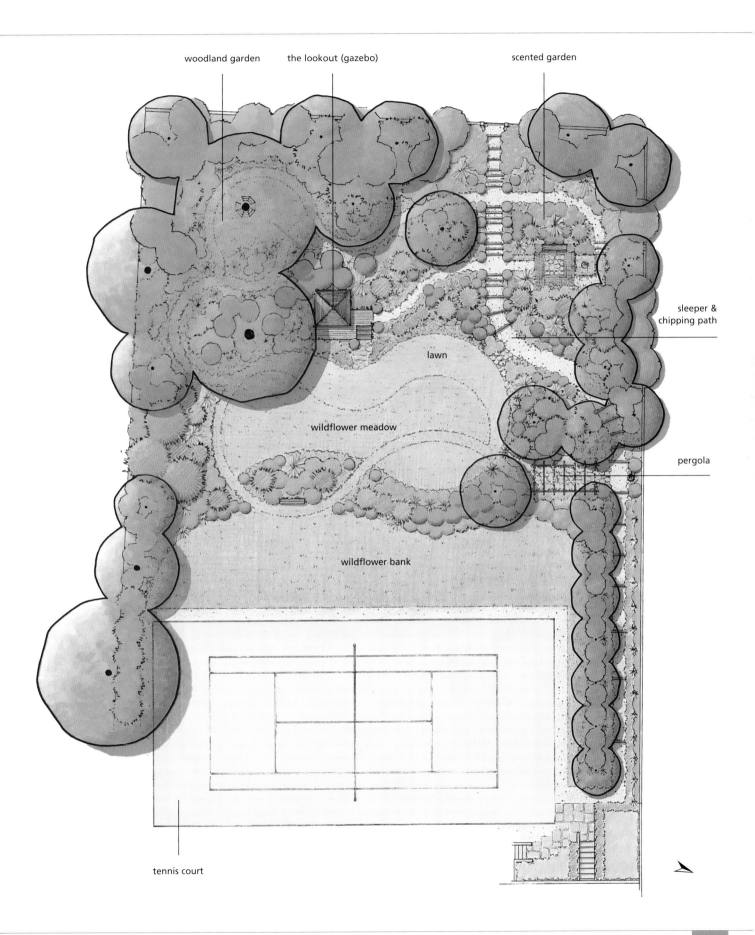

woodland garden   the lookout (gazebo)   scented garden

sleeper &
chipping path

lawn

wildflower meadow

pergola

wildflower bank

tennis court

A New Zealand Garden

Anthony Paul

dimensions: **80 x 70m (262 x 230ft)**
soil: **clay**
aspect: **north facing (south facing in Northern hemisphere)**
key features: **natural swimming pool, deck**

above *This terrace is a combination of tufted groundcover and sharply defined pathways, creating an architectural effect that also links with the grasslands beyond the boundaries.*

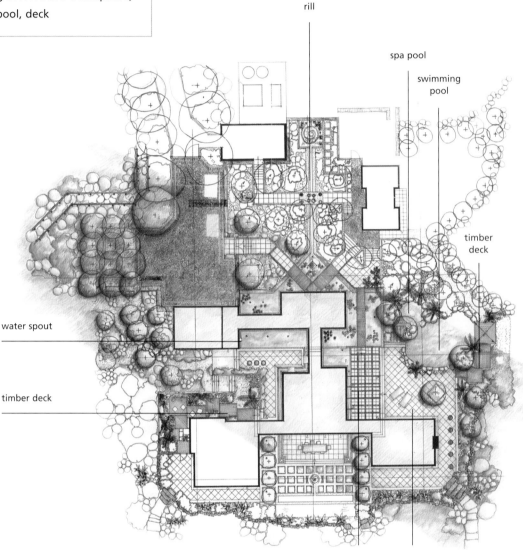

rill

spa pool

swimming pool

timber deck

water spout

timber deck

pergola   paved terrace

The brief was to create a contemporary garden with an emphasis on water, including a natural swimming pool, for a house on the North Island of New Zealand. The owners wanted a large number of trees planted on the the site, and they requested that the garden should be planted with native plants as much as possible. The design should link the newly built house with the garden, and it should also capitalize on the view over a bay, which was spectacular.

The garden formed a small area of a much larger plot of land. It had a slope towards the sea but no existing trees or plants because it was a new garden on what was originally a green field site. A strong sea wind presented constraints, and the very heavy clay soil also had to be considered in the design. A paved terrace was laid near the natural-style pool and spa pool, which was positioned to provide views from the house. Paving was also used to link to other areas of the garden. A timber decking for relaxing and entertaining was situated where the owners could also enjoy views of the bay. Other features included a water spout, rill, and spiral, a pergola, and plants in containers on the terrace.

A grouping of trees were planted to create a wind barrier, and the general planting scheme of shrubs and other planting materials conformed with the owners' request to use as many native New Zealand plants as possible.

"Fiveways"

John Moreland

dimensions: **43 x 40m (141 x 131ft)**
soil: **acid**
aspect: **sunny, sheltered from prevailing winds**
key features: **pergola, *Escallonia* hedging**

The owner of this garden required an area for outdoor eating and entertaining friends. She also required a play area and small "paddock" areas for the children's Shetland ponies and a rescued donkey. A single-storey office block and storage area adjoining the property needed screening.

The garden lies alongside a fairly busy country road and runs into a small field; it is surrounded on three sides by semi-mature woodland which provides it with good protection from the prevailing winds.

A mixture of Marshalls "Brindlebrown" Tegula pavers and Atlas Buff pre-cast slabs were laid in banded patterns to form a level area, and the pathways consisted of pea gravel. Granite retaining walls around the "moulded" area had raked-out joints to create a dry-stone effect. Simple overhead beams and a pergola were stained to match the door and window finishes of the house. To screen the office block and storage areas, earth was mounded

up and planted with a mixture of dogwood, willow, and butterfly bush, with alders (*Alnus*) and willows (*Salix*) as screen planting.

Low clipped box formed a boundary around the vegetable garden, and flowing lines of evergreen *Escallonia* hedging were used to enclose and define different areas of the garden. The client particularly wanted to create an orchard with a variety of local West Country apple varieties, and this was incorporated in the planting scheme. Generally, the planting was to be a mixture of flowering shrubs and perennials which the owner wished to plant herself.

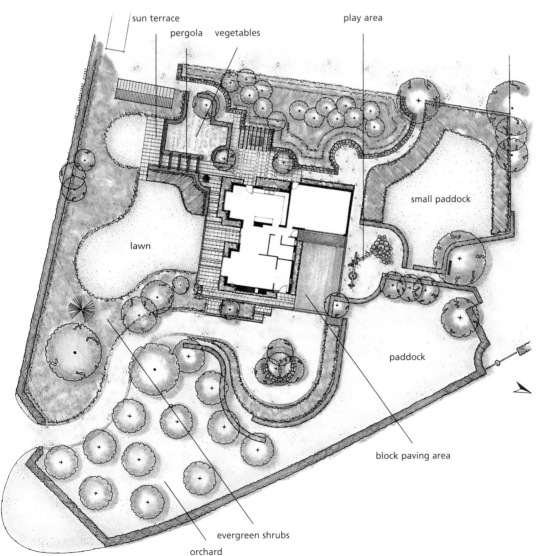

sun terrace
pergola   vegetables   play area

small paddock

lawn

paddock

block paving area

evergreen shrubs
orchard

above *Among the trees and shrubs suggested in the scheme for this garden was the sumach tree, Rhus typhina – here showing in its striking autumn colouring.*

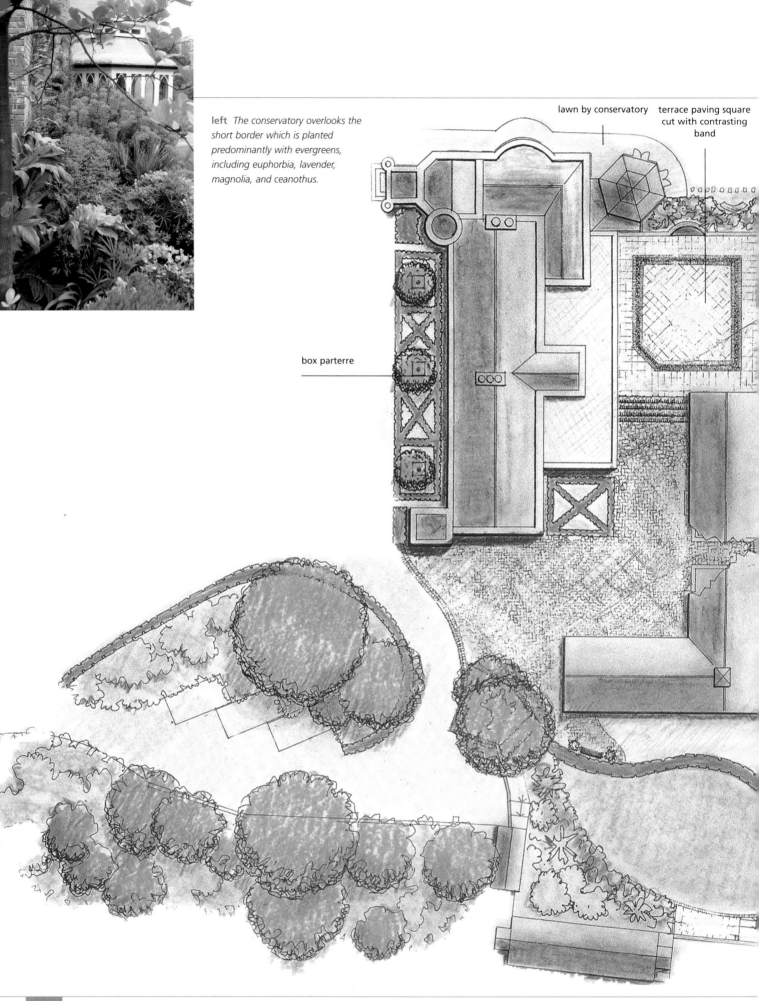

left *The conservatory overlooks the short border which is planted predominantly with evergreens, including euphorbia, lavender, magnolia, and ceanothus.*

lawn by conservatory

terrace paving square cut with contrasting band

box parterre

Walled Country Garden

Clarke Associates

dimensions: **7 hectares (17.5 acres)**
soil: **loam and silty clay on chalk**
aspect: **sheltered**
key features: **listed wall, pool garden, kitchen garden**

The formal gardens were inspired and shaped around one of the key historic elements – a weathered brick wall which extended from the house into the woodland which wraps itself around the whole site. With the addition of a new yew hedge, the Grade II listed wall encloses the splendid double border of the "Vista Garden" which gives access to the pool garden, the east lawn, the children's garden, and the kitchen garden beyond, thereby being the primary link between the house and the walled gardens.

The short border on the east side of the wall is overlooked by the conservatory and was planted with evergreens such as lavender, magnolia, and ceanothus, as well as *Acanthus spinosus* and *Cynara cardunculus* for added drama. The pool garden was planted with prolific vines on the sunny side and fragrant honeysuckle, *Elaeagnus* x *ebbingei*, and late-flowering clematis on the shady wall.

The double border was packed with a mixture of herbaceous perennials, ornamental grasses, shrubs, and trees. Structure was provided by *Amelanchier lamarckii*, several varieties of *Viburnum plicatum*, and *Cotinus*, and *Hydrangea quercifolia* and *Corylus* at the shadier end. Large flowered *Clematis*, Virginia creeper, and dinner plate vine colonized the long wall.

The kitchen garden was built in raised beds wrapped in hurdles. The rabbit-proof enclosure was warm and sheltered, and an ideal environment for growing vegetables. Box and yew were used effectively on the approach to the main entrance.

short border

double border with 12 ornamental trees, shrubs & perennials

swimming pool

vegetable garden with 20 raised planters

right *The historic weathered brick wall protects the kitchen garden's raised beds from the woodland area behind.*

A Variety of Gardens

Balston & Co

dimensions: **5,679sq m (1½ acres)**
soil: **free draining, sandy soil**
aspect: **gardens facing south, west, north, and east**
key features: **rose garden, ha-ha, kitchen garden**

right *The framing of views in country gardens is particularly important. Here, the cropped box (Buxus) spheres and hedges beyond emphasize the distance.*

At first the owners wanted a decision on where to plant the hedging that was already on order. They were keen to create a comprehensible structure which could contain a number of different types of plantings such as mixed borders and a rose garden.

The gardens were all round the house with the kitchen garden facing south and west. Extended western gardens also faced west, with borders to the north, and a swimming pool and herb gardens to the east. The principal views were to the north and west, although there was an important view from the kitchen garden to the south.

A start had already been made with a kitchen garden and a rose garden, but later a green garden, a garden of paving plants, and a gravel garden were developed. The designer also created a converted a stone barn into a banqueting hall, as well as a barbecue area with a pizza oven. Careful manipulation of space using structure provided views, filters, and barriers. Ha-has to the north and west gave a clear view over fields to a lake and the distant horizon. A fruit garden with a strong timber framework made good use of the unusual elliptical space next to the kitchen garden.

Within a large enclosure of walls and yew hedges, mixed borders have a strong framework of juniper, amelanchier, and *Pyrus* 'Chanticleer' (an upright form of pear). The shrub and hebaceous plantings had a strong emphasis on texture – *Cortaderia*, *Daphniphyllum*, and *Acanthus*, There was also a strong emphasis on late flowering, including such plants as *Caryopteris*, *Penstemon*, *Sedum*, *Gaura*, and *Lavatera*.

left *Clipped box (Buxus sempervirens) provides a unifying feature plant in this expansive garden. The architectural forms frame views or soften the raised pool to create a fine green tapestry.*

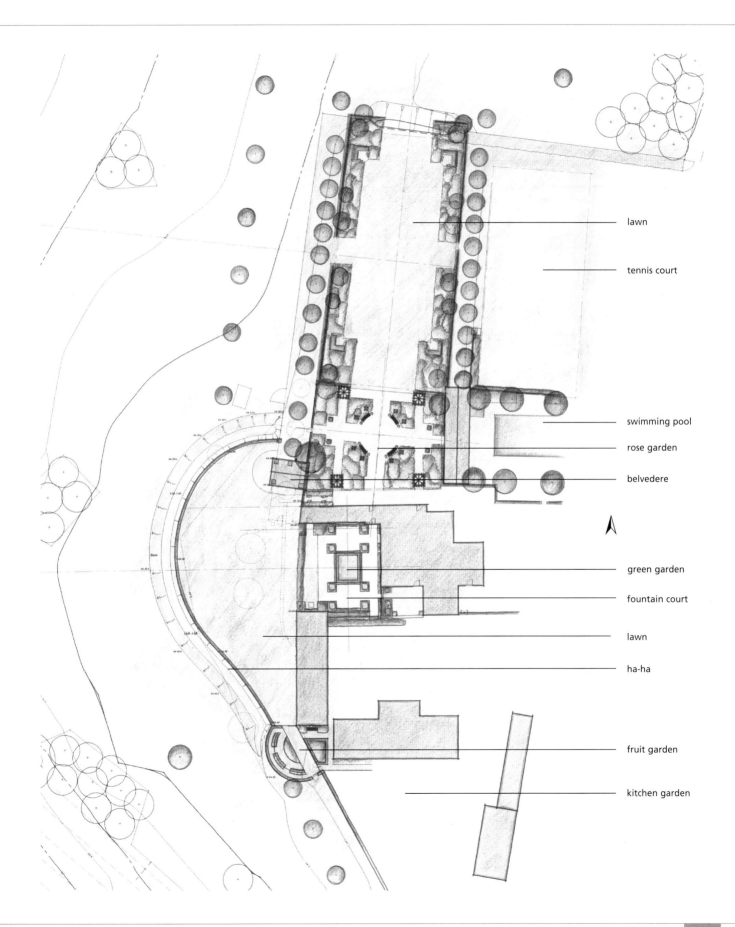

lawn

tennis court

swimming pool

rose garden

belvedere

green garden

fountain court

lawn

ha-ha

fruit garden

kitchen garden

Cliff-Top Garden

Naila Green

dimensions: **25 x 12m (82 x 39ft)**
soil: **sandy**
aspect: **southeast facing**
key features: **decks, gravel gardens**

Situated on a cliff, this low-maintenance garden had to look good all year round, have an informal feel with lots of plants, discreet hard landscaping, and retain its spectacular sea views. Various sitting areas were required but, expressly, no lawn.

A simple structure of straight gravel paths cut through the garden. Apart from leading users to and from the garden, the paths were also to lead the eye to the garden's ultimate focal point – the sea. An area of decking under the verandah was used as a sheltered sitting/dining area. Another, sited almost on the edge of the cliff, had two timber loungers, and was devoted solely to sunbathing. Other seating was strategically placed around the garden. A circle of gravel with edging bricks created another focus point. A second gravel garden in a semi-circular shape was decorated with a nautical theme, and it included original lobster buoys and shells.

With regard to planting, consideration was given both to the garden's views and its exposure to full sun and salt-laden winds, and its poor, free-draining chalky soil. Consequently only plants which did not obscure the view and were suited to the conditions were used. Order was created by the use of a strong evergreen structure of flowering shrubs. This was softened and made more interesting by adding a variety of perennials, self-seeding biennials, and bulbs. Large mature specimen shrubs were planted singly, but also as repeat incidents. Perennials were planted in groups or drifts and allowed to self-seed.

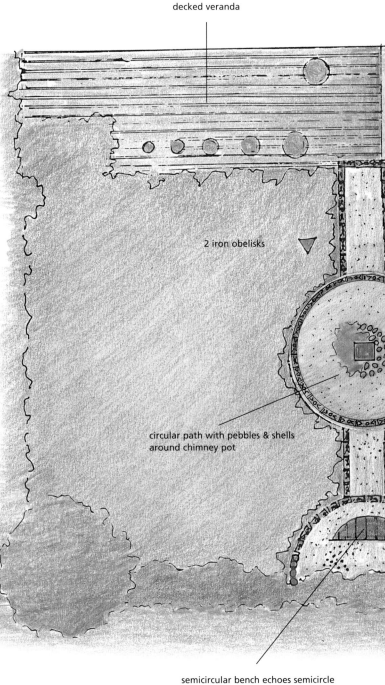

decked veranda

2 iron obelisks

circular path with pebbles & shells
around chimney pot

semicircular bench echoes semicircle
of gravel

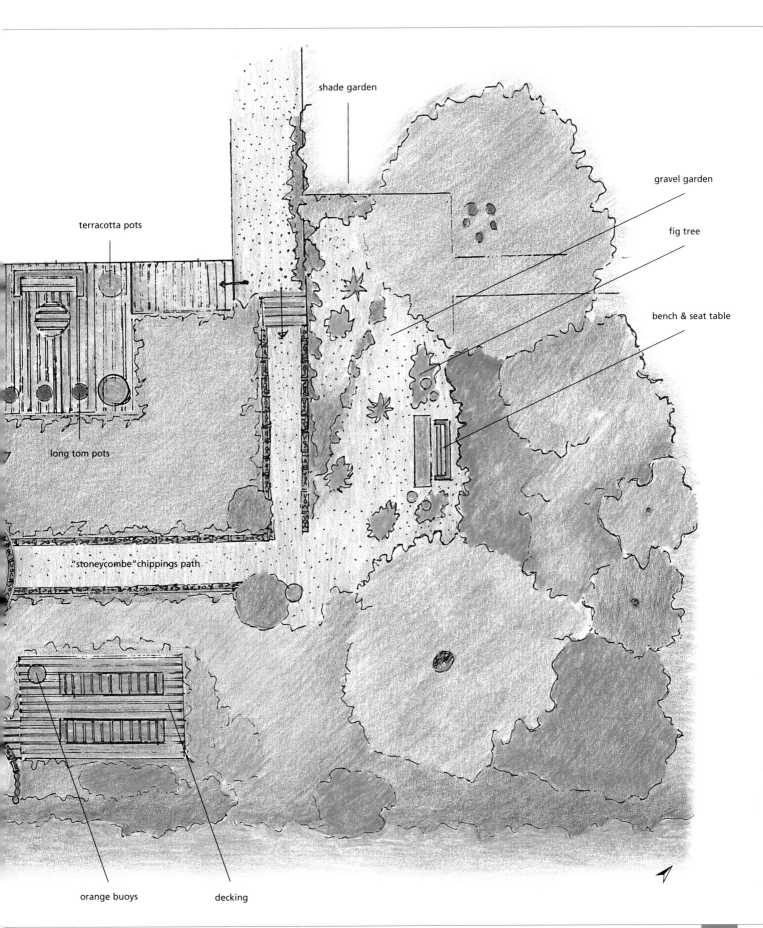

shade garden

gravel garden

fig tree

terracotta pots

bench & seat table

long tom pots

."stoneycombe"chippings path

orange buoys

decking

Rural Cottage Garden

Rachel Myers Garden Design

dimensions: **2000sq m (½ acre) approx**
soil: **sandy, neutral, improved with well-rotted manure**
aspect: **north facing**
key features: **willow footbridge, terrace, pergola**

above *The deciduous shrub* Sorbus cashmiriana *not only has attractive flowers in late spring but interesting white berries.*

right Rosa *'Fru Dagmar Hastrup' is a strong-growing rugosa rose whose pink summer flowers are followed by red hips in the autumn.*

The owners wanted a garden to complement their 16th-century Grade II listed cottage. An area for entertaining was requested, together with a pond and pergola. Numbered among their favourite plants to be included were roses, geraniums, flowering cherry trees, philadelphus, and jasmine. A cutting garden was also desired. The car park should be concealed from the house.

They owners indicated a preference for gravel and brick for the hard landscaping, and these were used as paving materials to form a terrace. In keeping with the cottage setting, a footbridge structure was created that has willow woven into it. It will need regular attention by pruning back and weaving new growth into place among the handrails and balusters to provide a healthy and rigid framework.

The planting, particularly the trees, needed to fit gently into the landscape to harmonize the scale of the cottage with a dominant surrounding woodland. On approaching the garden through the quiet planting of the west garden, the planting in the north garden by comparison was luxurious, with grasses mixed among flowering perennials, creating movement and softness. The east garden comprised principally roses and geraniums, with moss roses being used in abundance. The colour scheme moved from electric pinks, bright blues, plums, and deep purples, to creamy whites and pale blues in the south garden. The terrace garden found space for culinary herbs and salad crops, while on the slope facing the kitchen window, annual and biennial cutting flowers mingled with winter-flowering shrubs.

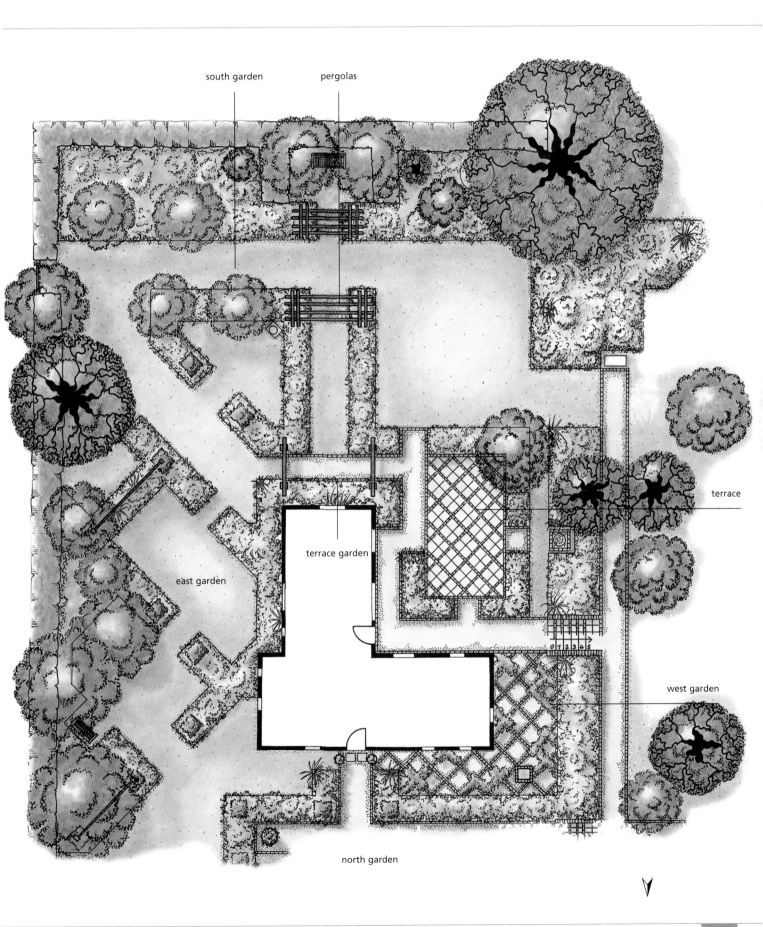

south garden

pergolas

terrace

terrace garden

east garden

west garden

north garden

0 1 2 3 4 5

"The Pottery"

Simon Dorrell

dimensions: **70 x 50m (230 x 164ft)**
soil: **clay**
aspect: **southeast and southwest facing**
key features: **canal, topiary, orchard, nuttery**

The owners of a pottery wanted a garden designed for dual purposes. The garden had to have an area for the private enjoyment of the family; however, it was also to serve as an area open to the general public to display the many and varied uses of terracotta in a garden setting. They also requested fruit and vegetable gardens, as well as an orchard and a nuttery, and they requested an area for communal bonfires. They wanted a garden with minimal maintenance, and an existing hedgerow was to be retained.

The garden is bordered by a stream on it's western boundary. A broad hedgerow dissects the plot, roughly south west to northeast. The design further compartmentalized the garden by creating a water canal and extensive use of hedging, topiary, and terracotta pots. The style of the fruit and vegetable gardens, orchard, and nuttery was formal, with plantings set in angular geometric plantings. Yew, beech, and box were used as hedging to create boundaries. A bonfire site was also established in a formal style, set off with topiary satellites. In contrast a stream garden was designed in a more relaxed informal style.

Pleached limes, apple trees for the orchard, hazels for the nuttery, and Irish yews were among the trees planted. Yew, box, and Portugal laurel were chosen to form topiary. A mixed planting of deciduous and evergreen shrubs – predominantly viburnums, hydrangeas, philadelphus, and magnolias – as well as hardy perennials and tender annuals – formed the planting scheme.

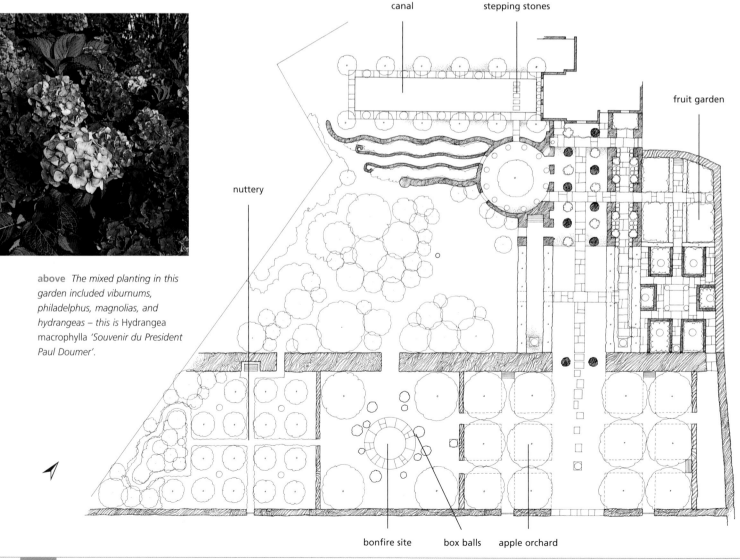

above *The mixed planting in this garden included viburnums, philadelphus, magnolias, and hydrangeas – this is* Hydrangea macrophylla *'Souvenir du President Paul Doumer'.*

canal   stepping stones

fruit garden

nuttery

bonfire site   box balls   apple orchard

Expanding Garden

Barbara Lumsden Landscape & Garden Design

dimensions: **60 x 30m (197 x 98ft)**
soil: **chalky clay**
aspect: **north facing slope**
key features: **kitchen garden, terrace**

right *A wild cherry – here* Prunus avium *'Plena' – was among the ornamental trees incorporated into this garden.*

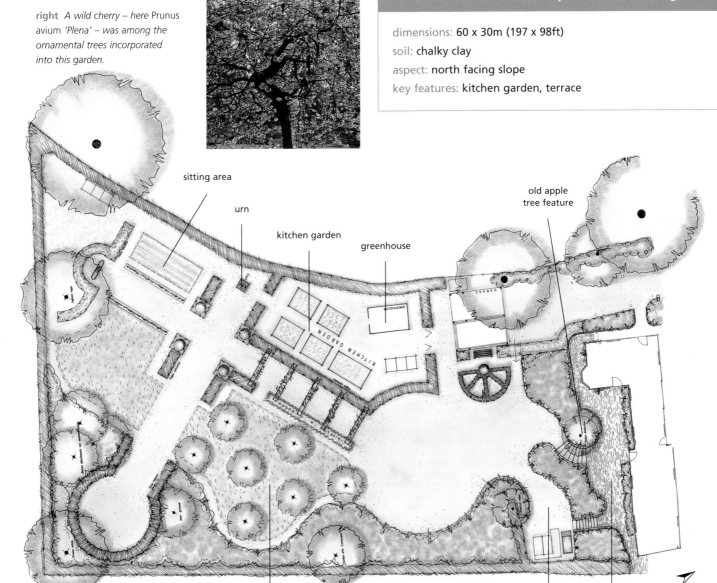

sitting area

urn

kitchen garden

greenhouse

old apple tree feature

orchard

play area   terrace

The owners wanted to integrate the existing garden with newly acquired land which slopes up away from the house to open farmland. They requested a country garden with as little hard landscaping as possible, but allowing for paths in the kitchen garden. Good overall structure so that it looks good in winter was important, and there should be areas that conceal and reveal so that all the garden is not seen at once. An existing oak and apple tree were to remain. It was important to take into consideration the view from the neighbouring house across the garden.

The existing terrace was resurfaced with brick pavers and the brick retaining wall reshaped to make a feature of the existing old apple tree. New brick steps were built to curve round the tree.

Flower borders located along the top of the retaining walls by the terrace received the most sun. Existing steps to the children's play area and playhouse were also rebuilt, and a sand pit was added to the play area.

An area was levelled to form a kitchen garden with cold frames and a greenhouse. A fruit cage was supplied for soft fruit, and apple and pear trees were espaliered. An orchard was planted with medlar, mulberry, quince, and plum trees. Ornamental trees, a herb garden, flower borders, arches for roses, and an area with long grass and wild flowers and bulbs were also incorporated into the garden. A sitting area was created at the top of the garden to catch the evening sun, and afford views over the village to the church.

An Executive Garden

Christopher Maguire

dimensions: **373sq m (1223sq ft)**

soil: **alkaline**

aspect: **northeast facing**

key features: **ponds divided by deck**

right *The simple geometric lines of the deck open the garden to the expansive meadow views beyond the boundary.*

Apart from providing somewhere to sit, somewhere for washing, and a small greenhouse, the owners were completely open to suggestions. This was the garden of a newly completed "executive" house so there was no existing planting except for the remains of a natural hedge along the boundary with the adjoining property. The principal feature of the garden is the view. The plot is on the edge of the development overlooking arable land and a small hill in the distance.

The orientation of the garden meant that any sitting area close to the house would soon be in shade. This, along with the view, suggested a principal sitting area further away from the house towards the boundary. This sitting area forms the dominant features of the garden. It consists of two large ponds divided by a deck

sitting area and a deck walkway axis which directs the eye to the fields and hill outside the site. The boundary wall was kept low to emphasize the view. Dense massing of grasses of miscanthus and pheasant's tail grass (*Stipa arundinacea*) along the boundary and round the deck and pond further reinforce the link between the garden and the wider landscape beyond. Water plants, such as irises and water lilies, were planted around the ponds.

The gardens on either side of the walkway were quite different. On the southeast side there was a lush lawn that has been laid to the edge of the pond. On the opposite side there were gravel walks bordered by a planting of a variety of shrubs, perennials, and climbers. Both of these areas were planted with specimens of mountain ash to provide vertical focus points.

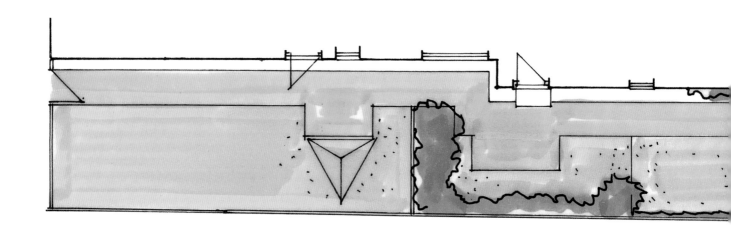

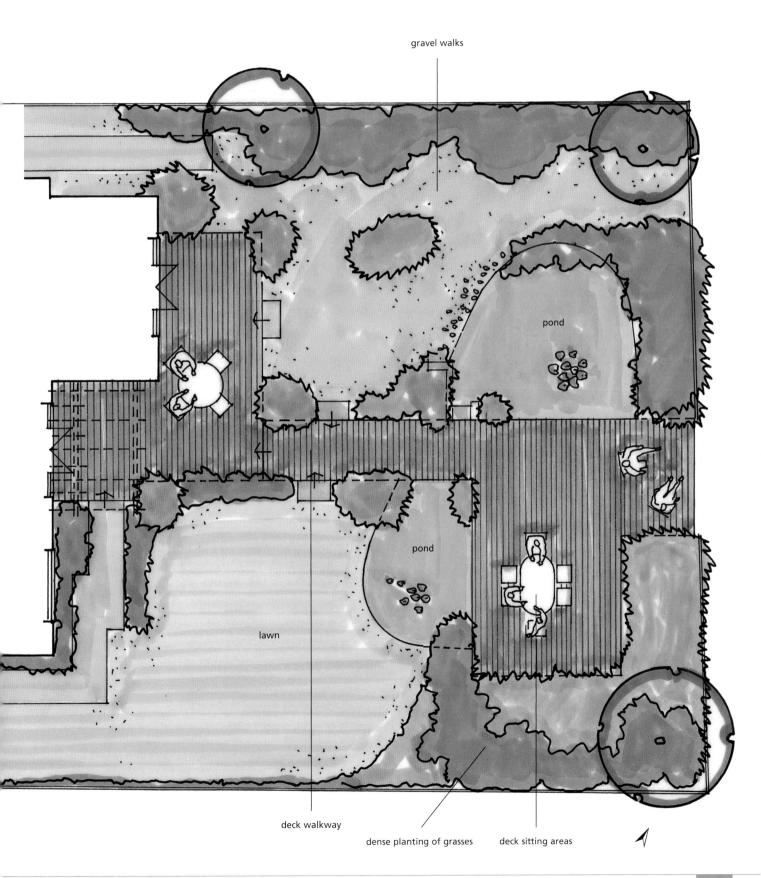

gravel walks

pond

pond

lawn

deck walkway

dense planting of grasses

deck sitting areas

Two Gardens Into One

Jan King

dimensions: **3000sq m (¾ acre) approx.**
soil: **clay subsoil, neutral**
aspect: **southeast facing**
key features: **terrace, pond**

right *The low perennial border planting makes the most of the views from the garden. The arching trees provide dramatic foreground interest.*

The brief for this garden was to draw the front and back garden together. The hard landscaping had already been designed, so the issue was to make sense of these existing features by shaping lawns and flower beds and using plants in keeping with the surrounding fields. There was an existing terrace and various trees, including an apple, a cherry, two mountain ashes, birches, a goat willow, some plums, and other ornamental trees in the front garden. There was also a clay-lined pond lying at a 45-degree angle to the house.

Before the planting could begin, the nutrient-rich clay soil had to be improved to lessen its density by adding sharp sand, horticultural grit, and mushroom compost. This helped the plants to absorb the nutrients. The planting was designed to complement the arable fields around the garden. It was also designed to be interesting year round, but to come to a peak in the late summer and autumn. *Lavandula angustifolia* 'Hidcote' was planted in large drifts, and *Amelanchier lamarckii* as individual specimens. Perennials include plants that keep their form over the winter. *Anaphalis margaritacea*, *Cynara cardunculus*, and *Phormium* 'Sundowner' were planted in large clumps, and *Artemisia pontica*, *Echinacea purpurea*, *Eryngium bourgatii*, and *Macleaya microcarpa* 'Kelway's Coral Plume' in drifts. Grasses, mostly planted in drifts, were chosen for their ability to withstand the winter.

left *Large drifts of perennials provide a structured but relaxed quality to the border planting. The flat plates of Sedum and Achillea provide horizontal emphasis against the taller shrubs to the rear.*

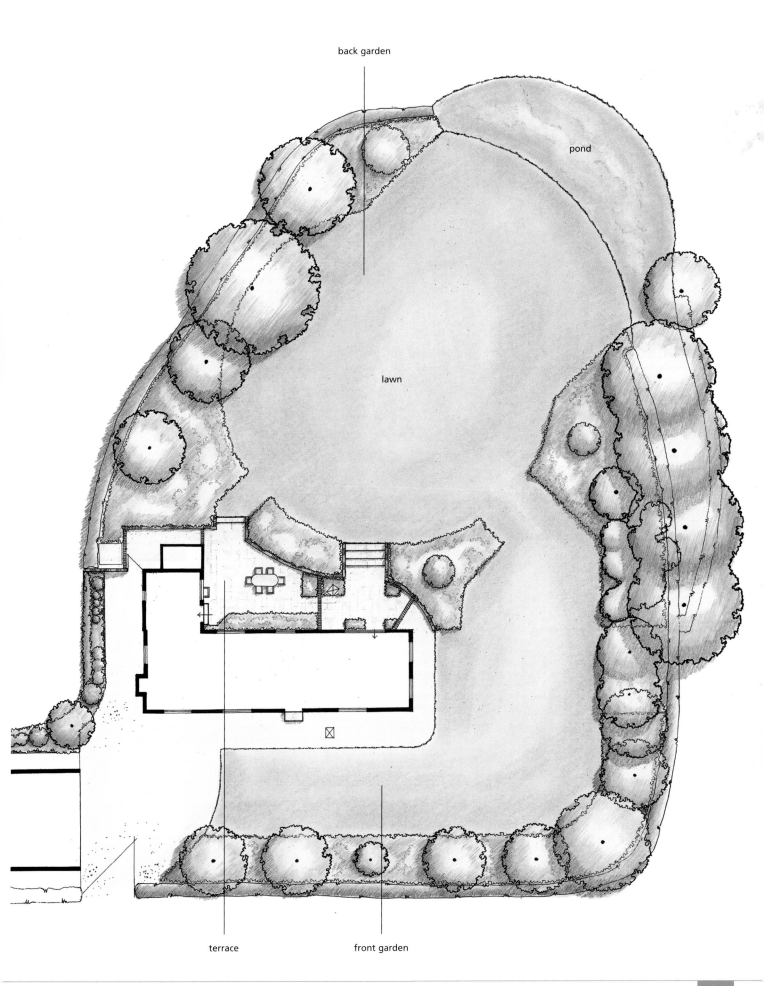

back garden

pond

lawn

terrace

front garden

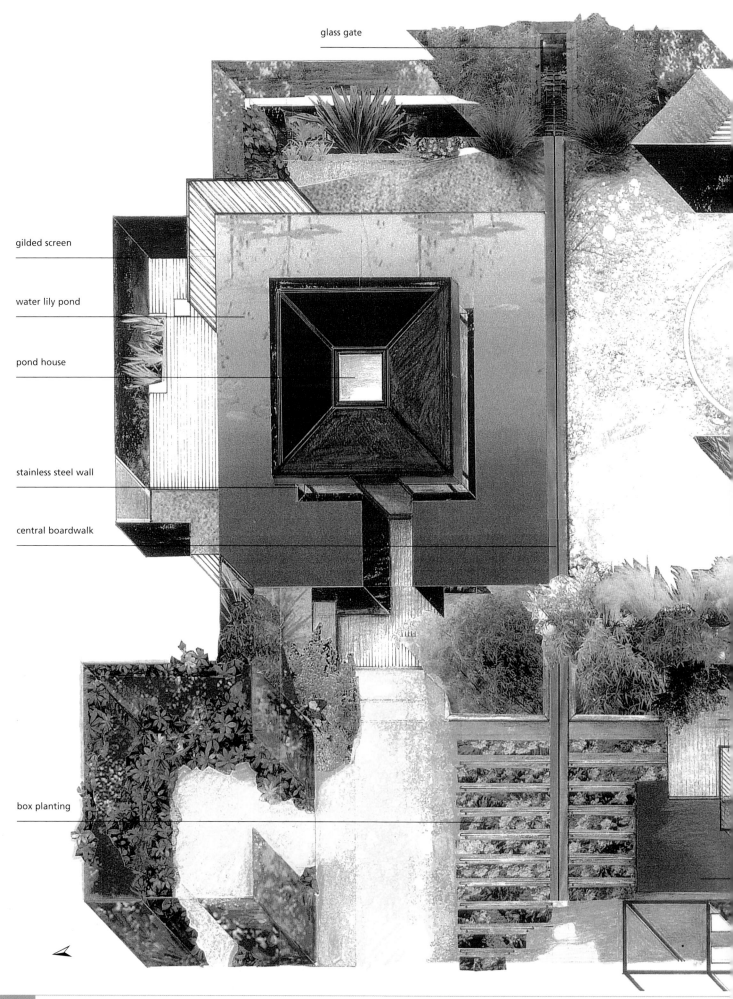

glass gate

gilded screen

water lily pond

pond house

stainless steel wall

central boardwalk

box planting

A Reflective Garden

Jenny Jones, Highwater Jones Limited

dimensions: 800sq m (2600sq ft) approx
soil: various, but predominantly clay on chalk
aspect: open, sunny
key features: water basin, glass pavilion, and screening

The garden is located on two terraces that have been built on a gently sloping site. The owner wanted to create a garden in contrast to the cultivated farmland surrounding it and was willing to allow a degree of experimentation. Strong winds and rural predators necessitated a protective screening around the entire site.

All the garden elements, plants, and structures were designed to integrate – none were regarded as focal points. Built features included a series of glass and metal enclosures and screens. Glass is an ideal reflective material for providing discreet screening, and the reflective opaque, mirrored, and transparent glass screens sheltered the planting.

There was also a water basin surrounding a glass pavilion, with the water in the basin reflecting light into the glass surface of the pavilion. The pavilion acted as a pivotal point from which to view the garden and countryside beyond. A playful "water harp" was suspended over the lower terrace pond, and a central boardwalk with steps served to disect both terraces.

Grasses, including *Stipa* and *Miscanthus*, as well as *Phormium* and bamboo predominate the planting scheme. Static *Buxus sempervirens* was planted to provide a contrast to the fluid grasses on this windy site.

shade house

black glass wall

polished aluminium circle set in gravel

deck

bench

pond

right *In this axonometric photo-montage the different spaces of the garden read well, showing their specific qualities and characteristics.*

An Italian Hillside Garden

Bernard Trainor Design Associates

dimensions: **4 hectares (11 acres)**
soil: **mountain clay**
aspect: **from full sun to shady**
key features: **sunken garden, wild garden**

The owner of this Californian garden wanted to create the atmosphere of an Italian hillside garden, but keeping contemporary principles in mind. The new design also had to integrate features from the existing c.1930 garden.

A landscape of transitions, this large project exemplifies harmony between old and new, natural and constructed. The site consisted of many garden sections containing arid region plantings that flowed into the natural terrain and blended with the extended views of the wooded hills beyond. The garden was designed to seamlessly meld with the architecture and the indigenous landscape. Among the features were a swimming pool garden, entrance courtyard, sunken garden, Californian wild garden, and expansive plantings of experimental dry-climate materials – an important consideration in this arid landscape.

A Mediterranean planting theme was created by using materials from dry climates from around the world. A wall to the entrance courtyard was trained with ceanothus. The sunken garden provided a suitable atmosphere for olives and lavender, two plants often associated with the Mediterranean. To create a more unified whole, a limited selection of trees, shrubs, and perennials were chosen, but they were used in larger quantities.

entrance
courtyard

swimming pool garden

sunken garden

above *Retained planting beds cascade down the hillside, providing a soft backdrop to the main sitting areas.*

wild garden

"The Flow Garden"

Barbara Hunt & Jill Billington

dimensions: **60 x 20m (197 x 66ft)**
soil: **alkaline, chalky loam**
aspect: **open aspect to east, south, and west**
key features: **terrace, yew hedging**

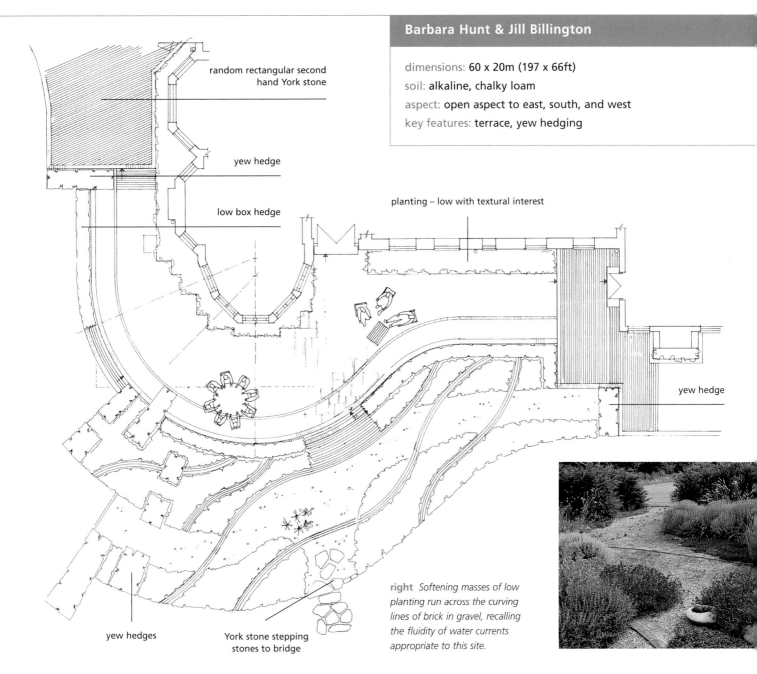

random rectangular second
hand York stone

yew hedge

low box hedge

planting – low with textural interest

yew hedge

yew hedges

York stone stepping
stones to bridge

right *Softening masses of low
planting run across the curving
lines of brick in gravel, recalling
the fluidity of water currents
appropriate to this site.*

The house was built in a mixture of periods, the latter and dominant part being early 1900s. A large area of paving for family use and entertaining was required for the rear of the house. The owner was enthusiastic about plants and employed a full-time gardener. He wanted a scheme that would be sympathetic to the house and its surroundings, and he was keen to break away from a traditional design treatment.

This portion of the site was part of a much larger garden, and it lay between the rear of the house and a gently flowing river. Elsewhere on the site were mature yew and beech hedging, an old curving wall, and several minor streams, suggesting a softly curving, linear theme for the design.

The new terrace, made of reclaimed York stone, was edged with low box hedge. The layout of the terrace was designed to link it to the architecture of the house. The arcs of the curved terrace stemmed from a setting out point located in the projecting bay, as did the radiating axial lines, along which ran wedges of yew hedge. The yews frame glimpses of both river and planting, and separated them from the more gentle, more organic, curving lines of brick, gravel, and plants within the garden itself.

The planting scheme, apart from the structural box and yew hedging, comprised of mainly sub-shrubs and herbaceous plants, set out to echo the curving lines of the underlying design. Grasses provided accent planting.

Garden by the Sea

dimensions: **30 x 22m (98 x 72ft)**

soil: **sandy loam, free-draining, alkaline**

aspect: **west facing, sunny**

key features: **Pool with pebble beach, deck**

The brief was for an easy going, laid back garden which would lead out from the back door of the cottage to a deck by a pool, where the owner could sit and enjoy the setting sun. The garden was to provide a haven of relaxation without the demands of high maintenance. As the garden is near the sea shore, the owner also wanted the garden to reflect the sweeping shapes of the bay and to be built from some of the materials found there: boulders, pebbles, and timber.

The proximity to the sea has given this garden its lovely quality of light, but the strong winds and free draining soil restricted planting choices to those plants tolerate of the exposed conditions. The sloping nature of the site allowed for exposed rock strata to be incorporated in a water cascade.

The main feature was the pool with pebble beach which meandered towards the house as a dry stream bed, eventually becoming a single path through which timber steps ran down to a timber terrace outside the patio doors. A timber deck sitting area overlooked a large informal pond. On the higher side of the pond was a rock cascade with running water. The deck terrace outside the back of the cottage hid a drain which ran all around the cottage.

Ornamental trees and structural grasses formed the main architectural elements within the garden. The dense planting included trees, shrubs, herbaceous plants, and grasses, aquatic plants, oxygenators, and gravel planting. The sloping margins of the pond were ideal for wildlife.

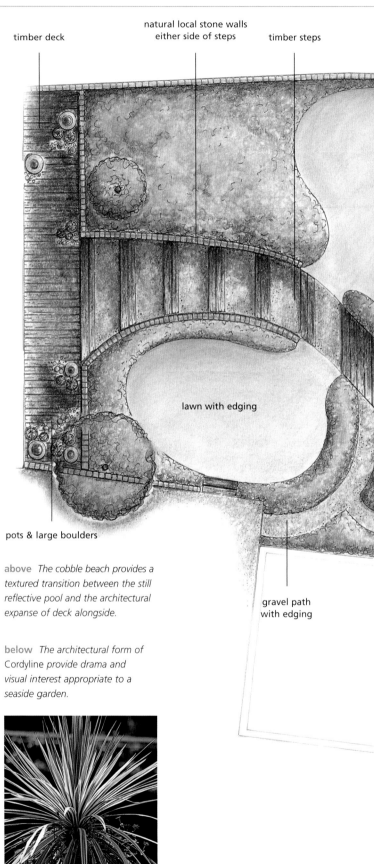

above *The cobble beach provides a textured transition between the still reflective pool and the architectural expanse of deck alongside.*

below *The architectural form of Cordyline provide drama and visual interest appropriate to a seaside garden.*

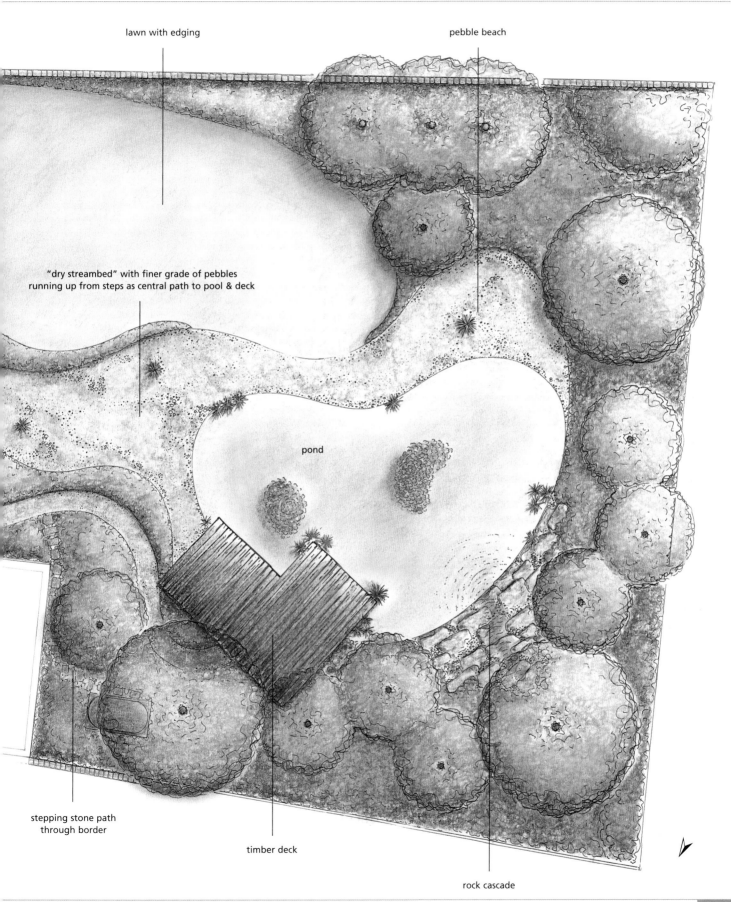

lawn with edging

pebble beach

"dry streambed" with finer grade of pebbles
running up from steps as central path to pool & deck

pond

stepping stone path
through border

timber deck

rock cascade

Woodland Garden

Sasha Kennedy Svensson

dimensions: **2 hectares (5 acres)**
soil: **sandy, acid**
aspect: **sheltered**
key features: **terrace, swimming pool**

The owners wanted the garden to consist of different spaces with different characteristics. They wanted to relax in their garden and to be able to stroll through it. A water feature and swimming pool were requested, as were a large entertainment area for formal and informal lunch and dinner parties, and more parking space. They also needed some sort of storage area.

The site is situated on top of a valley and has a lot of dense woodland around it. It has a few old existing structures on it such as a potting shed and a walled garden. It is a sheltered and isolated site, and due to the tall trees there is a sense of adventure about it. The garden is on a sloping site which could be used to an advantage in certain parts but also provided constraints to the design of the garden. Neighbours could be seen and traffic heard from the road on one of its boundaries, so providing a barrier to these were also considerations for the design.

York stone was chosen for the terrace, while concrete paving slabs and rendered concrete were used around the pool area. A swimming pool was placed inside the wall garden. Gravel provides a suitable drive and was also used in the walled garden and in the lower part of the garden. Bark chippings provide a softer surface for the small woodland paths. The shed and garage where designed to echo the architecture of the house and guesthouse, which overlooks a meadow.

An undulating line of trees drew the eye across the garden. Radiating blocks of trimmed box (*Buxus*) or yew (*Taxus*) were a key focal point. It was also intended that the walled garden and swiming pool area would be planted with luxurious exotics. Woodland planting consisted of conifers, beech, and birch. Native plants provided additional interest.

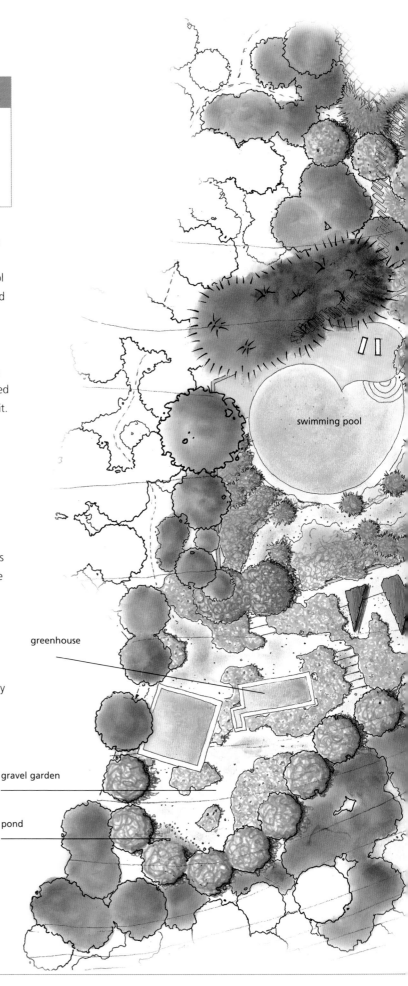

swimming pool

greenhouse

gravel garden

pond

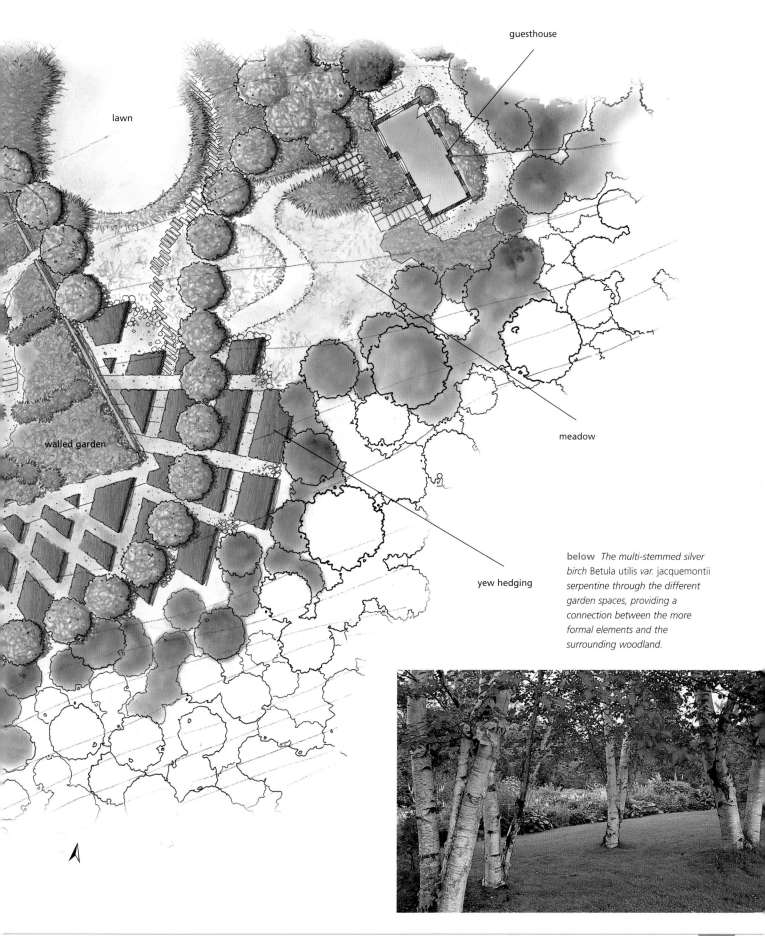

terrace

lawn

guesthouse

walled garden

meadow

yew hedging

below *The multi-stemmed silver birch* Betula utilis *var.* jacquemontii *serpentine through the different garden spaces, providing a connection between the more formal elements and the surrounding woodland.*

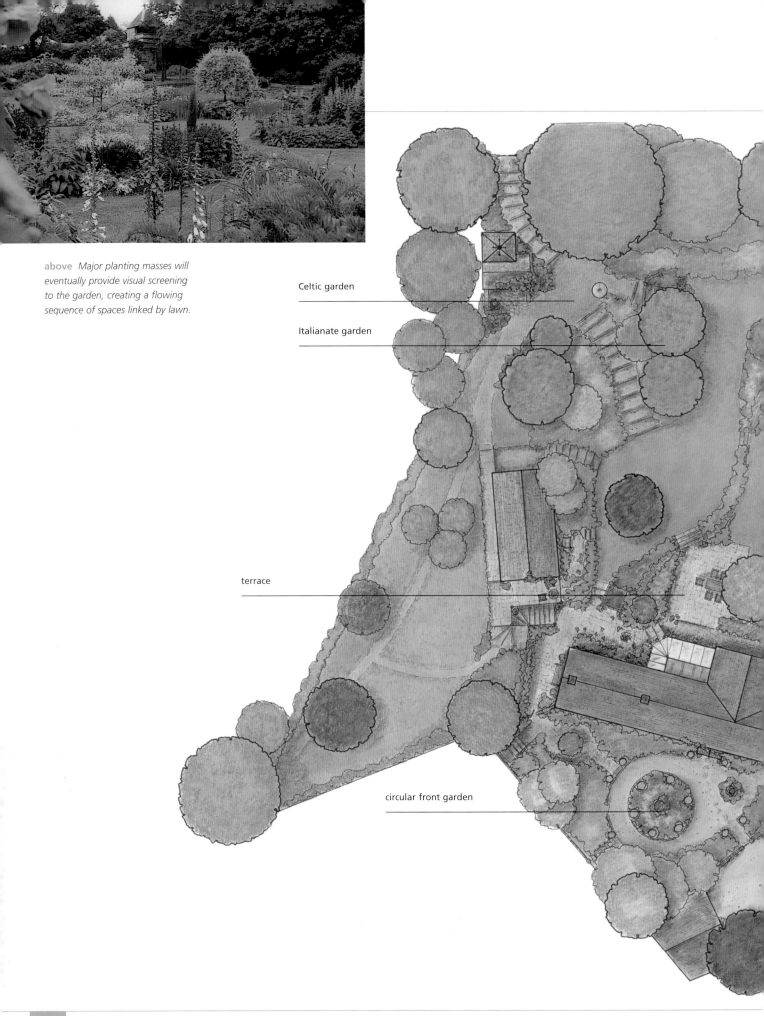

above *Major planting masses will
eventually provide visual screening
to the garden, creating a flowing
sequence of spaces linked by lawn.*

Celtic garden

Italianate garden

terrace

circular front garden

Hillside Garden

Liz Davies Garden Design

dimensions: **1 hectare (2 acres) approx**

soil: **netural**

aspect: **exposed**

key features: **terrace, raised beds, Celtic garden**

The original farmhouse was built into the side of the hill, and during renovation excavated soil was used to create level sitting areas. The soil in the front garden is insufficient for planting so raised beds were constructed around the house and the front gravelled.

The back garden is exposed to northerly winds that blow along the valley, so a windbreak of poplars, oaks, and pine was planted. This made a fantastic backdrop to the garden and an invaluable windbreak. The design of the garden took advantage of the different levels of the land. Three sets of steps led to the top of the garden, constructed from reclaimed flagstones, old stone tiles, and railway sleepers. Paths, patios, and terraces were constructed from flags or pea gravel, and raised beds were constructed from local pennant and uncoursed stone to match the farmhouse.

The garden was divided loosely into different areas by groups of mixed conifers, ornamental trees, pleached limes, or low stone walls. There was a semi-formal circular front garden; a large lawn; a natural pond surrounded by moisture-loving plants and mixed herbaceous borders; an Italianate garden with steps, terrace, and grotto; a wild meadow garden; and a Celtic garden with a folly.

The planting was varied, concentrating on form and texture. Bold, large-leaved architectural plants and exotics were a favourite, and used wherever possible. Borders were loosely colour themed, although always undergoing change. Large plantings of perennials and grasses gradually replaced the herbaceous borders.

pond

lawn

swimming pool

right Soft and expansive perennials surround more formal clipped box and border edges to create an atmospheric and peaceful corner in this large garden.

"Holly Meadow"

Michael Roberts Garden & Landscape Designs

dimensions: **20 x 16m (66 x 52ft)**

soil: **neutral, compacted**

aspect: **southwest facing**

key features: **arbour, gazebo, wild flower meadow**

right The open gazebo within the "wildflower" meadow. The photograph was taken shortly after the garden was finished and before the planting had developed.

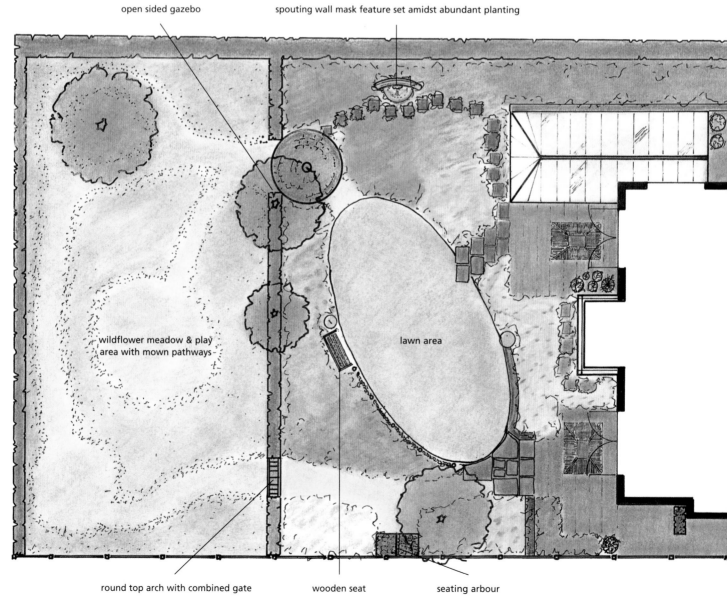

open sided gazebo

spouting wall mask feature set amidst abundant planting

wildflower meadow & play area with mown pathways

lawn area

round top arch with combined gate

wooden seat

seating arbour

The owners wanted a cottage garden surrounded with native species hedging to blend into the rural surroundings. A small play lawn was required, as well as paved entertaining areas immediately outside the French windows. Two small water features were required, one to be viewed from the kitchen window and the second from within the garden and conservatory.

The house was set slightly lower than the garden, within a retaining wall, to lessen the visual impact on the surrounding area. Apart from an imposing hawthorn hedge there were no existing landscape features.

A small arbour was positioned to the south side of the garden to provide shaded seating with a stone wall and pool surround. The gravel pathway to the front of this arbour led to an arched gateway giving ingress to the "wild flower" meadow. This meadow was also accessed via a small open gazebo, with tumbled block flooring, reached by a stepping stone pathway through the planting, or from across the lawn and a second gravel path. The old garden retaining wall was removed and rebuilt, following the curve of the new lawn, with new access steps constructed at either end of this wall. Two metal wall arches and one free-standing arch were positioned along the north side of the house, to create an entrance and frame a piece of statutory or art selected by the owner at a later date. The design was adjusted during construction to follow a complete change to the shape and style of the conservatory.

An amalgam of evergreen and deciduous shrubs and herbaceous and evergreen perennials were chosen for both their fragrance and flower, and small decorative trees were planted as specimen plantings.

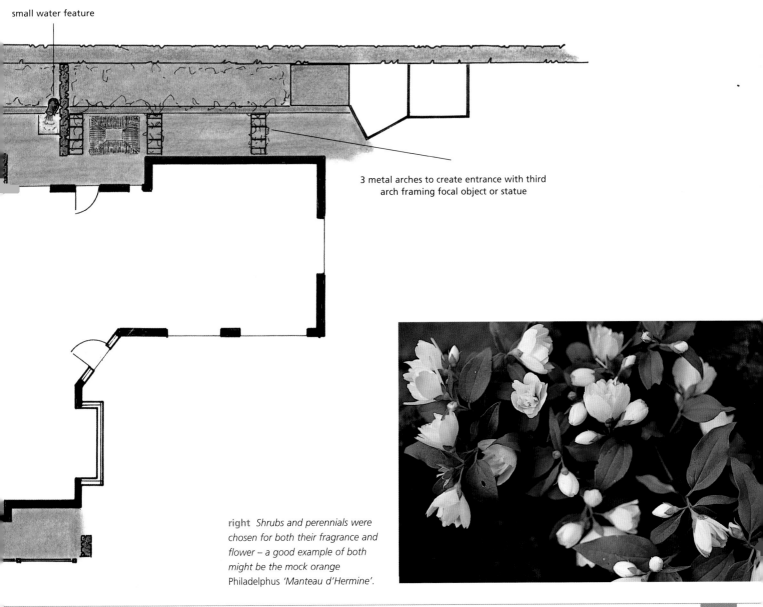

small water feature

3 metal arches to create entrance with third arch framing focal object or statue

right *Shrubs and perennials were chosen for both their fragrance and flower – a good example of both might be the mock orange* Philadelphus *'Manteau d'Hermine'.*

List of Designers

Acres Wild – Debbie Roberts and Ian Smith
110 High Street, Billingshurst,
West Sussex RH14 9QS
Tel/Fax: 01403 785 385
Email: enquiries@acreswild.co.uk

James Aldridge
61 Bellenden Road, Peckham SE15 5BH
Tel/Fax: 020 7732 8959
Email: gardens@jamesaldridge.net

Alistair Baldwin
Clematis Cottage, Main Street,
Grewelthorpe, Ripon, HG4 3BT
Tel: 0776 4221569
Email: abaldwin@lmu.ac.uk

Diana Balmori – Balmori Associates
451 Broome Street, Ste 11W New York,
NY 10013, USA
Tel: 001 212 431 9191
Email: dbalmori@balmori.com

Balston & Company
Long Barn, Patney, Devizes, Wiltshire SN10 3RB
Tel: 01380 848 181
Email: admin@balston.co.uk

Elizabeth Banks – Elizabeth Banks Associates
10-11 The Dove Centre, 109 Bartholomew Road,
London NW5 2BJ
Tel: 020 7482 4545
Email: EBA@eba.co.uk

Helen Billetop Garden Design
58 Northcote Road, St Margarets,
Twickenham TW1 1PA
Tel: 020 8892 3825
Email: helen@helenbilletop.com

Jill Billington
100 Fox Lane, London N13 4AX
Tel/Fax: 020 8886 0898
Email: jill.billington@btinternet.com

Bonita Bulaitis
6 Watton Road, Ware, Hertfordshire SG12 0AA
Tel: 01920 466 466
Email: bonita@gardendesignstudio.co.uk

**Del Buono-Gazerwitz Landscape Architecture
– Tommaso del Buono and Paul Gazerwitz**
1 Leinster Square, London W2 4PL
Tel/Fax: 020 7243 6006
Email: info@delbuono-gazerwitz.co.uk

John Brookes Landscape Design
Clock House, Denmans, Fintwell,
Nr Arundel, West Sussex BN18 0SU
Tel: 01243 542 808
Email: denmans@denmans-garden.co.uk

George Carter Garden Design
Silverstone Farm, North Elmham,
Norfolk NR20 5EX
Tel: 01362 668 130
Email: grcarter@easynet.co.uk

Clarke Associates – Marie Clarke
1-5 Offord Street, London N1 1DH
Tel: 020 7700 2027
Email: enquiries@clarkeassociates.cc

Douglas Coltart
The Cottage, Wallceton, Maybole,
Ayrshire KA19 8LU
Tel: 01465 811 244
Email: d.coltart@au.sac.ac.uk

Paul Cooper
Ty Bryn, Old Radnor, Presteigne, Powys LD8 2RN
Tel: 01544 230 374
Email: paulcooper58@hotmail.com

Cheryl Cummings Garden Design
The Coach House, 13 St James Mews,
Monmouth NP25 3BW
Tel/Fax: 01600 719 014
Email: cherylcummingsgd@aol.com

Liz Davies Garden Design
Croesllanfro Farm, Rogerstone, Newport,
Gwent NP1 9GP
Tel: 01633 894 343
Email: lizplants@aol.com

Michael Day
The Chalet, Marston Meysey,
Swindon, Wiltshire SN6 6LQ
Tel: 01285 810 486
Email: michaelday@gardendesign24.fsnet.co.uk

Simon Dorrell
Bryan's Ground, Nr Stapleton,
Presteigne, Hertfordshire LD8 2LP
Tel: 01544 260 001
Email: all@hortus.co.uk

Alison Dove
Partridge Hall Farm Cottage, Sandon,
Buntingford, Hertfordshire SG9 0RA
Tel/Fax: 01763 287 643
Email: alisondove@gardendesignuk.net

Paul Dracott Garden Designs
Poppy Cottage, 68 London Road,
Sawston, Cambridge CB2 4XE
Tel: 01223 830 904
Email: enquiries@pdgardendesigns.co.uk

Sarah Eberle, Hillier Landscapes
Ampfield House, Ampfield, Romsey,
Hampshire SO51 9PA
Tel: 01794 368 855
Email: hillierlandscapes@btinternet.com

Andrew Fisher Tomlin
74 Sydney Road, Wimbledon, London SW20 8EF
Tel: 020 8542 0683
Email: a@andrewfishertomlin.com

Julia Fogg/David May
56 Park East, Bow Quarter, London E3 2UT
Tel: 020 8980 3999
Email: julia@juliafogg.com

Jane Follis Garden Design
Blithe Cottage, Eythrope Road, Stone,
Buckinghamshire HP17 8PH
Tel: 01296 747 775
Email: jfgdndesign@aol.com

Nigel Fuller
Lower Burrow Farmehouse, Kingsbury,
Episcopi, Somerset TA12 6BS
Tel: 01460 242 760
Email: nigel.fuller2@btopenworld.com

Naila Green, Corporate Gardens
Highover House, Lady's Mile, Exeter Road,
Dawlish, Devon EX7 0XA
Tel: 01626 888 598
Email: naila@corporate-gardens.co.uk

Roderick Griffin, Sutton Griffin & Morgan
The Long Barn, Welford, Newbury,
Berkshire RG20 8HZ
Tel: 01488 657 657
Email: newbury@sgm_architects.co.uk

Annie Guilfoyle, Creative Landscapes
Daisy Cottage, 40 Lutener Road, Easebourne,
Midhurst, West Sussex GU29 9AT
Tel: 01730 812943
Email: annie@creative-landscapes.com

Catherine Heatherington Designs
9 Cecil Road, Muswell Hill, London N10 2BU
Tel: 020 8374 2321
Email: gardens@chdesigns.co.uk

Dene Hohwieler
28 Multon Road, London SW18 3LH
Tel: 020 874 8418

Barbara Hunt, Hunt Design
91 Church Street, Staines, Middlesex TW18 4X5
Tel/Fax: 01784 452 919
Email: bahunt@waitrose.com

Alex Johnson
4 Grove Road, Blackboy Hill
Bristol BS6 6UJ
Tel: 0117 973 0023
Email: enquiries@elemental.freeserve.co.uk

Jenny Jones, Highwater Jones Limited
Garstons, Gatcombe, Newport,
Isle of Wight PO30 3EQ
Tel: 01983 721 752
Email: **all@highwaterjones.com**

John Kenny
50 Otterfield Road, Yiewsley,
West Drayton, Middlesex UB7 8PE
Tel/Fax: 01895 420 344
Email: ja.kenny@virgin.net

Lotti Kierkegaard
Charlotte Kierkegaard Design,
34 Boileau Road, London SW13 9BL
Tel: 020 8255 7633
Email: lotti@kirkegaard-design.com

Jan King
The Mill House, Lane Road, Wakes Colne,
Colchester, Essex CO26 2BP
Tel: 01787 222 540
Email: jan@floralking.co.uk

Sarah Layton at Allium Gardens
13 Purley Avenue, London NW2 1SH
Tel/Fax: 020 8450 1862
Email: sarah@alliumgardens.co.uk

Arabella Lennox-Boyd
1–5 Dells Mews, Churton Place, London SW1V 2LW
Tel: 020 7931 9995
Email: office@arabellalennoxboyd.com

**Barbara Lumsden Landscape &
Garden Design**
Little Becketts, Arkesden, Saffron Walden,
Essex CB11 4HG
Tel/Fax: 01799 550 238
Email: barbara.lumsden@virgin.net

Mark Lutyens
Clifton Little Venice, 3 Warwick Place,
London W9 2PX
Tel: 020 7432 1890
Email: mlutyens@dircon.co.uk

Christopher Maguire
15 Harston Road, Newton,
Cambridge CB2 5PA
Tel: 01223 872 800

John Moreland
Bay View, Alma Terrace, Penzance,
Cornwall TR18 2BY
also Studio Flat
47 Wickham Road
Brockley, London SE4 1LT
Tel: 01736 367 525
Email: johnmoreland@supanet.com

Rachel Myers Garden Design
56 Marsh Road, Temple Cowley,
Oxford QX4 2HH
Tel/Fax: 01736 367525
Email: info@rachelmyersgardendesign.co.uk

Robert Myers – Elizabeth Banks Associates
10-11 The Dove Centre,
109 Bartholomew Road,
London NW5 2BJ
Tel: 020 7482 4545
Email: EBA@eba.co.uk

Anthony Noel
36 Parkview Court, Fulham High Street,
London SW6 3LP
Tel: 020 7736 2907
Email: anthony.noel@virgin.net

Ryl Nowell – Cabbages & Kings
Alexander Barn, Sotterley,
Beccles, Suffolk NR34 8EZ
Tel/Fax: 01502 575 524
Email: ryl@ckings.co.uk

Olin Partnership – Dennis McGlade
The Public Ledger Building, Suite 1123,
150 S. Independence Mall W.,
Philiadelphia PA, 19106, USA
Tel: 001 215 440 0030
Email: dmcglade@olinptr.com

Anthony Paul
Black & White Cottage,
Standon Lane,
Ockley, Surrey RH5 5QR
Tel: 01306 627 677
Email: apaul1945@aol.com

Nigel Philips Landscape & Garden Design
Station Studio, Cooksbridge,
Lewes,
East Sussex BN8 4SW
Tel/Fax: 01273 400 983
Email: post@nigelphilips.co.uk

**Christopher Pickard Garden &
Landscape Design**
11 Tanners Yard, 239 Long Lane,
London SE1 4PT
Tel: 020 7378 7537
Email: christopher.pickard@btinternet.com

Keith Pullan Garden Design
1 Amotherby Close, Amotherby, Malton,
North Yorkshire YO17 0TG
Tel: 01653 693 885
Email: keithpullan@email.com

**Michael Roberts Gardens &
Landscape Designs**
7 Caernarvon Close, Chesterfield,
Derbyshire S40 3DY
Tel: 01246 209 609
Email: michael@garden-creators.com

Natalya Scott
30 Jasper Street, Bedminster, Bristol BS3 3DU
Tel: 01179 634 118
Email: talyascott@hotmail.com

Victor Shanley
6 Eastry Avenue, Hayes Bromley,
Kent BR2 7PF

David R. Sisley
Straight Mile Nursery Gardens,
Ongar Road, Pilgrim's Hatch, Brentwood, Essex
CM15 9SA
Tel: 01277 374 439

Vladimir Sitta
Terragram Pty Ltd,
105 Reservoir Street,
Surry Hills NSW 2010, Australia
Tel: 0061 292 116 060
Email: room413@tig.com.au

David Stevens
Well House, 60 Well Street,
Buckingham,
Buckinghamshire MK17 0HE
Tel: 01280 821 097
Email: gardens@david-stevens.co.uk

Tom Stuart-Smith Landscape Design
43 Clerkenwell Road, London W1T 2RF
Tel: 020 7631 3185
Email: tom@landskip.com

Andy Sturgeon Garden Design
15 Clermont Road, Brighton,
East Sussex BN1 6SG
Tel: 01273 553 336
Email: andysturgeon@andysturgeon.com

Sasha Kennedy Svensson
c/o Guy & Sophie Williams
20 Spedan Close
London NW3 7XF
Email: sasha@mail.nu

Joe Swift /Sam Joyce – The Plant Room
47 Barnsbury Street,
London N1 1TP
Tel: 020 7700 6766
Email: info@plantroom.co.uk

Julie Toll
Business and Technology Centre,
Bessemer Drive, Stevenage,
Hertfordshire, SG1 2DX
Tel: 01438 310 095
Email: info@julietoll.co.uk

Bernard Trainor Design Associates
PO BOX 60127, Palo Alto,
California 94306, USA
Tel: 001 650 569 3163
Email: contact@btdaonline.com

Mark Anthony Walker Associates
4 Station Road,
Haddenham,
Ely, Cambridgshire CB6 3XD
Tel: 01353 749 007
Email: mark.a.awalker@btinternet.com

Andrew Wenham
38 Hitchin Road, Weston,
Hertfordshire SG4 7AY
Tel: 01462 790 079
Email: gardens@ryan-wenham.net

Cleve West
20 Blagdon Walk,
Teddington,
Middlesex TW11 9LN
Tel: 020 8977 6470
Email: clevewest@btconnect.com

**Andrew Wilson – Pockett Wilson
Garden Design**
Laurel Cottage,
12 Bridge Road,
Chertsey, Surrey KT16 8JL
Tel: 01932 563613
Email: info@pockettwilson.co.uk

Steven Woodhams – Woodhams Landscape
378 Brixton Road,
London SW9 7AW
Tel: 020 7346 5656
Email: design@woodhams.co.uk

Index

Page numbers in *italics* refer to illustrations

A

activity areas *46*, 93, 144
alcoves 32
antipodean plants 92, 224
arbours 33, 251
arches 35, 104, 182

B

bamboo *25*, 56, *57*, *90*, 96, 110, 133
beach areas 36, 73, 95, 113, 188, 244
benches 36, 40, 68, 83, 133, 149, 166
boardwalks 59, 92, 181
bridges 180, 188, 232
buildings 18, 52, 170, 180, 181

C

canals 39, 54, 74, 186, 234
ceramic poles 187
child-friendly gardens 36, 68, 113, 121, 136, 168–9
cobbles *59*, 160, 244
companion plants 21
concrete 46, 54, 84, 92, 137
conservatories 42, 46, 96, 107, 129, 142, 227
containers 70, 79, 90, 118, 130, 160, 166
country gardens 216–51
courtyards 46, 64–5, 69, 76, 82–3, 154–5, 178, 180

D

decking
    beach effect 73
    coloured 70, 107
    diagonal 136, 151
    dining areas 80, 230
    for entertaining 58, 80, 83, 88, 224
    over water 52, 58, 95, 188, 236, 244
    raised 80, 139, 166, 187
    split-level 90, 95, 144, 146
    for sunbathing 64, 88, 111, 156–7, 230
dining areas 46, 56, 70
dry gardens 46–7, 167, 242

E

entertainment areas 58, 63, 64, 68, 80
"The Eros Garden" 33
espaliers 21, 197
evergreens 27, 39, *93*, 121, 162, 194
experimental gardens 28–9

F

ferns *24*, *25*
"Fire Garden" 17, 18–19
fires 18, 53, 73, 170, 234
formal gardens 27, 140–1, 156–7, 192–215, 226–9
fountains 66, 80, 107, 108, 129, 132, 151, 167

G

garden plans explained 10–15
garden rooms 21, 84–5, 115, 129, 134, 198, 201
gazebos *see* summerhouses
granite 24, 25, 59
grasses 30, 40, 46, 110, *138*, 164, 241
gravel areas 80, 104, 113, 230, 246, 249
greenhouses 102, 122

H

hedges
    box 76, 93, 100, 137, 158
    Escallonia 225
    as focal points 20, 23, 106, 122
    living 33
    meandering 208
    screening 66
    yew 53, 141, 212, 218, 243
herb gardens 46, 64, 158, 194, 201
herbaceous plants 122, 125, 173

I

informal gardens 86–125

J

jungle areas 36–7, 53

K

kitchen gardens 194, 235

L

"Land of Contrasts" 92
landscape installations 28–9, 35, 40–1, 70, 172, 187
lawns 54, 90, 116, 130, 134, 186, 194
"Life's Journey Garden" 34–5
lighting 45, 76, 118, *119*, 142, 163, 178
limestone 74, 176
low-maintenance gardens 46–7, 50–1, 63, 104, 113, 136–7, 160, 230–1

M

mazes 190, 208
Mediterranean-style gardens 46, 62, 100, 115, 151, 167, 242
"Millennium Garden" 30–1
mirrors 40, 64, 76, 139, 153, 161
"The Moon Garden" 26
moss walls 77

N

native plants 30, 92, 224
"No Strings Attached" 40–1

O

orchards 54, 146, 194, 200, 218, 225, 234
oriental themes 49, 181

P

parterres 194, *195*, 200
paths 20, 35, 96, 134, 162
patios 68, 170, *171*
patterns 21, *59*, 147
paved areas 60, 130, 147, 154, 160, 204, 214
pavilions 202, 218, 228, 241
"Peace Garden" 20
pebbles 26, 51, 59, 76, 83, 113, 146
pergolas
    concrete 54
    curved 62, 104
    metal 59, 133, 152, 178
    wire 84–5, 151, 178
    wooden 32, 97, 102, 104, 140, 225
playhouses 36, 68
ponds
    with beach areas 95, 188
    with decking 95, 188, 236
    diagonal-shaped 110
    for fish 190
    formal 199
    ornamental 146
    planted 108, 188, 236
pool gardens 225, 228
pools
    with beach areas 73, 244
    care of 149
    with decking 244
    formal 228
    geometric shapes 27
    grill-covered 58, 179
    infinity edge 114
    large 173, 176
    reflecting 23, 73, 77, 114, 116, 180

still 23, 59, 70, 176
tiled 26
with water features 24, *25*, 173
see also ponds; swimming pools
privacy 48, 56, 66, 98, 102, 113, 127, 132

R
raised beds 24, *25*, 51, 66, 157, 197, 249
ramps 102, 153
reclaimed materials 27, 32, 94–5, 104
rocks 90, 107, 146, 164, 185
roof gardens 30, 45, 70–1, 78–9, 118–19, 152–3
roof terraces 72–3, 163
rose gardens 194, 199

S
"Sanctuary Garden" 22–3
screens
    glass 70, 241
    hedging 66
    perspex 118, *119*
    projection 58
    steel 39
    walls 42, 114
    wooden 73
sculpture 39, 59, 66, 70, 92, 154, 186, 212
"Sculpture Garden" 38–9
seaside gardens 36–7, 50–1, 112–13, 170–1, 208–9, 230–1, 244–5
seating 32, 63, 73, 74, 90, 122
    see also benches
secret gardens 20, 53, 90–1, 100
sheds 66, 68, 90, 95, 96, 154
show gardens 17, 22–3, 28–9, 38–43, 74–5, 92
slate 18, 56, 111, 153, 166, 186
sloping sites 26, 53, 62, 94–5, 100, 102–3, 106, 122–3
small gardens 21, 45, 76–7, 83, 98, 107, 126–73
sound absorption 56, 58
Spanish-style gardens 115, 167
split-level gardens 36, 48–9, 63, 88–9, 146
"Square Roots Garden" 27
    steel
    arches 35
    beams 42
    containers 118, 160, 166
    espaliers 197
    screens 39
    on walls 26, 28, 176
    in water curtains/walls 23, 142, 207
    water features 56, 60, 118, 132,153, 178, 212

stepping stones *25*, 186, 201
steps 63, 68, 98, 182, 202
streams 108
succulents 46, 164
summerhouses 36, 121, 149, 182, 222, *250*, 251
sunken gardens 102, 132, 140–1, 142, 201, 242
swimming pools 46, 220, 224, 246

T
terraces
    with "beds" 42
    brick 106, 235
    circular 137, 143, 199, 202
    decking 244
    gravelled 249
    sandstone 125
    slate 56
    split-level 62, 100, 106, 161
    sunken 201
    York stone 66, 210, 243, 246
topiary 27, 39, 74, 130, 198, 204, 207, 234
trees
    arboretums 69
    avenues 214
    existing 18, 62, 80, 125
    as focal points 18, 20, 64, 68, 74, 88, 106, 186
    fruit 54, 214, *215*
    for nuts 234
    pleached 210, *211*, 212
trellises 21, 76, 154, 161, 162, 168

U
urban gardens 24–5, 30–1, 44–85, 166

V
vegetable gardens 62, 200, 202
vertical gardens 77

W
walls
    cladded 24, 25, 74
    coloured 28, 74, 139
    curved 46, 52, 96, 132, *148*, 149, 150
    espaliered 21
    moss 77
    rendered 22, 23, 52, 96
    screening 42, 114
    with steel 26, 28, 176
    stucco 28
    weathered 227
    wooden *148*, 149

water bowls/basins 115, 180, 241
water columns 60, 76, 163
water curtains 35, 58, 142
water features 27, 59, 96, 104, 158
    concrete 137
    in pools 24, 25, 173
    in steel 56, 60, 118, 132, 153, 178, 212
    wall-mounted 51
water sculpture 186, 212
    see also individual features
water gardens 174–91
water rills 33, 178, 180, 212, 228
water spillways 185
water troughs 125
water walls 23, 207
waterfalls 24, *25*, 33, 56, 108, 182
wellheads 74
wheelchair-friendly gardens 97, 153, 182
wildflower meadows 122, 125, 220, *250*, 251
wildlife gardens 173, 242
wind/wind features 36, 59, 70, 73, 241, 249
woodland areas 116, 134–5, 144, 181, 246–7
woven structures 33, 172, 173, 232

Picture Acknowledgments

Mitchell Beazley would like to acknowledge and thank the following for supplying photographs for inclusion in this book.

Jacket: Front, top left Joe Swift & Sam Joyce, top right Helen Billetop Garden Design, centre left Youn-sun Chun, centre right photo Andrew Lawson, design Tom Stuart Smith, bottom photo Marianne Majerus, design Joe Swift; Back, top photo Marianne Majerus, design Jill Billington & Barbara Hunt, bottom Liz Davies Garden Design.

All photographs and plans have kindly been supplied by each featured garden designer, with the exception of the following:

Key: AL Andrew Lawson, GPL Garden Picture Library, HGL Harpur Garden Library

Page 14 GPL/Marie O'Hara, 20 AL, 24 left HGL/Marcus Harpur, 24 right, 27 HGL/Jerry Harpur, 38, 39 left Marianne Majerus, 39 right Marianne Majerus, design George Carter, 40, 41 left and right HGL/Jerry Harpur/Bonita Bulaitis, 49 AL, 52 HGL/Marcus Harpur, 53 AL, 57 left GPL/Jerry Pavia, 57 right Mise au Point/Yann Monel, 58 Jonathan Buckley, design Paul Cooper, 59 Mise au Point/Arnaud Descat, 60 GPL/Sunniva Harte, design Nigel Phillips, 61 HGL/Marcus Harpur, 62 AL, 65, 68 HGL/Marcus Harpur, 69 Clive Nichols Garden Pictures/Clive Nichols, 73 AL, 74 AL, design Mark Anthony Walker, 76 GPL/Brian Carter, 79 left GPL/Linda Burgess (Gardens/Plants), 79 right GPL/Brigitte Thomas, 83 HGL/Jerry Harpur, 85 Marianne Majerus, design Joe Swift, 90 HGL/Jerry Harpur, 92, 96 AL, 102 GPL/Ron Sutherland, 106 AL, 107 GPL/J S Sira, 113 HGL/Jerry Harpur, 125 bottom AL, 128 HGL/Jerry Harpur, design Doug and Sue Band, 130, 131 AL, design Anthony Noel, 135, 136, 137 HGL/Marcus Harper, 141 GPL/Gary Rogers, 142, 144 Clive Nichols Garden Pictures/Sarah Layton, 150 GPL/John Glover, 156 AL, 162 HGL/Jerry Harpur, 173 AL, 176 HGL/Marcus Harpur, design Beth Chatto, 187 Derek St Romaine, 188 HGL/Jerry Harpur, 200 HGL/Marcus Harpur; 204 photos David Markson; 205 AL, 211 AL, Rofford Manor, Oxford, 215 left AL, 215 right HGL/Jerry Harpur, 218 GPL/Brigitte Thomas, 220 AL, 225 HGL/Jerry Harpur, 232 left AL, 232 right HGL/Marcus Harpur, 234 AL, 235 HGL/Jerry Harpur, 243 Marianne Majerus, design Jill Billington & Barbara Hunt, 251 Octopus Publishing Group, 247 AL.

Additional credits:

Pages 4–5 photo Ian Green, design Naila Green, 25 photo Francis Ware, 26, 230 photos Ian Green; 28–29 photos Kraig Beck; 46–47 photos Bernard Trainor Carolyn Clebsch; 108–9, 115 photos Bernard Trainor, Carolyn Clebsch; 90 photo Liz Davies; 222 photos Ian Smith; 226–27 Marie Clarke; 242 photo Kraig Beck; 248–249 photos Liz Davies, Ruth Chivers.